# Mornings
## with the Lord

# ALSO BY DOREEN VIRTUE

## Books

*Father Therapy* (with Andrew Karpenko, M.S.W.)
*10 Messages Your Angels Want You to Know*
*Awaken Your Indigo Power* (with Charles Virtue)
*Veggie Mama* (with Jenny Ross)
*The Courage to Be Creative*
*Nutrition for Intuition* (with Robert Reeves, N.D.)
*Don't Let Anything Dull Your Sparkle*
*Earth Angel Realms*
*Living Pain-Free* (with Robert Reeves, N.D.)
*The Big Book of Angel Tarot* (with Radleigh Valentine)
*Angels of Abundance* (with Grant Virtue)
*Angel Dreams* (with Melissa Virtue)
*Angel Detox* (with Robert Reeves, N.D.)
*Assertiveness for Earth Angels*
*How to Heal a Grieving Heart* (with James Van Praagh)
*The Essential Doreen Virtue Collection*
*The Miracles of Archangel Gabriel*
*Mermaids 101*
*Flower Therapy* (with Robert Reeves, N.D.)
*Mary, Queen of Angels*
*Saved by an Angel*
*The Angel Therapy® Handbook*
*Angel Words* (with Grant Virtue)
*Archangels 101*
*The Healing Miracles of Archangel Raphael*
*The Art of Raw Living Food* (with Jenny Ross)
*The Miracles of Archangel Michael*
*Angel Numbers 101*
*Solomon's Angels* (a novel)
*My Guardian Angel* (with Amy Oscar)
*Angel Blessings Candle Kit* (with Grant Virtue; includes booklet, CD, journal, etc.)
*Thank You, Angels!* (children's book with Kristina Tracy)
*Healing Words from the Angels*
*How to Hear Your Angels*
*Signs from Above* (with Charles Virtue)
*Fairies 101*
*Daily Guidance from Your Angels*
*How to Give an Angel Card Reading Kit*
*Angels 101*

*Crystal Therapy* (with Judith Lukomski)
*The Crystal Children*
*Earth Angels*
*Messages from Your Angels*
*Angel Visions II*
*Eating in the Light* (with Becky Black, M.F.T., R.D.)
*The Care and Feeding of Indigo Children*
*Angel Visions*
*Divine Prescriptions*
*Healing with the Angels*
*"I'd Change My Life If I Had More Time"*
*Divine Guidance*
*Angel Therapy*®
*Constant Craving A–Z*
*Constant Craving*
*The Yo-Yo Diet Syndrome*
*Losing Your Pounds of Pain*

## Audio/CD Programs

*10 Messages Your Angels Want You to Know* (unabridged audio book)
*The Courage to Be Creative* (unabridged audio book)
*Don't Let Anything Dull Your Sparkle* (unabridged audio book)
*The Healing Miracles of Archangel Raphael* (unabridged audio book)
*Angel Therapy*® *Meditations*
*Archangels 101* (abridged audio book)
*Solomon's Angels* (unabridged audio book)
*Fairies 101* (abridged audio book)
*Angel Medicine* (available as both 1- and 2-CD sets)
*Angels among Us* (with Michael Toms)
*Messages from Your Angels* (abridged audio book)
*Divine Prescriptions*
*The Romance Angels*
*Connecting with Your Angels*
*Manifesting with the Angels*
*Healing Your Appetite, Healing Your Life*
*Healing with the Angels*
*Divine Guidance*

## DVD Program

*How to Give an Angel Card Reading*

# Calendar

*Angel Affirmations 2018 Calendar*
*Daily Blessings from Heaven Calendar*
(for 2019 and each year thereafter)

# Card Decks

*Crystal Angels Oracle Cards*
*Butterfly Oracle Cards for Life Changes*
*Loving Words from Jesus*
*Archangel Gabriel Oracle Cards*
*Angel Answers Oracle Cards* (with Radleigh Valentine)
*Cherub Angel Cards for Children*
*Flower Therapy Oracle Cards* (with Robert Reeves, N.D.)
*Indigo Angel Oracle Cards* (with Charles Virtue)
*Angel Dreams Oracle Cards* (with Melissa Virtue)
*Mary, Queen of Angels Oracle Cards*
*The Romance Angels Oracle Cards*
*Life Purpose Oracle Cards*
*Archangel Raphael Healing Oracle Cards*
*Archangel Michael Oracle Cards*
*Angel Therapy® Oracle Cards*
*Magical Messages from the Fairies Oracle Cards*
*Daily Guidance from Your Angels Oracle Cards*
*Saints & Angels Oracle Cards*
*Magical Unicorns Oracle Cards*
*Goddess Guidance Oracle Cards*
*Archangel Oracle Cards*
*Magical Mermaids and Dolphins Oracle Cards*
*Messages from Your Angels Oracle Cards*
*Healing with the Fairies Oracle Cards*
*Healing with the Angels Oracle Cards*

All of the above are available at your local bookstore, or may be ordered through Hay House USA: www.hayhouse.com®; Hay House Australia: www.hayhouse.com.au; Hay House UK: www.hayhouse.co.uk; Hay House South Africa: www.hayhouse.co.za; Hay House India: www.hayhouse.co.in

Doreen's website: www.AngelTherapy.com

# Mornings
## with the Lord

A Year of *Uplifting* Devotionals
to Start Your Day on the Right Path

## Doreen Virtue

**HAY HOUSE, INC.**
Carlsbad, California • New York City
London • Sydney • Johannesburg
Vancouver • New Delhi

**Published and distributed in the United States by:** Hay House, Inc.: www.hay house.com® • **Published and distributed in Australia by:** Hay House Australia Pty. Ltd.: www.hayhouse.com.au • **Published and distributed in the United Kingdom by:** Hay House UK, Ltd.: www.hayhouse.co.uk • **Published and distributed in the Republic of South Africa by:** Hay House SA (Pty), Ltd.: www .hayhouse.co.za • **Distributed in Canada by:** Raincoast Books: www.raincoast .com • **Published in India by:** Hay House Publishers India: www.hayhouse .co.in

*Interior design:* Bryn Starr Best

The author of this book does not dispense medical advice or prescribe the use of any technique as a form of treatment for physical, emotional, or medical problems without the advice of a physician, either directly or indirectly. The intent of the author is only to offer information of a general nature to help you in your quest for emotional and spiritual well-being. In the event you use any of the information in this book for yourself, the author and the publisher assume no responsibility for your actions.

Unless otherwise indicated, all scripture quotations are taken from the Holy Bible, New Living Translation, copyright © 1996, 2004, 2007, 2013, 2015 by Tyndale House Foundation. Used by permission of Tyndale House Publishers, Inc., Carol Stream, Illinois 60188. All rights reserved.

Scripture quotations marked *WEB* are taken from the World English Bible, a Bible in the public domain (http://ebible.org/web): *January 9; March 11; May 13; June 3, 11, 18; July 14, 15; August 2, 3, 20, 23; September 5, 11, 21, 25, 27, 30; October 11, 30, 31; November 13; December 3.*

Scripture quotations marked *ASV* are taken from the Holy Bible, American Standard Version, a Bible in the public domain (www.biblegateway.com): *August 30.*

### Library of Congress Cataloging-in-Publication Data

Names: Virtue, Doreen, date, author.
Title: Mornings with the Lord : a year of uplifting devotionals to start your
    day on the right path / Doreen Virtue.
Description: 1st edition. | Carlsbad, California : Hay House, Inc., [2017]
Identifiers: LCCN 2017027594 | ISBN 9781401955120 (hardcover : alk. paper)
Subjects: LCSH: Devotional calendars.
Classification: LCC BV4811 .V57 2017 | DDC 204/.32--dc23 LC record available at
https://lccn.loc.gov/2017027594

ISBN: 978-1-4019-5512-0

10 9 8 7 6 5 4 3 2 1
1st edition, October 2017

Printed in the United States of America

*To Jesus Christ of Nazareth,*
*who expresses a love that is beyond*
*what words can describe.*
*Thank you for saving me!*

# Introduction

Starting your day with uplifting reading sets a positive tone for your mind-set, which then leads to positive experiences. In fact, one reason why I'm committed to reading the Bible and other inspiring material in the morning is that whenever I've skipped this positive practice, I've felt "off" and my day didn't go as well.

After all, God doesn't promise us a perfect life, only his perfect support and love. Having God's support, combined with your positive outlook, helps you cope with life's twists and turns.

If you're guided to begin each day with positive reading, the Lord will clear the path for you to have enough time for your morning devotionals. All you need to do is express your desire to do so, and then make a commitment to devote your first few moments to talking with and listening to God. This may involve waking up earlier, delaying doing anything else first, or substituting a former morning ritual.

Avoid arguing with yourself or others about whether or not you have enough time to commune with God. Set this activity in the same category as other must-dos, like brushing your teeth or hair.

Consciously connecting with the Lord strengthens your communication lines, helping you notice and understand the divine messages sent to you. The more often you deliberately commune with God, the more your faith and sense of peace increase.

The devotionals in this book are dated so that you can read a page to begin your morning. Each entry offers a contemplative topic, a prayer to the Lord, and a relevant scriptural passage. My prayer is that these pages serve as stepping-stones to meditation, worship, and further biblical study.

You are certainly encouraged, if you are guided, to open the book to a random page for a message at any time. I also encourage you to personalize the prayers in this book so that they are from your heart and applicable to your current situation.

May each page in this book be a catalyst for you to develop an ever closer personal relationship with God. May you enjoy hours of heartfelt conversations with the Lord. And may your heart be filled with the immense love, peace, and sense of purpose that he sends to all who invite him into their lives.

*With Love,*
*Doreen*

---

*A note on references to God:* In this book, I refer to God with masculine pronouns such as *he* because of tradition and to reflect my own spiritual experiences. If you feel more comfortable substituting gender-neutral pronouns, please do so.

In scripture, God is respectfully referred to by many names—including *Yahweh, LORD, Adonai,* and *God*—which you will see in this book. Often the name *Lord* specifically denotes Jesus. In some Christian faiths, the Holy Trinity of the Father, Holy Spirit, and Jesus are all called *God* or *Lord.* In others, the Father is the only God, and Jesus is the Son and not God. My prayer is that you won't allow any confusion or controversy to arise while reading the pages of this book, but perhaps use any theological questions as a springboard for further study and pray for guidance to settle your own beliefs.

# A Note If You Are Healing Your Relationship with Jesus

If you've had painful experiences with organized religion, then I congratulate you for taking the healing step of opening this book. Many people associate Jesus with guilt, emotional pain, rejection, judgment, and hypocrisy. I'm proud of you for having the courage to move past these perceptions in order to reconnect with Jesus in a new way.

While I personally receive great comfort from attending church (I'm a member of a church of the Episcopalian/Anglican denomination, known for being nonjudgmental and inclusive of all lifestyles), it's also possible to have a personal relationship with God and Jesus outside of organized religion.

Please don't allow negative experiences with organized religion to disconnect you from a true best friend who wants to help you now and always. Yes, some people in organized religions have acted in very hurtful ways, but *Jesus would never hurt you.*

Yes, the Bible has been translated, rearranged, and used to justify evil actions. But Jesus never did any of those things.

Yes, the paintings of Jesus often portray him as Caucasian instead of reflecting his cultural heritage. But those are artists and rulers who are responsible for those portrayals, not Jesus.

Yes, patriarchy has done horribly oppressive and cruel things to women. But Jesus never did. Let's stop confusing the historical actions of people with the actions of Jesus.

If, while reading this book, you find yourself believing that you are being judged, please take some time to meditate and pray, as this belief is possibly linked to old, unhealed wounds from your past. Or perhaps you've engaged in actions that you know, deep down, aren't the right path for you. If so, you have a beautiful opportunity to heal something that may have been deeply hidden.

The ego doesn't want us to know Jesus, because the ego is terrified of the powerful healing love he offers. So the ego may try to distract you from reading this book. Please don't allow the ego to interfere (or should I say "inner fear") with your spiritual path!

If you're feeling lonely or lost, please take the Lord's hand and let him help you. Jesus is real, and he *wants* to help you. Don't push away what could be your greatest friendship and the cure for loneliness: the one who will help you to love and take care of yourself, and find your life purpose and a clear connection with God—the greatest feeling of blissful comfort imaginable.

The following prayer may help:

*Lord, I want to know the real you,*
*but I'm nervous about getting hurt, judged, or disappointed.*
*Can you help me overcome my fears about you so that*
*I can feel your guidance, healing, and love?*

As Jesus said in John 16:33: "I have told you all this so that you may have peace in me. Here on earth you will have many trials and sorrows. But take heart, because I have overcome the world."

---

## CELEBRATE NEW LIFE IN THE NEW YEAR

All around the world, family and friends gather to celebrate the arrival of a new year. You can probably sense a collective excitement and anticipation for new intentions and dreams, as well as the relief that comes from letting go of things that weren't serving you. You may also have some questions: *Will this year go better than last? Will my soul mate arrive? Will my career change? Will my health hold up? Will my big break come?*

Darling, as you head into this year, rest assured that God is on your side. He wants you to trust that he cares for you. He's made a way for his children to live a new kind of life in Jesus Christ: a life filled with peace and joy, the kind of life in which you commune with him at a deeper level, resting in his peaceful presence.

Will trials come? Perhaps. Will things go as planned? Maybe not. But each morning, rise giving praise to the Almighty Creator for his goodness, mercy, and faithfulness. Make a commitment to do your best to live from a centered place in him each day, mindful of his presence. Resolve to dig deep into his holy Word, inviting Spirit to fill you with renewed love, peace, and joy.

May this be the year when your heart opens more to the pure love and strength that God offers to you!

### Good Morning, Lord

*Please help me maintain my optimism and faith throughout this year, and stay by my side at each moment.*

*"This means that anyone who belongs to Christ has become a new person. The old life is gone; a new life has begun!"*

2 CORINTHIANS 5:17

# Refresh Your Soul-Garden Daily

Gardeners understand the law of sowing and reaping. Sow good seeds, water them regularly, pull the weeds, and you'll reap an abundant garden. The Word of God states that, as a believer, you're much like a garden. If you, being the good seed that you are, regularly hydrate yourself with the water of the Word, you'll grow a spiritual garden bursting with blessings. On the other hand, if you neglect God and the Word, you may be left with a bare plot of land.

Jesus of Nazareth is the Master Gardener. He is the nutrient that your spiritual garden needs to grow healthy, abundant fruit. He rains down his Spirit in times of drought and upholds you when the strong winds blow.

Refresh your soul-garden each morning with God and his Word. If you're weary, soak in his life-giving presence. If you're sad, allow his spiritual rain to wash away your tears. If you're not sure what to do in a situation, allow the wind of his spirit and angels to direct your path. Today, allow God to be your spiritual sustenance.

### Good Morning, Lord

*Please nourish my soul and replenish my body
with your pure love, compassion, and understanding.*

*"The Lord will guide you continually, giving you water when
you are dry and restoring your strength. You will be like a
well-watered garden, like an ever-flowing spring."*

Isaiah 58:11

# WHEN IN DOUBT, BELIEVE ANYWAY

Along life's journey, you may sometimes find yourself struggling with doubt. You may doubt yourself, others, and maybe even your faith. It may feel as if you're lost in the wilderness, hungry and thirsty, awaiting some sort of sign from God. The heart can certainly feel heavy at such times.

You may wonder how you can replace that doubt with faith. How can you have assurance that God is real and present—that Jesus is alive and well, and interested in a personal relationship with you?

In a letter written to believers and skeptics alike, the apostle John states that he is an eyewitness to the reality of Jesus Christ of Nazareth. He's seen the "Word of life" in person and urges those who struggle with doubt to trust his testimony. He welcomes them into fellowship with God and the church, assuring them that even if they haven't seen Jesus in person, they can believe based on his own firsthand account.

Dear one, you too can hold on to faith even when you experience confusion or don't feel that God is near. Even when you're lost or heavy hearted. Begin each morning with God's Word, and take time regularly to enjoy the fellowship of believers. Just as a hot coal can ignite fire in those nearby, so too can the Word and the witness of another inflame your heart.

## Good Morning, Lord

*Please guide my day so that I can feel your presence, surrounding me with other believers and your reassuring Word.*

---

*"We proclaim to you the one who existed from the beginning, whom we have heard and seen. We saw him with our own eyes and touched him with our own hands. He is the Word of life. This one who is life itself was revealed to us, and we have seen him. And now we testify and proclaim to you that he is the one who is eternal life. He was with the Father, and then he was revealed to us."*

1 JOHN 1:1–2

# GOD'S WORD IS THE
# ULTIMATE INSTRUCTION MANUAL

Some people think the Bible is composed of old stories that have no relevance today. In fact, the sacred text is full of wise teachings that are useful for navigating life. Sure, humans may have penned it, and it has been translated many times, but it was the Spirit of God writing through the authors and guiding the translations. It was "God-breathed," with God using people to record a practical instruction manual for humankind.

The wisdom and guidance in the Bible applies to plenty of practical issues that humankind contends with regularly. Scripture has answers regarding relationships, parenting, finances, communication, emotions, business, temptation, and so much more.

The Word of God can illuminate and guide your path. It will serve as your instruction manual, equipping you to be who you are in God and do what he has called you to do. The more you consistently read it, the more it supernaturally speaks to you and provides protective insulation.

So, dear friend, please dig into the Bible and seek direction for your life. Hold fast to the truths you learn, as they are practical, relevant, and good. The Bible is a paradise replete with glorious nuggets of wisdom. Sit with it daily with an open heart and allow it to strengthen and guide you in all your ways.

## Good Morning, Lord

*Please guide my scriptural reading and learning,
and show me my best path of spiritual study.*

*"All Scripture is inspired by God and is useful to teach us what is true and to make us realize what is wrong in our lives. It corrects us when we are wrong and teaches us to do what is right."*

2 TIMOTHY 3:16

# FAITH IS MORE THAN POSITIVE THINKING

As we reviewed in yesterday's devotion, scripture is inspired by God and can help us as believers navigate life here on Earth. The book of Romans states that as we attend to the Word of God, our faith will increase. Our confidence will soar. Who couldn't use more faith and confidence in their lives?

After all, living in doubt, lack, and fear is certainly *not* living up to our potential. We can't inspire others if we're cloaked in fears.

Perhaps you've skipped reading the Word of God for a while; perhaps you had issues with the Book. But if you take the time to nourish your soul with it, you'll notice your faith growing. You'll be able to look at your problems with a new perspective—with *God's* perspective, knowing that he is well able to help you through them.

Faith is more than positive thinking; it is stepping into God's power, knowing for certain that he will do as he says. Faith is learning God's promises and standing on them even if the mountain you're facing is enormous. Faith, dear one, is your ticket to peace and joy, and the good news is that you can grow it each day as you direct your attention to the Word of God.

## Good Morning, Lord

*Please guide my steps today so that my words,*
*thoughts, and actions are testimonies of faith.*

*"So faith comes from hearing, that is,*
*hearing the Good News about Christ."*

ROMANS 10:17

# Praise God for His Greatness

The psalmist David was a master of celebration, and scripture records him belting out praise and worship to God quite often. David knew how powerful and grand God was. He'd witnessed God's mighty acts, and as a result, he couldn't help but resound with enormous praise.

God is so much bigger than we can even imagine. No matter how many things we discover about him on this journey, we'll never really understand the depths of him while we're in this earthly body. He's like a fathomless ocean whose depths cannot be measured.

Just as David set his heart on giving great praise to God each day, let this be your aim. Whether you're alone or with a community, let your heart burn with passion for the Creator. Thank him for his mercy and proclaim his mighty acts, for he is worthy of praise!

Great is God, and greatly to be praised!

### Good Morning, Lord

*Please help me feel your vast limitlessness and to understand that with you, everything is possible.*

---

*"Great is the Lord! He is most worthy of praise!
No one can measure his greatness. Let each
generation tell its children of your mighty acts;
let them proclaim your power."*

Psalm 145:3–4

# What Is the Reason for Your Happiness?

When someone asks me how I can walk in peace and joy even when trials come, I am delighted to tell them that my faith in God is the reason. Even during challenging times, I choose to put my hope in our Heavenly Father, Jesus, Holy Spirit, and God's beloved angels.

Chances are that people are observing you too, including your family, friends, and coworkers. There may come a time when you're questioned about your faith or why you believe what you do. Some may even wonder how you can walk around so optimistic and full of joy. What will you tell them? To what or whom will you give credit for your demeanor?

Scripture tells us to be ready to respond to such questions in humility. Offer up a gentle answer. Let others know that it's God's Spirit in you that fills you with hope, faith, and joy. There's absolutely no shame in proclaiming the goodness that your Heavenly Father bestows on you.

Today, as you go about your day, keep your heart set on God. Allow his joy to fill you to overflowing. Trust that he's with you every moment. Should others ask you about your joy, gladly share with them the reason for your happiness.

## Good Morning, Lord

*Thank you for filling my life with your presence, your love, and your peace.*

*"Instead, you must worship Christ as Lord of your life. And if someone asks about your hope as a believer, always be ready to explain it."*

1 Peter 3:15

# Resist the Temptation to Worry

Do you worry about things more often than you'd like? Is your anxiety level high? Beloved one, the fear associated with chronic worry can paralyze you. It can sap your energy and even cause health issues. Fortunately, worry is a mental habit that can be broken when you put your full trust in God. It's a lower energy that can be washed away with God's Word.

The story of Peter stepping out of the boat onto water is a great example here. When his eyes were on Jesus, he miraculously walked on the water, but when he turned his attention to the fierce winds, fear overtook him and he began to sink. Jesus, being the Rescuer that he is, reached out and saved Peter.

In the same way, when you're afraid of "sinking," worried about your relationship, job, finances, health, and so on, pause and ask yourself, "Am I looking at Jesus here or the problem? Where is my trust?"

Scripture tells us to live in the present moment, leaving the future to God. Resist the temptation to worry today. Trust that no matter what is going on in your life or in the world, you can lean on Spirit each moment for peace. Worry will not help you, but God will! His Spirit can give you internal power that will calm your nerves. Let this truth buoy you up as you go about your day, keeping your eyes fixed on Jesus.

## Good Morning, Lord

*Please hold my hands, support me, and keep
me above the water safely with you.*

*"So don't worry about tomorrow, for tomorrow will bring
its own worries. Today's trouble is enough for today."*

**Matthew 6:34**

# LET YOUR WORDS SUPPORT YOUR ACTIONS

Staying true to your promises can make such a positive impact on others. You've likely experienced someone giving you their word but not following through with it. This may have left you feeling sad, mad, bitter, or distrustful. It's not always easy to tell the truth or commit to promises, but doing so exemplifies good character and pleases God. Just as God is faithful to his promises, so he desires his children to do the same.

James tells us, "Let your 'yes' be 'yes,' and your 'no,' 'no.'" This means that when you commit to do something for someone, see it through. If you commit to stop doing something, stop.

Granted, following through might not always happen. Sometimes we change our minds or realize we bit off more than we can chew. A good practice is to sit with each issue before you make a promise or commitment. Really gauge whether you can be true to your word before answering. If you don't want to do something, respectfully decline and feel good about your decision. That's practicing self-care.

This week, pay attention to how you respond when others ask you for something. If you're not sure, ask God for direction and tune in to your own truth.

## Good Morning, Lord

*Please help me follow through on the promises
that I make to you, myself, and others.*

*"But above all things, my brothers, don't swear—
not by heaven, or by the earth, or by any other oath;
but let your 'yes' be 'yes,' and your 'no,' 'no';
so that you don't fall into hypocrisy."*

**JAMES 5:12 (WEB)**

# CONSIDER THE WISE WAYS OF THE ANTS

Have you ever taken time to stop and observe ants? Have you noticed how they tend to march aligned in a single file? How they rebuild their mound within a few days after it's been knocked down? We can learn so many valuable lessons from ants. They're diligent, work together, plan ahead, store surplus, and travel high and low in order to establish stable resources. They work long hours in the summer, gathering plenty of food to sustain them through the winter.

God's Word tells us to consider the ways of the ant, as we can glean valuable life lessons by doing so. Yes, God is faithful to provide for our needs, but we also have a part to play. To thrive and to achieve goals, observe the ants and apply their work ethic to your life. Make a commitment to model traits like discipline, self-motivation, and drive.

Consider the ant's ways in your personal and spiritual life. Procrastination will not get anyone far. Choose a solid work ethic, performing each task as if for the Lord. Be wise with your finances, doing your best and trusting God for the rest. As believers, we can individually and collectively work together, just like the ants, to continue building God's Kingdom here on earth.

### ❧ *Good Morning, Lord* ❧

*Thank you for helping me feel motivated and confident about my
work projects, and helping me have the energy and
time to focus upon my priorities.*

---

*"Take a lesson from the ants, you lazybones.
Learn from their ways and become wise!"*

PROVERBS 6:6

## SET YOUR HEART ABLAZE FOR GOD

In the book of Luke, we find Cleopas and another disciple walking toward Emmaus shortly after Jesus had been crucified. They were discussing the crucifixion, concerned that maybe Jesus wasn't really the Messiah who was sent to redeem Israel. Jesus, who was alive and well, joined them on their walk, but they did not recognize him.

Once Jesus broke bread with them, the disciples' eyes were opened and they recognized him. Jesus shared many things about scripture and God's plan. Later that evening, they remembered how their hearts had been burning when they were walking with Jesus on the road. They could feel something was different about this man.

There's something about spending time with Jesus and the scriptures that will get *your* heart burning, too. It's like Jesus is the match that can set fire to your heart in a way that helps you passionately serve God and man.

If you find yourself struggling with apathy or lack of zeal, get into God's Word and spend some quality time with Jesus of Nazareth. As you do, God's Spirit will ignite you. You'll feel a love-burn within your heart throughout the day, knowing that Jesus is alive and fully present with you.

### Good Morning, Lord

*Please help me open my heart to your love
and feel your presence near me always.*

---

*"They said to each other, 'Didn't our hearts
burn within us as he talked with us on the road
and explained the Scriptures to us?'"*

LUKE 24:32

# Protect Yourself in God's Armor

There's no doubt we're going to face things in this world that are deceptive or dangerous. Spiritual attacks can certainly occur. Now, I know this contradicts the idea that positive thinking is all we need to live in safety and bliss, but the truth is that there *are* lower energies out to thwart God's plans.

How do we move forward while protecting ourselves? Well, just as a soldier dons protection from head to toe, so should we put on the whole armor of God to shield us from the lower energies of the world. There is a battle upon Earth, with positive and negative spiritual forces clashing. There are real powers of darkness looking to conquer vulnerable and trusting people. The Word tells us to therefore clothe ourselves in God's armor so that we can walk in safety and confidence each day. This armor can protect us from people or circumstances that might cause pain or suffering.

Every morning, consciously ask Holy Spirit to help you suit up with the full armor of God, clothing yourself in righteousness, truth, peace, and faith. This will help you to better discern things like whom you should spend time with, what business connections to make, whom to date, where to go, and whom to set firm boundaries with.

Right now, protect yourself with God's armor, so you can go forth today confident that God's got you covered.

### ∼ Good Morning, Lord ∼

*Please help me be shielded and protected from darkness in all ways.*

---

*"Put on all of God's armor so that you will be able to stand firm against all strategies of the devil. For we are not fighting against flesh-and-blood enemies, but against evil rulers and authorities of the unseen world, against mighty powers in this dark world, and against evil spirits in the heavenly places."*

Ephesians 6:11–12

# There Is No Fear in God

Living in fear can really take a toll. Granted, there are times when life throws some mighty big things our way, but fear is an energy we can conquer with God. Imagine a little boy, scared and alone. Then his dad shows up, and suddenly that little boy stands tall, all fear gone.

The psalmist David faced plenty of frightening moments, oftentimes surrounded by enemies. He had every logical reason to be afraid, but he leaned on God for his protection and strength. He looked at his enemies and acknowledged them; rather than cowering in fear, he boldly declared that his faith rested in the God of Israel.

There are countless things people fear, including rejection, sickness, not having enough, divorce, and death. But, darling, God loves you so much that he does not want you going around holding on to fear. He wants you to lean on him and trust that he will stand up for you. He will make a way. He will help you release fearful emotions, trusting that he has everything under control.

You're not alone. You may have enemies or challenging circumstances surrounding you, but you can put your hope and trust in the Lord. You can place your faith in God, choosing to believe that all things are working out for you. God is the fortress that will protect and defend you. Today, child of God, let your Heavenly Father stand up for you so you can go about your day in peace and joy.

## Good Morning, Lord

*I feel worried about* [describe fears], *and I need your help, please, to lift these fears and restore my faith and peace.*

---

*"The Lord is my light and my salvation—so why should I be afraid? The Lord is my fortress, protecting me from danger, so why should I tremble?"*

**Psalm 27:1**

# In Christ Jesus, You Are Enough

Chances are, you've felt guilty about something you've said or done in the past. Maybe you made a decision that hurt another, or maybe you regret not doing something. Over the years, many people have come to me carrying long-term guilt that was robbing them of their peace and joy.

We know that judgment is frowned upon, and spiritual people are usually pretty good at avoiding it. The toughest part for many is self-condemnation. It's that part of you that feels like you're never doing enough or, worse, that *you're* not enough.

Are you carrying around guilt from the past? Are you working hard to try to earn approval from others or God yet always coming up short? Do you condemn yourself for making mistakes, not *doing* "enough good," or not *being* "good enough"?

The apostle Paul talks about wanting to do good but sometimes finding himself caving to temptation or missing the mark. The same thing can happen to us, too, at times. We can certainly miss the mark. We can say or do things that hurt others and ourselves, but God is a merciful and gracious Father. He is compassionate, dispensing mercy over judgment.

Right now, dear one, please let that guilt go. Give it to God, and in return receive grace and mercy. God knows your heart. He sees that you are good. In Christ Jesus, you are loved and you are enough.

### Good Morning, Lord

*Thank you for your mercy and compassion, and please help me show myself mercy and compassion.*

*"So now there is no condemnation for those who belong to Christ Jesus. And because you belong to him, the power of the life-giving Spirit has freed you from the power of sin that leads to death."*

**Romans 8:1–2**

# STRIVE TO BECOME MORE LIKE JESUS

All of us come into this world innocent and pure. Look at any baby, and you see preciousness and purity. Over time, personalities or egos are formed; as we grow up, we can get lost in a sea of forgetfulness about our true spiritual identity. We were created with a mind, body, *and* spirit, yet we can lose sight of the spiritual part of us at times.

God sent his Son, Spirit, and Word to help us recover what we think we've lost: our core essence. He desires that, as followers of Jesus, we grow spiritually, becoming more like Jesus. Part of this spiritual-growth process is adopting values and attributes that Jesus modeled. As we conform to Jesus's image, we exchange anger for peace, selfishness for generosity. We replace pride with humility, hate with love, insecurity with confidence in God.

Sweetheart, the flesh will be tempted to hold on to the lower energies, so remember that you're here on God's mission. This life *is* about you, but it's *more* about God's will for your life. You're here to learn lessons that can aid you in your spiritual transformation, becoming more like Jesus.

Today, as you continue your journey with God, ask Holy Spirit to help you become more like Jesus. Embody the fruits of the Spirit as you go about your day, offering love, peace, patience, kindness, and gentleness to all you meet.

## Good Morning, Lord

*Thank you for showing me the way to a life of joy,*
*purpose, and meaning. I aspire to be like you.*

*"For God knew his people in advance, and he chose them*
*to become like his Son, so that his Son would be the*
*firstborn among many brothers and sisters."*

ROMANS 8:29

# GROWING MORE LIKE JESUS EVERY DAY

A large part of Jesus's ministry was teaching, but he didn't approach the leaders of the day to become his disciples. Instead, he approached common men and requested that *they* follow him. The men could have refused, but they had a sense that Jesus was no ordinary man. When they made a commitment to follow Jesus, they opened their hearts to learn a new way of life. They had to leave their jobs, homes, and families. They had to face persecution, stretch out of their comfort zone, and trust that Jesus was telling them the truth about our Father and helping them grow spiritually.

Regardless of what spiritual path people are on, there will be those who teach harmful material. Spiritual maturity helps us not to chase after every new guru who seems to have all the answers, yet may not necessarily be on the path that leads to God.

God wants his children to grow up spiritually, conforming to the image of Jesus of Nazareth. The Spirit of God is here to work in us, helping us become more loving and compassionate. Just as Jesus's disciples made a commitment to follow him and model his ways, please make a fresh commitment each morning to do the same. In the 1990s, it became widely popular for Christians to ask themselves, "WWJD: What Would Jesus Do?" The question is equally valid today.

 *Good Morning, Lord*

*Please help me be a true follower of your ways
and model you in all that I say, think, and do.*

---

*"Then we will no longer be immature like children. We won't be
tossed and blown about by every wind of new teaching. We will
not be influenced when people try to trick us with lies so clever
they sound like the truth. Instead, we will speak the truth
in love, growing in every way more and more like Christ,
who is the head of his body, the church."*

EPHESIANS 4:14–15

# TRIALS CAN BECOME A SPRINGBOARD INTO AN AWAKENING

This life journey we all share can sometimes involve problems and pain. The question is: How will you choose to *be* in the midst of your trials? Will you complain and worry, or will you turn your attention toward God? Will you ask him to be with you in the fire and show you the opportunity for growth?

Even in the darkest night of the soul, God is helping behind the scenes. Our problems can both draw us closer to God and ultimately bring deeper levels of joy. Many have told me that their biggest trial in life later became the springboard to their spiritual awakening. Sure, the outside was rough, but what was going on inside them was miraculous. They were able to dig deep and get to the root of some big issues; heal old wounds; and form a stronger connection with God, Jesus, Holy Spirit, guardian angels, and other people.

Yes, trials may come, but God will not let them overtake you. You're building spiritual maturity gradually and learning lessons. Trust that God is with you, steering you away from harmful things or attachments that don't serve you. This mountain you're approaching may be challenging to climb, but Holy Spirit will help you ascend step-by-step. And once you reach that peak, you'll better see the larger picture. You'll be jubilant in your "Aha" moment, understanding why you had these experiences.

## Good Morning, Lord

*Thank you for helping me have the grace*
*of acceptance and trusting in God.*

*"For our present troubles are small and won't last very long. Yet they produce for us a glory that vastly outweighs them and will last forever!"*

**2 CORINTHIANS 4:17**

# DO YOU LOVE OUTSIDE YOUR CIRCLE?

Jesus loved to teach large crowds the ways of the Kingdom of God. He wanted to see change effected in individual hearts as well as the collective. In the Sermon on the Mount, Jesus paints a portrait of characteristics that believers ought to exemplify. He wants his followers to understand that they are called to be a light in the darkness. Hope for the hopeless. A friend for the lonely.

Essentially, he says, "If you only accept and love your circle of friends, how are you different from anyone else?" True. Loving people you like is easy, but the kind of love that God calls us to is *unconditional* love for all people. It's going the extra mile even for those who are not your friends. It's the commitment to make a difference in people's lives. Make someone's day by giving them a compliment or help them out in some way. Invite them over for fellowship. *Pray for them.*

It's this type of love that we are to extend to the world. It's this kind of love that strips us of ego, or pride. It reduces selfishness and judgment. Thus, God's Kingdom is built one by one, with men, women, and children seeing and feeling God's love through us. Today, allow God's light to shine through you. Lavish his kind of love on *all* you meet.

## Good Morning, Lord

*Thank you for loving all beings through my open heart, and reminding me that everyone is part of my spiritual family.*

*"If you love only those who love you, what reward is there for that? Even corrupt tax collectors do that much. If you are kind only to your friends, how are you different from anyone else?"*

MATTHEW 5:46–47

# EVERY LETDOWN IS AN OPPORTUNITY FOR GROWTH

Life doesn't always go as planned. There are times when we may stumble, become disheartened, hit a wall, or take a wrong turn. Yet the spiritual truth is that everything we experience is an opportunity for growth. Every letdown, mistake, rejection, heartache, emotional breakdown, and harsh word can help us learn valuable life lessons. They're also opportunities to increase faith.

You may be in a challenging situation right now. Maybe you're going through a breakup, or your kids are struggling. Perhaps you're concerned financially or healthwise. You're not sure what to do. You wonder how much longer you can take it.

Sweetheart, God is with you. He's aware of everything going on in your life right now. Rest assured that he is supporting your steps. He's got your back. He sees your heart. He hears your prayers. This may be uncomfortable, but you've got to move forward in faith. Remain confident that God is watching over you today, that his Spirit is in you, and that guardian angels surround you with their loving presence.

### ✑ *Good Morning, Lord* ✑

*Please give me the strength to face my challenges, and help me to stay filled with the faith that you are supporting me.*

*"The Lord directs the steps of the godly.
He delights in every detail of their lives."*

**PSALM 37:23**

# FOLLOW JESUS CHRIST OF NAZARETH

There are spiritual teachers and philosophies out there that lead people astray. Even with good intent, their messages can be confusing or offer false promises that leave people feeling disheartened or disillusioned. The Word of God states that we should not believe every spirit or teaching that comes our way, as there are those lower energies or powers that are rooted in darkness. These spirits can blind people from the absolute truth found in God and his Son, Jesus.

Just as a good parent sets boundaries and guidelines for children, so did our Heavenly Father send Jesus to set guidelines for humankind. For even the freest of spirits out there, having guidelines can be very helpful. Is there more than one pathway to love? Yes, but if a teaching denies that Jesus was both divine and human simultaneously, it may lead people to believe in something less than the truth.

Jesus of Nazareth is God's Son, who came to walk among men and women, teaching them about his Father and the Kingdom of God. It is this Jesus, through the power of his Spirit, that will lead you back to your Heavenly Father. If you've been wandering or drifting, not sure what to believe, please follow the ways of Jesus Christ, Son of God. God assures you that in doing so you'll never be led astray.

## Good Morning, Lord

*Thank you for teaching me how to be spiritually discerning so that I follow only God's will.*

---

*"This is how we know if they have the Spirit of God: If a person claiming to be a prophet acknowledges that Jesus Christ came in a real body, that person has the Spirit of God."*

1 JOHN 4:2

# Consciously Cultivate Community

Loneliness is common in every age-group. In general, most people feel lonely at times, but *chronic* loneliness can cause intense suffering. It can lead to apathy, depression, anger, and more. In an age where so many are isolating themselves due to technology, God desires his children to commit to cultivating authentic community or fellowship with others. This, dear one, is a way we can all join to help alleviate loneliness.

The first-century church was highly devoted to taking time to develop fellowship. Followers committed to sharing meals, learning together, and simply getting to know each other on a personal basis. They understood that God desired his children to spend quality time together.

Sure, life gets busy. But let's remember that sharing the journey with others delights our Heavenly Father. Cultivating authentic community is a discipline that God wants us to commit to on a regular basis. As we do, more love will be shared, more hearts will feel fulfilled, and loneliness will be abated.

As you begin this day, gauge the quantity and quality of your fellowship with others. If it has been lacking, make a fresh commitment to reach out to those whom God lays on your heart's doorstop. If you've been lonely, take that first step of reaching out to another; they may be lonely, too! Together, my friend, with God as our Source, we can all make a big difference in the world as we consciously cultivate community.

### Good Morning, Lord

*Please guide me to meaningful and healthy friendships with a foundation of sharing God's love.*

*"All the believers devoted themselves to the apostles' teaching, and to fellowship, and to sharing in meals (including the Lord's Supper), and to prayer."*

ACTS 2:42

# REMAIN JOYFULLY STEADFAST IN GOD

Have you ever been with someone who seems to have it all together, but when a challenge comes their way, they lose it? They freak out, whine, yell, curse, or shut down while you stare in amazement at their reaction.

Tests and trials occur in life, and that's when someone shows their true colors. It's during these difficult periods that we can grumble and give up—or see hardship as an opportunity to turn to God. The pain, anger, confusion, or anxiety we feel can be transformed into something meaningful for the good of all.

James tells us that as followers of Jesus, we should choose to feel optimistic and joyful when tests and trials knock on the door. Why? Because those are the times that God can teach us incredible things about him, ourselves, and others. It is then that we can choose to walk in faith, seeing with God's eyes instead of our own. We can remain mindful of God's ways and gauge just how mature our spirituality really is.

Dear one, if you're going through a trial right now, choose to trust that God will see you through it. His Spirit and angels are with you, strengthening you and helping you persevere. Through this trial, you're growing spiritually. You're learning lessons that you might have never learned had it not shown up. Today, remain joyfully steadfast in him, knowing that you are indeed becoming more like Jesus each day.

## ∽ *Good Morning, Lord* ∾

*Please hold me steady during the trials of my life; remind me to trust in the blessings, support, and lessons that God is offering to me.*

*"Dear brothers and sisters, when troubles of any kind come your way, consider it an opportunity for great joy. For you know that when your faith is tested, your endurance has a chance to grow."*

JAMES 1:2–3

# GOD IS WATCHING OVER YOU

You can feel confident that whatever happens, you will be supported by God's strength. He doesn't promise a perfect life from earthly standards, but he does promise a spiritually perfect life. As long as you continually check in with God through prayer and meditation—and follow his guidance—you have nothing to worry about.

God has equipped you with so much help, available the moment that you ask for and accept it. Consider the monumental team that your Creator has assigned to you: the Holy Spirit, Jesus, Archangel Michael, your guardian angels . . . They're all available 24 hours a day, seven days a week, free of charge.

With all this help, how could you doubt? The more you ask for help, the more confident you grow. The more often you pray, the safer and more secure you feel.

### *Good Morning, Lord*

*Please hold me tightly and help me feel safe and secure. Please help me trust, have confidence, and be filled with faith that you are guiding and watching over all of us.*

*"For God has not given us a spirit of fear and timidity, but of power, love, and self-discipline."*

2 TIMOTHY 1:7

## ADOPT GOD'S MIND-SET

Do you ever look back on a period of your life and ask, *What was I thinking?* Most of us have shaken our heads (hopefully with a smile) at something we've said or done, and wondered what was going on in our minds.

Having an optimistic mind-set is certainly advantageous. However, just thinking positive thoughts isn't enough to bring forth the deeper spiritual transformation you desire. This is why someone who recites affirmations daily may still struggle with negativity, emotional issues, and core wounds year after year. Positive thinking keeps you in your head, but God's Word and ways can drop down into your heart, fostering authentic change that lasts.

God tells us to renew our minds according to his Word. He instructs us to resist the temptation to adopt the ways of the world. The truth is, as a follower of Jesus, you may lead a life that looks different from others', and that's all right. People may ridicule or judge you, but as you commit to becoming increasingly like Jesus, more love and light will spread throughout the world. I think we can *all* welcome that.

Ask God to reveal to you whether you're giving more thought to the ways of the world or to his will for your life. Is how you spend your time helping you show up in the world as God desires? Take an honest inventory. Commit to renewing your mind-set according to God's Word, allowing Holy Spirit to guide and assist you.

### *Good Morning, Lord*

*Thank you for helping me focus upon spiritual priorities and trust that you will guide me and support my earthly needs.*

*"And I will give you a new heart, and I will put a new spirit in you. I will take out your stony, stubborn heart and give you a tender, responsive heart."*

EZEKIEL 36:26

# Divine Order through God's Wisdom

If you ever accidentally disturb an ant mound, please take a moment to watch the ants. Observe their chaotic behavior. Underground, they have highly ordered, choreographed colonies where they're committed to working in harmony. However, when they're threatened, it's pandemonium.

Perhaps this is how our Creator sees humanity at times. Sure, he's in control. Yet, as freewill beings, we don't always look to God for wisdom or to his Word for guidance. And at times, we succumb to fear and forget to turn to God for help.

Fortunately, God has promised to guide everyone through his Word and Spirit. As you turn toward him and the scriptures, you receive clear direction, inspiration, support, and helpful guidelines. When tests, trials, and turmoil show up in your life, God sends the Holy Spirit to reveal the wisdom you need in order to get through or take the next step.

God is *omnipresent*, meaning "everywhere." He cares about you. If you need wisdom and guidance, ask him right now and expect to hear from him today. The message may come through his Word, your guardian angel, a good friend, or a strong feeling, but rest assured, he *will* direct you.

## Good Morning, Lord

*Thank you for walking beside me today,
reminding me to pause and pray for God's guidance
before making decisions or taking action.*

*"If you need wisdom, ask our generous God, and he will
give it to you. He will not rebuke you for asking."*

**James 1:5**

# Trust Even When You Don't Understand

Chances are, you've been hurt by people. You may be familiar with how the sting of betrayal can prompt people to distrust and build sturdy walls to protect their hearts. Some have a tough time trusting God, too. They may feel hurt because God could have prevented something painful but didn't. Some might have strong negative feelings about patriarchy, people within the church, or the history of religion. Regardless of the reason, they've distanced themselves from God.

If there's one thing I've learned, it's that we will never fully understand God or this life while we're in these earthly bodies. Yes, we can gain insight and revelation. Yes, we can tap into the heavenly realms and feel the presence of Jesus and our guardian angels. However, no one can fully wrap their heads around the vastness of God's divine nature and ways of being. No matter what we do, sometimes we just won't understand why certain things happen.

You may be struggling with confusion, distrust, or skepticism right now. Your faith level might be super low. But, dear one, God wants you to fully trust that he is on your side. He wants you to lean on him even when you have no idea what's going on and there seems to be no way out.

Today, exercise your faith muscles regularly. Resist the temptation to seek intellectual comprehension. Go to your Father like a child runs to their daddy, innocently believing he is working all things out for the greater good. Because, beautiful soul, he is.

### ∼ Good Morning, Lord ∼

*Please help me restore my faith and trust in God,*
*and learn to lean upon him for guidance and support.*

*"Trust in the Lord with all your heart; do not depend on*
*your own understanding. Seek his will in all you do,*
*and he will show you which path to take."*

Proverbs 3:5–6

# FAITH ALLOWS YOU TO REST IN GOD

"Just have faith, dear. Everything will be all right."

We hear these words at times from those who want to help us feel better. You might hear them and think, *But you don't know what's going on! You don't know that for sure! Things right now are* horrible! Yes, doubt creeps in at times, even for those whose faith seems insurmountable.

Paul talks about faith in Romans. He tells readers that God has given every person a measure of faith, and when it is exercised, God's Kingdom will grow. Why? Because when we're walking in faith in God, we can let go. We can take a deep breath and exhale all anxiety and stress. This frees up our mental and emotional energy so we can go about doing what God has called each of us to do, such as teaching, serving, encouraging, or lavishing love.

Maybe you think it's too challenging to believe God over your visible circumstances, but Jesus said faith, even as tiny as a mustard seed, can move mountains. Don't be concerned if you feel that your faith is low; you can certainly grow it. Consciously practice putting your faith in God when it comes to small *and* big things today. Believe that God is at work behind *every* scene.

Spending time with his Word will also increase your faith, so commit to regular devotion time. Surrender to God each morning, relying on him fully, and give yourself permission to rest in God. This, dear one, makes for a beautiful day.

## Good Morning, Lord

*Please help me feel your presence and strength in order to build a solid foundation of faith and trust in God's support.*

---

*"'You don't have enough faith,' Jesus told them. 'I tell you the truth, if you had faith even as small as a mustard seed, you could say to this mountain, "Move from here to there," and it would move. Nothing would be impossible.'"*

MATTHEW 17:20

## LET COMPASSION LEAD YOU

Jesus was a very popular man in his time. People near and far had heard about this prophet who claimed to be the Son of God, sent to redeem mankind. Many people wanted to check him out for themselves. Some were skeptics, while others believed his claims, often going to him for prayer, healing, or advice. Although people had different motives for seeking Jesus, the truth is that masses went to him in need of *something*.

He could have been annoyed by the fact that he couldn't go anywhere without someone tugging on his sleeve. He could have disguised himself when out and about. But do you know what he did? He saw the masses with his heart. He saw that so many of them were discouraged, weary, sick, and hurting.

The Word says he was moved with compassion for them. He was attuned to their suffering and instead of just saying, "Oh, you'll be okay," he spent time with them. He sat with them; shared meals with them; and laid his healing hands on them, ministering empathy, kindness, tenderness, hope, and love.

Empathetic altruism can certainly help lessen suffering in the world. Dear one, be like Jesus and consciously choose to embody compassion. See those who are lost, miserable, sick, or suffering as Jesus sees them, and offer empathy, comfort, and encouragement.

### Good Morning, Lord

*I am dedicating today to walking and working beside you in order to help and heal others who are in need.*

---

*"When he saw the crowds, he had compassion on them because they were confused and helpless, like sheep without a shepherd."*

MATTHEW 9:36

# GOD'S WISDOM VS. EARTHLY WISDOM

Have you ever wanted to do something but didn't feel you had enough training, knowledge, or skills to do it? A lot of people go around saying, "If only I had the [*degree, resources, connections,* etc.], I could do so much good in the world."

I imagine that men and women in the days of Jesus's earthly ministry felt the same. They may have thought, *If only I were a scholar, I could be a disciple of Jesus.* But God's wisdom is not the world's wisdom. God looks beyond titles, education, age, appearance, and income when it comes to using people in powerful ways to advance his Kingdom.

The apostle Paul addresses this in his letter to the Corinthians. He reminds them that God called them, even though most of them were ordinary, common people. They were not leaders or well-known celebrities. They were tradesmen, slaves, fathers, and mothers who might have been easily overlooked by someone using human achievements as qualifications.

But Jesus saw their hearts. He saw their willingness to rely upon God and not upon themselves. And this is how God looks at you, darling. He sees your humble heart seeking to live a life that is pleasing to him. No matter what your background, God has chosen you to be his beloved. Trust that as you rely on his Spirit, you can and will show up in mighty ways in your world.

 *Good Morning, Lord*

*Please help me release self-doubts and
believe in myself as you believe in me.*

---

*"Remember, dear brothers and sisters,
that few of you were wise in the world's eyes or
powerful or wealthy when God called you."*

1 CORINTHIANS 1:26

## REPLACE FEAR WITH FAITH

Not many people talk about their deepest, darkest fears. They may share some of their concerns, but their gravest worries oftentimes lie silent within. It could be an immense fear of death or perhaps a paralyzing fear that if their partner ever really gets to know them, they'll face rejection. Other common fears include sickness, failure, commitment, poverty, and stepping out of the comfort zone.

These lower-energy feelings can take a toll on a soul over time, causing emotional and physical distress. Sometimes the fear may dwell beneath the surface. You may not even realize it's there, yet it can subtly manifest in your attitude or the choices you make.

Dear one, the Son of God came and conquered all the lower energies, including fear. God made a way for us to transmute fear into faith, trusting that he is ultimately in control. God knows your deepest fears and acknowledges them. However, he also says, "Fear not, because I am with you." Today, release every fearful thought to him. Affirm your faith in God alone and let his Spirit of peace abide richly as you go about your day.

### Good Morning, Lord

*Thank you for being with me every minute, boosting my spirits and faith, ensuring a beautiful day.*

*"Don't be afraid, for I am with you. Don't be discouraged, for I am your God. I will strengthen you and help you. I will hold you up with my victorious right hand."*

ISAIAH 41:10

# WELCOME SPIRITUAL GIFTS DESIGNED JUST FOR YOU

Doesn't it feel nice to receive a gift? It helps us feel loved and appreciated. God offers everyone a remarkable gift—the indwelling presence of his Spirit. What a joy to be able to invite God to work through us by Holy Spirit's power!

You may wonder why we need God's Spirit. Isn't intention and hard work enough to do what God wants us to do?

Setting goals and taking action is important, but doing things in our power alone can cause confusion, burnout, or discord. God gives his Spirit graciously to equip and empower believers to share the love of Jesus with the world in a big way. God's Spirit is the vast energy behind the words, teaching, and actions that transform lives and communities.

Each person has been given gifts that will help build the Lord's Kingdom of love. Through the gift of the Spirit, we're able to tap into those gifts, hone them, and exercise them for humanity's and God's sake. Maybe you feel led to teach or preach, to encourage the hopeless or heal broken hearts. Maybe you have a bent for leadership, casting a vision for a better future, offering hospitality to the lonely, or giving to the needy.

If you're not sure what gifts you've been given, ask God to reveal them to you. Then invite Spirit to help you manage and operate in those gifts so that others can be served and God can be glorified.

## Good Morning, Lord

*Thank you for helping me notice, appreciate,*
*and utilize all the gifts that God has given to me.*

*"In his grace, God has given us different gifts for doing certain things well. So if God has given you the ability to prophesy, speak out with as much faith as God has given you. If your gift is serving others, serve them well. If you are a teacher, teach well."*

ROMANS 12:5–7

## KEEP AN ATTITUDE OF PRAYER

Do you think prayer really makes a difference? Do you take the time to pray regularly? The subject of prayer is found throughout scripture, as God desires for his children to relate to him on a personal level. Prayer is a pipeline to the Father, who adores us. The apostle Paul emphasizes prayer in Ephesians 6, advising believers to equip themselves with spiritual armor and then pray without ceasing.

If you struggle with prayer, know that you're not alone. Many people feel like they should pray harder, more often, or "better." The truth is that prayer, just like any type of communication, can vary in form. Prayer is simply talking to God as if you were talking to a close friend. Prayer is revealing your feelings, making requests, offering praise, or silently adoring the Heavenly Father.

God declares that he hears every prayer and that prayer indeed makes a difference. This month, be mindful to keep the lines of communication open between you and God. Each morning, shield yourself with the armor of God and spend some quality time communing with him. Then, as you go about your day, continue to share with your Father, confident that he is listening and responding.

### Good Morning, Lord

*Could you please remind me to pray more often?*

---

*"Pray in the Spirit at all times and on every occasion.*
*Stay alert and be persistent in your prayers*
*for all believers everywhere."*

**EPHESIANS 6:18**

# LET GO AND LET GOD

Many people like the popular recovery slogan "Let go and let God." It's simple to remember and can be quite helpful, but for those who tend to struggle with control issues, it can be more challenging than that. For example, do you ever have "if only" syndrome? *If only _____ would happen, I'd be happy. If only I could have that career, lose weight, or find a good man to marry, I'd smile more. If only I had more money, joy would be my friend.*

This type of thinking sets you up for frustration and disappointment. It's you, trying to control your circumstances rather than allowing God to have full rein. It's you, anxiously striving rather than feeling content where you are, on the way to where you're going.

God desires that we let go of our own will and trust him no matter what we're dealing with. Trust that even if we never achieve our human-made goals, God is leading us to what will truly bring lasting happiness.

Darling, please take a moment to see if you've been entertaining the "if only" mentality, believing that joy lies in externals and in the future. If so, truly let go and allow God's will. This frees you up so you can go about each day in peace, trusting in the goodness and grace of Almighty God.

### ⤖ *Good Morning, Lord* ⤖

*Thank you for helping me shift my intentions
to that which is divinely guided.*

---

*"So humble yourselves under the mighty power of God, and at
the right time he will lift you up in honor. Give all your
worries and cares to God, for he cares about you."*

1 PETER 5:6–7

# BE CONTENT NO MATTER WHAT

If you have children, you may have asked them a time or two, "Why can't you just be content with what you have?" The "more is better" mentality seems to be prevalent—and, yes, it does feel nice to get those things you desire. However, if you're basing your happiness on acquiring "things," you're probably dealing with discontent.

The newest gadget just doesn't thrill you anymore. Looking in your closet full of clothes, you feel you have nothing to wear. This yearning for more (money, vacations, love, toys, and so forth) is common, and you may not even realize you're contending with it.

If you take an honest inventory, Holy Spirit will show you the truth. Things and experiences can never satisfy at a deep and lasting level. Yes, they bring *temporary* happiness or a *momentary* thrill, but that feeling won't last. Things pacify, but God satisfies. Only God can bring enduring contentment. We all want peace, and when we can trust him for that peace over everything else, then we can really sit back and relax, basking in contentment.

How about you? Do you find yourself reaching for something more to satiate a deep hunger within? Do you accumulate more things in an attempt to feel happiness? God says we can learn how to be content in him, no matter what's going on in life. So, dear one, the next time you feel discontentment arise, remember that true peace and joy comes from the Lord.

## Good Morning, Lord

*Thank you for holding my hand and guiding me to true and lasting happiness.*

*"Not that I was ever in need, for I have learned how to be content with whatever I have."*

**PHILIPPIANS 4:11**

# God Provides Trustworthy Answers

How do we know the difference between trustworthy divine guidance and the whims of the ego? Many of us have been diverted down the path of distraction by the ego's instructions, with its hallmark adrenaline-pumping impulsive energy.

In contrast, God's true guidance lands softly in our hearts as a quiet wisdom of knowing what to do. Sometimes there's an inner battle, when the ego argues in favor of a different way. The ego says that its way is easier and more fun than that of true divine guidance.

Fortunately, God's guidance is steady, patient, and repetitive. And deep down, we know it's the right path for us. We may delay following divine guidance, but eventually (sometimes after learning a hard lesson by following the ego), we end up on the path of God's great love.

### *Good Morning, Lord*

*Please help me discern true guidance
and act only as God guides me.*

---

*"But when the Father sends the Advocate as my
representative—that is, the Holy Spirit—he will
teach you everything and will remind you
of everything I have told you."*

John 14:26

# Know Who You Are in Christ Jesus

Over the years, I've met many who battled insecurity, unsure of how to overcome it. Perhaps you can relate. Do you ever feel as if you are not worthy of approaching God? That you're bothering him? Maybe you feel like you're never good enough in his eyes. Fortunately, the Word of God can help combat such feelings. When we turn to the scriptures, we find out just who we are in Christ: a righteous son or daughter of the living God.

Do you find your identity in him or in outward things, like looks, status, or material possessions? Are you prone to self-absorption, thinking mainly about yourself, your problems, or how others perceive you? Darling, overcoming insecurity *is* possible when you become a student of the Word, learning the truth about your nature.

If you rely on people or things to establish your worth, you'll end up disappointed; people constantly change their opinions, and things don't last. But God is steadfast, immovable, and unchangeable, and he wants you to learn who you are in him. You do that by reading his Word, taking what he says and meditating on it until it drops from your head to your heart.

As you align your mind with the mind of Christ, God will begin to heal wounds at the root of your insecurity, helping you become whole in him. Then, over time, when insecurity arises, you'll be able to recognize and resist it, knowing that your worthiness comes solely from the Lord.

### Good Morning, Lord

*Thank you for shining your bright healing light*
*upon the darkness of my insecurities, helping me*
*feel safe and secure within myself.*

*"But the person who is joined to the Lord is one spirit with him."*

1 Corinthians 6:17

## YOUR BODY IS A TEMPLE

"We're spiritual beings having a human experience." This popular statement serves as a great reminder that this life journey on Earth is temporary. Once our time here is complete, the spirit does not die but lives on. It also reminds us that we are having experiences *as* a human.

We are spirit, and we are human. God, in his infinite wisdom and majesty, has given his Holy Spirit freely to dwell inside those who ask to receive it. He has made a way for his presence to find its home in the innermost sacred space of our hearts.

We find Paul talking about this to the Corinthian church. He tells believers that God wants them to take the way they treat their bodies seriously because it is where Spirit abides. Just as you strive to take care of your home, so God wants you to take care of your body, his home.

God desires that every believer consider the body to be his dwelling place. He desires his children to take care of it, including eating nourishing foods, exercising, getting enough rest, and resisting the temptation to do harm to it. He has given his Spirit to help you do this, as it brings glory to him.

Today, as you go about your day, be mindful that God's Spirit resides in you. Your Heavenly Father has given your physical being to you for your life purpose. Commit to taking care of it the best you can, allowing Holy Spirit to assist you as needed.

### Good Morning, Lord

*Thank you for the guidance, support, and motivation*
*of the Holy Trinity in taking good care of my body.*

---

*"Don't you realize that your body is the temple of the Holy Spirit, who lives in you and was given to you by God?"*

1 CORINTHIANS 6:19

# Whose Approval Are You Seeking?

If you worry about what others think of you, rest assured that this is something God can help you with. Living in a state of anxiety over others' perception of you can be exhausting: mentally, physically, and spiritually.

I understand the desire to be accepted and loved by others; this yearning is inherent to all. However, God's Word says that he wants us to find our identity, worth, and peace in him alone. he says that if we are walking his path, with the power of his Spirit dwelling within, we will be able to live in a state of peace despite what anyone thinks.

For the next several days, we're going to study the Word on this topic, because worrying about others' opinion of you hinders your peace. Sure, you may be doing a lot, but if you're doing, doing, doing for others or working so hard to be likable, your energy reservoir may run low. Eventually, you'll tap out, because when your primary focus is on self or others before God, your "busyness" can lead you into spiritual barrenness.

And, darling, our loving Father desires that we serve him and humanity from a pool of grace, overflowing with the fruits of his Spirit. The more you come to know who you are in Christ Jesus, the more you're able to walk in a state of peace, no matter what others think.

## Good Morning, Lord

*Please show me if I am attaching my worth to what others think of me. Help me rest in your truth: that in you, I am all that I need to be and can show up as peace and love everywhere I go.*

*"Obviously, I'm not trying to win the approval of people, but of God. If pleasing people were my goal, I would not be Christ's servant."*

**Galatians 1:10**

## Approved by God

How did it go yesterday? Did you notice if you were saying or doing things, hoping to get people's approval? Or did you show up with the peace and love of God, knowing that regardless of what they thought of you, your worth rested on your identity in Christ?

Part of the spiritual-maturity path includes digging into God's Word and spending time with the Heavenly Father to get to the point where you're not moved by what others think. You determine that you're not going to agree with the majority out of fear of rejection or ridicule. You aren't going to live in a constant state of anxiety or fear.

Yes, at times it can be challenging to brush off judgments or harsh words. After all, we are human, and we do desire love from others. However, over time, we can begin to solidify our identity in God's love and approval alone. We can more easily recognize when we're operating in the head space as opposed to the sacred space.

Today, dear one, if you catch yourself getting caught up in concerns over what others think of you, switch your thoughts immediately to prayer. Ask your Heavenly Father to take away the temptation to alter your behavior in an attempt to gain approval. Ask him to show you his amazing love and acceptance in a deeper way. Then, simply rest in him.

### Good Morning, Lord

*Thank you for supporting my self-esteem and self-confidence, and reminding me throughout the day that you love me.*

*"For we speak as messengers approved by God to be entrusted with the Good News. Our purpose is to please God, not people. He alone examines the motives of our hearts."*

1 Thessalonians 2:4

# How Do Others See You?

My hope, dear one, is that you've now gotten insight as to whether you're more concerned with pleasing man or God. Scripture states that what others think about you *can* matter, but only insofar as God desires that they see Christ's love in you. God desires that people look at you and think, *Wow. She genuinely cares.* God's Spirit in you will lead you to show up in the world as a servant of God, full of his light, love, peace, compassion, and generosity.

Jesus desired that all would come to know him, but he never changed his behavior, which would dishonor his Father, in an attempt to win approval from those who rejected and persecuted him. He knew who he was, and was devoted to fulfilling his Father's will. So, too, can we as Christ followers live in such a way as to faithfully shine God's beauty and love onto a world that needs it. Not to win anyone's approval, but to draw people to the goodness and mercy of God. To give from a place of God's compassion and generosity, over the temptation to give out of approval seeking. To love with God's vast love, rather than love from a place of neediness or unworthiness.

As you go about your day, ground your identity in God. Contemplate how others might be drawn to Christ through you. Show up, walking in the power and fruits of his Spirit, and just watch how God will reach and bless others through you.

## Good Morning, Lord

*Thank you for shielding me from negativity
and helping me be impervious to criticism.*

*"Be careful to live properly among your unbelieving neighbors. Then even if they accuse you of doing wrong, they will see your honorable behavior, and they will give honor to God when he judges the world."*

1 Peter 2:12

# THE MASTER COUNSELOR HAS COME

If you had access to an excellent counselor or spiritual director for free, 24 hours a day, do you think you'd worry less? Well, friend, the good news is that God's Spirit is available to be your "go-to" person for guidance and support; he can counsel and comfort you every moment of every day. Yes, you can receive the Holy Spirit and allow him to be your helper in times of trouble. Your comforter in times of sorrow. Your strength in times of weakness.

You may wonder how God's Spirit can fill you. Well, think of how electricity travels from a power source to an outlet. You can't see the source or the electricity itself, but you know that if you plug your lamp into the outlet, the electricity will flow from the source, through some wires, to that outlet, and cause light to shine.

In the same way, God is our Source, and his Spirit is like electricity flowing from him. We can choose to plug into Spirit, which connects us to Source. This connection with Spirit allows him to show up in our lives as Counselor, Advocate, Comforter, and Deliverer, ultimately liberating us from having to navigate life in our own power. This is great news, especially for those who are worn-out and weary.

Today, be sure to plug into the ultimate Source of strength and power, allowing Holy Spirit to lead and guide you throughout your day as your Counselor and Comforter.

## Good Morning, Lord

*I'm coming to you with my arms and my heart wide-open, asking for the Holy Trinity to fill me with confidence and peaceful energy.*

---

*"But I will send you the Advocate—the Spirit of truth. He will come to you from the Father and will testify all about me."*

JOHN 15:26

## HOLY SPIRIT IS PRAYING FOR YOU

Sometimes, even when we know that we've got the resurrection power of Holy Spirit living within, we can still find ourselves in times of struggle. Relationship problems arise, there are issues at work, money is tough to come by, and so on. We want our faith to soar. We want our hard work to pay off. We want to bat a thousand, but in reality we sometimes feel like we're striking out.

Then what? When you find yourself tired, weary, disillusioned, or aimless, what can you do? What *will* you do?

If we turn to the Word, we learn that it is the Spirit of God that will help us when we're feeling weak. When we don't understand the "whys" or feel like God has disappeared, the Word says that Holy Spirit will intercede or pray for us. In fact, Spirit is continually conversing with God on our behalf!

What does this mean? Dear one, when your spirit is low or your energy depleted and you don't know what to pray for, be assured that Holy Spirit is standing in the gap for you, holding sacred space, praying that God's will be done in your life. That way, you'll be steadfast with hope, trusting that he and the angels are working on your behalf.

Go ahead and lean into the arms of Spirit as you go about your day.

 *Good Morning, Lord*

*Thank you for breathing life into me, for praying
on my behalf, and for boosting my faith.*

*"And the Holy Spirit helps us in our weakness. For example, we don't
know what God wants us to pray for. But the Holy Spirit prays
for us with groanings that cannot be expressed in words."*

ROMANS 8:26

# DETOX YOUR MIND REGULARLY

There's a lot of talk about detoxing the body of harmful substances and chemicals. I agree that there's value in cleaning up our diet. Likewise, it's important to clean up our *mentality* as well, as the thoughts we let run through our minds can help or hinder us. This *mental detox* helps us become more like Jesus. When our minds are aligned with God's mind, we can go about our days at peace, able to be led by his voice more readily.

To detox mentally means to be mindful of the kinds of thoughts you're thinking, and choosing not to dwell on negative ones. When you dwell on negative thoughts, your mood and actions reflect negativity. However, if you share your thoughts with God, you'll be able to discern what's truth and what's not.

This is more than just positive thinking. It's lining up your thoughts with God's thoughts and choosing to believe his Word over any other. For example, when guilty thoughts come knocking at your door, lasso those thoughts and rein them in. Compare them to what God's Word has to say about the matter.

The more you become a student of God's Word, the more likely that you'll be able to turn negative, defeating thoughts over to God. Start each morning by cleansing your mind with God's Word, knowing that it is the absolute truth.

 *Good Morning, Lord*

*Please help me think like you and guide
my focus to what really matters.*

*"We use God's mighty weapons, not worldly weapons, to knock
down the strongholds of human reasoning and to destroy false
arguments. We destroy every proud obstacle that keeps people
from knowing God. We capture their rebellious
thoughts and teach them to obey Christ."*

2 CORINTHIANS 10:4–5

## LET GOD'S PEACE RULE

Good morning, dear child of God. So, how did yesterday go regarding detoxing your mind? Were you able to take your negative thoughts and turn them over to God? Were you able to realize the connection between your thoughts and anxiety, moodiness, fears, or doubts?

See, when you capture those lower-energy thoughts and check them against God's Word, you diminish their ability to take root. Instead, you allow God's Word to take root in you, giving you a clear picture of *God's* reality—not the ego's reality. You invite Spirit to remind you who you really are in God's sight. How blessed you are. How righteous, courageous, loving, and peaceful you are. How strong you are in Christ Jesus.

Darling, when you align yourself with God's Word and ways, you live in a state of peace. People, situations, and errant thoughts may attempt to get you off track, but when you stand on the Word of God, you'll be able to take a deep breath and relax into his promises. Take a moment right now and feel his peace from head to toe.

### Good Morning, Lord

*I am inviting you into my heart and mind, and into every activity during my day ahead. Please help me feel your steady support, love, and presence, that I may be peaceful.*

---

*"And let the peace that comes from Christ rule in your hearts. For as members of one body you are called to live in peace. And always be thankful."*

COLOSSIANS 3:15

## EMBRACE AND EXTEND GOD'S LOVE

Love is a theme throughout the scriptures. If you read all the chapters of the Bible, you'll see a central motif of God showing his abundant love for his people. The apostle John, ministering with a spirit of love, urges believers to love one another with God's kind of unconditional love. He distinguishes this from other types of love, like the friendly or romantic variety.

The kind of love born of God is supernatural, extraordinary, inclusive, and abundant, radiating effortlessly. The Word says that God *is* love, and those who follow him ought to extend his loving nature to others, whether they feel like it or not. Is it always easy? No, but Jesus will guide you to love unconditionally, as he modeled in the Gospels.

Dear one, the more you get to know God, the deeper your love connection becomes. Thus, you'll gladly love God and others above all else. Today, celebrate God's beautiful love for you, receiving it with gratitude and allowing it to flow out into the world. In this way, *others* can experience God's amazing love through you.

### Good Morning, Lord

*Thank you for filling my heart with so much
healing love that I exude it wherever I go.*

*"Dear friends, let us continue to love one another,
for love comes from God. Anyone who loves is
a child of God and knows God."*

1 JOHN 4:7

## QUIET YOUR SOUL

You may know someone who's a real chatterbox, a person with a knack for one-sided conversations. You extend patience and do your best to listen attentively. However, when they're done talking, you may truly enjoy the silence that follows.

Sometimes silence really is golden. It allows for relaxation, reflection, and a time to draw inward strength. God loves it when we talk with him, but he also desires that we go to him and sit in silence and listen. It is in the silence that we can fully *disconnect* from distractions and *connect* with God in our innermost being. It is there that we can cultivate a greater intimacy with our Father, feeling a depth of love that cannot be expressed in words.

This "secret place of the most High," as the Bible describes it, is found in communion with God. In this sacred space, you can rest in God's gracious river of love and goodness. Here, God's Spirit will wash away fears, doubts, and ego-based concerns, and fill you with all that is good. Here, you and God meet in the center of divinity, sharing a connection your heart has yearned for since time immemorial.

Dear one, take time daily to turn within and meet God in silence. For often in the silence, God speaks the loudest.

### Good Morning, Lord

*I pray to have the strength and courage to be silent and listen to you. Please help me hear you, dear Lord.*

---

*"I have calmed and quieted myself, like a weaned child who no longer cries for its mother's milk. Yes, like a weaned child is my soul within me."*

PSALM 131:2

# JESUS MAY BE A WANDERER, BUT HE'S ALWAYS PRESENT

When Jesus was 12, he wandered off to the temple courts so he could listen to the teachers of the law. His parents worried, just like any mother or father does when they can't find a child. The Word in the Gospel of Luke says that Mary and Joseph were "frantic" and "didn't know what to think" when they found Jesus sitting at the feet of scholars as a student. Mary asked her Son, "Why have you done this to us?" (Luke 2:48) as if Jesus were trying to cause her and Joseph grief. Mary didn't realize that Jesus, now a young man, was drawn to diligently study the scriptures, as it was very important to his earthly ministry.

Maybe at times you feel the same way Mary did, asking, "Jesus, why have you done this to us? While you were off wandering, this horrible thing happened in my life. If you had been here, you could have prevented it." Dear one, we just don't always understand God's ways. Jesus is always carrying out his Father's business. Even if it may appear as if he is absent, he isn't. The Holy Trinity is forever with you, through the good *and* challenging times.

You may not understand why troubled times come, but trust that it's not personal. Dearest friend, Jesus is on your side.

### ◁──∞ *Good Morning, Lord* ∞──▷

*I need you so much, and pray that you'll help me feel
and know your steady presence by my side. Thank you
for giving me the strength to do my best.*

---

*"No, I will not abandon you as orphans—I will come to you. Soon the world will no longer see me, but you will see me. Since I live, you also will live. When I am raised to life again, you will know that I am in my Father, and you are in me, and I am in you."*

JOHN 14:18–20

# The Parable of the Sower

A *parable* is a story that illustrates a spiritual lesson. In Jesus's parable of the sower, a farmer scatters seed that represents the Word of God, able to produce a crop. Where the seed lands represents the heart of a person:

- First, there's the seed that lands on the path, and it's immediately snatched up by a bird. This is like those who hear the Word but dismiss it.

- Second, there's seed that falls on rocky ground. It starts to sprout but is not able to get firmly rooted in the soil, so it withers. This is like those who hear God's Word, get excited for a short time, and then forget about it.

- Third, there's seed that lands among thorns. It grows but gets choked up by the weeds. This is like those who hear the Word but do not abide by it.

- Last, there's seed that falls on good, fertile soil, taking root and yielding an abundant crop. This is like those who hear the Word, receive it gladly, and nurture it. Thus, they bear much fruit in their own lives and for the Kingdom of God.

This parable tells us that we can make room for God's Word to take root in our hearts. Each day, open your heart center to allow the seed to settle in. This way, you'll be able to show up in the world with an abundant harvest to share with those in need.

## Good Morning, Lord

*Please help me focus upon hearing, understanding, and living the Word of God, deep within my heart and soul.*

*"Listen! A farmer went out to plant some seed. . . .
Anyone with ears to hear should listen and understand."*

MARK 4:3–9

# THE WORD WILL FREE UP YOUR HEART

*I don't know why I did it.*

This is the response of many who do things they're not proud of. Now, the truth is that maybe they *don't* know why they did it. However, oftentimes people do things they know are wrong or hurtful according to the Word of God because they allow deceit, worry, addiction, fear of rejection, cares of the world, or lustful desires to choke or cloud their good judgment.

Yesterday, we talked about the parable of the sower, describing four types of soil where seeds fall. Recall that it's only the seed that falls upon good soil that takes root and grows wonderful crops. Dear one, the ways of the world may try to choke God's Word from producing an amazing crop in you. There are plenty of lower energies that will endeavor to keep you from enjoying a fruitful life—things like selfishness, competitiveness, unkind words, lying, addictions, infidelity, and greed.

Fortunately, you can fertilize the soil of your heart regularly by learning God's Word, praying, fellowshipping with those who encourage your walking with God, and more. Even if you dislike organized religion, there is a place for you in a healthy house of God, where you can benefit from the support and friendship of like-minded people. God will lead you there.

Nourish your heart-soil with God's Word daily, apply it to your life, and you'll enjoy an abundant spiritual harvest.

## Good Morning, Lord

*I pray for you to till any shallow ground in my heart today
so that it can be fertile and receptive to your Holy Word.
My desire is to bear much fruit for God's Kingdom.*

*"The seed that fell among the thorns represents others who hear
God's word, but all too quickly the message is crowded out by
the worries of this life, the lure of wealth, and the
desire for other things, so no fruit is produced."*

MARK 4:18–19

## TILL YOUR HEART-SOIL

In keeping with the parable of the sower, today let's look at a verse in Hosea that also talks about sowing and reaping. In chapter 10, Hosea speaks about the nation of Israel, who had allowed their spiritual heart-soil to be neglected and overrun by weeds. They were not living lives that pleased the Lord, so the prophet encouraged them to break up their hard, untilled ground so they could be ready to receive God's seeds of righteousness.

We can apply this instruction to our lives, too. Sometimes, in life, things happen that can cause you to feel pain or forget to pray. You may harden or numb your heart or refuse to let anyone in close. You may become angry or confused, but God asks his children to break up their hardened hearts in humility. Why? So that he can rain his goodness and righteousness upon you. So you can enjoy a heart that buds, blossoms, and bears the fruits of his Spirit: love, joy, peace, patience, goodness, faithfulness, gentleness, kindness, and self-control.

Dear one, uncultivated ground ends up barren, not fit to bless anyone. Therefore, ask Holy Spirit to help you keep your heart-soil tilled and weed-free so that your land will be soft and fertile, ready to receive God's seed in joy.

### Good Morning, Lord

*Please help me recognize and remove the weeds in my life, and support me in tending to my sacred garden.*

---

*"Plant the good seeds of righteousness, and you will harvest a crop of love. Plow up the hard ground of your hearts, for now is the time to seek the Lord, that he may come and shower righteousness upon you."*

HOSEA 10:12

## ABIDE IN GOD

This morning let's look at another parable used to teach believers how they can consistently produce the fruits of the Spirit. Jesus explains that he is like a vine and God is like the vinedresser, the cultivator of the vine. As a vine, he abides in God and, as a result, stays spiritually nourished and connected.

A significant key to living a life that is pleasing to God and embodying the fruits of the Spirit is to abide in God. Practical ways of doing so include spending time in prayer, learning the Word, being led by Spirit, and sitting in silence before God. Just as branches of a vine receive their nourishment and productivity from the roots, so shall we be spiritually nourished and productive when we abide in God.

Dear one, we've been grafted onto the Lord's vine by our faith, so let's abide in God through a loving and committed relationship. The result is that we'll enjoy the fruits of the Spirit, no matter what's going on around us.

### *Good Morning, Lord*

*I am setting the intention to consistently
communicate with you throughout each day;
if I forget, would you please remind me?*

---

*"Remain in me, and I will remain in you. For a branch
cannot produce fruit if it is severed from the vine, and
you cannot be fruitful unless you remain in me."*

JOHN 15:4

# Focus Less on Self, More on Others

If we look around, there's no shortage of self-centeredness going on. It seems as if we are living in a "me" generation. Sure, we've all acted selfishly occasionally, at times without even realizing it. But God desires his children to be centered less on self and more on others—not in such a way that we're lacking in self-care, but such that we seek to be of service.

See, God is a lavish giver. He wants us, as his creation, to consistently be on the lookout for how we can bless others. Living a self-centered life, consumed with "I want this and that," won't spread the love and light that God desires. It's shallow and ultimately leaves people feeling empty.

The ego can creep in subtly, so stay mindful of its tactics. Ask Spirit to show you whether you're spending your days thinking mainly about "me" or being led by God to be a source of blessing to others. Your blessing could be a phone call, an encouraging text or e-mail message, an invitation to someone for coffee, visiting an online forum to encourage those who are struggling, helping a person who needs a hand, and so on.

Friend, if *you* are struggling with something and find yourself thinking about it all the time, give it to God and reach out to bless another. Change your focus from "me" to others because, as you do, you will in turn be blessed. *Give*, and you shall receive much joy and fulfillment.

## ⤙ Good Morning, Lord ⤚

*I need your help, please, to be less self-involved and more focused upon how, with your guidance, I can bring blessings to this world.*

---

*"Don't look out only for your own interests,
but take an interest in others, too."*

Philippians 2:4

# GOD IS IN THE MIDST OF SUFFERING

If I were to tell you that everything that happens in your life—the triumphs and the tragedies—is all working for good, would you agree? Would you *feel* better when tragedy strikes? Could you remain calm and peaceful, assured that the pain you're feeling is somehow serving a worthwhile end?

The apostle Paul talks about this process in Romans 8:28, saying that all things work together for the good of those who love God. People often reference this verse when someone is going through something tough. They say, "Hey, it's going to be all right. God will use this suffering for your good. Someday you'll thank him for it." Perhaps, but when you're in seemingly insurmountable pain, sickness, misfortune, or grief, you may be shaking your head, wondering how anything good can come of it.

This verse doesn't mean that suffering *is* good or that all will be well if you just believe hard enough. You may in fact never understand why tragedy shows up, but one thing you *can* count on is that God is there before, in the middle of, and at the end of it all. He will never leave you, even in the darkest of times. He will hold you as a father holds his teary-eyed child—not promising them that "all will be all right," but that he will be there no matter what.

## ❧ *Good Morning, Lord* ❧

*Please hold on to me tightly, reassuring me that*
*I am safe and secure and that you will never leave my side.*

---

*"And we know that God causes everything to work together*
*for the good of those who love God and are called*
*according to his purpose for them."*

ROMANS 8:28

# If You Believe

When prayers don't get answered as you'd like or things don't turn out the way you want, how does it affect you? Do you get upset with God? Do you feel as if you can't trust him anymore? Or do you turn to God, even if you're confused, and trust that he is there with you? Do you trust that no matter what happens or doesn't happen, he is in control?

Because Jesus walked the earth, he understands suffering. In the Garden of Gethsemane, he prayed that he would not have to die to free humanity from its state of suffering, but he went to the cross anyway. The Word says he was in anguish, but he put God's will above his own, trusting that it was for the highest good.

Lazarus's grieving sister, Martha, turned to Jesus and questioned whether her brother would have died if Jesus had been there. Still, she believed and was bold enough to ask Jesus to do a miracle. Jesus, for the glory of his Father, revived Lazarus, and word of the miracle spread far and wide.

Just as Jesus said to Martha, "Didn't I tell you that you would see God's glory if you believe?" so he reminds you of the same, my dear. Even when prayers aren't answered in the time frame you desire, or things don't go as you wish, believe that God is working to draw you closer to him and bring him glory. You may not understand, but he will bolster your trust in his love.

### Good Morning, Lord

*Please help build my strength and trust, especially during negative events I seem to have no control over. In those moments, please help me remember that you are sustaining and supporting me.*

*"Martha said to Jesus, 'Lord, if only you had been here, my brother would not have died. But even now I know that God will give you whatever you ask.'"*

John 11:21–22

# Strengthen Yourself in the Lord

How many times have you been distressed because you felt as if people were throwing stones at you—condemning or judging you with their words and actions? Whether the disapproval comes from coworkers, family, friends, or even certain looks from strangers, there may be times when you just feel beaten down. Over time, this "stoning" can lead to emotional and health issues.

In the first book of Samuel, we find King David crying out in distress. An army had come while he was away and kidnapped his own and his army's wives and children. They burned his city to the ground. The people were not happy with David and wanted to stone him. Needless to say, things had not gone as planned.

But instead of getting bitter or giving up, the Word says, David strengthened himself in the Lord. He turned toward God, gaining the inner resources to overcome obstacles and do God's will. In fact, you can find instances of David turning to God for strength many times in scripture.

When you feel defeated, dear one, and stones are coming at you from all quarters, do as David did. Turn to God and strengthen yourself in him, for then you will be able to overcome.

## Good Morning, Lord

*Thank you for shielding and protecting me, and guiding my thoughts and actions to reflect God's love.*

---

*"David was now in great danger because all his men were very bitter about losing their sons and daughters, and they began to talk of stoning him. But David found strength in the Lord his God."*

1 Samuel 30:6

## DWELL IN GOD'S BEAUTIFUL PRESENCE

King David was a man after God's presence, yearning to dwell in it all the time. Granted, God's presence is not defined by locality—meaning, it doesn't have spatial dimension. However, in the times of David, God's presence was associated with the tabernacle in the wilderness (a portable tent for worship).

Today, we acknowledge that God's presence is everywhere. So when we say we want to come into his presence, this is essentially a metaphor. To experience God's presence is to arrive at a greater knowing of his reality. It's feeling him more intimately and deeply. It's taking the time to listen to his messages.

Does this mean we can feel him more at one time than another? Well, even though God is omnipresent, he can cause his presence to be felt more deeply as he wishes—to be more pronounced. And you probably know that you can more easily feel and hear God when your mind is quiet, clear, and sober.

Some say that when they get a deeper sense of God's reality, they're hit by a wave of tears. Others say deep joy overwhelms them. So, the experience can be different for each person.

Just as David yearned to dwell in God's presence continually, my prayer is that you, too, long to pursue God with the same devotion. Behold the beautiful presence of God no matter where you are—at home, work, church, and so on—for he is indeed everywhere.

### Good Morning, Lord

*Please help me see, feel, hear, and know that*
*your presence is with me, now and always.*

*"The one thing I ask of the Lord—the thing I seek most—is to live*
*in the house of the Lord all the days of my life, delighting in*
*the Lord's perfections and meditating in his Temple."*

PSALM 27:4

## HE'S REST FOR THE WEARY

Most days I feel strong, energetic, and joyful. However, there have been periods of my life when I needed more rest. Maybe I had a strict deadline to meet or my travel schedule was jam-packed. Like you, I've juggled multiple responsibilities.

Over time, I've learned to check in with myself and God regularly. At times when I notice myself feeling tired, I remember Jesus's Word: "Come to me, all of you who are weary and carry heavy burdens, and I will give you rest." Instead of plowing forward, exhausting my own strength and running the risk of burnout, I take time to rest in God's arms, even if it's just for a few moments. I ask God to help me take an inventory and set a doable pace. I ask, *Am I living in balance, or have I overextended myself?*

Dear friend, during the times you feel heavy, worn-out, or just plain exhausted, Jesus asks you to go to him. He doesn't require that you do anything for him. He simply wants you to rest your care-laden head on him and let him refresh and restore you. In this way, you'll be able to enjoy your life with your cup full—energized, at peace, and joyous.

### Good Morning, Lord

*Thank you for helping me balance my schedule
and reminding me of the importance of rest. Lord,
I am setting my burdens down before you
and leaning upon you to rest.*

*"Then Jesus said, 'Come to me, all of you who are weary
and carry heavy burdens, and I will give you rest.'"*

MATTHEW 11:28

## LET GO OF THE OLD

God's mercies are new every morning. His forgiveness wipes out the past. His love endures forever.

Child of God, this is your signal to let go of the old. Maybe you're holding on to guilt or shame. Maybe you're holding on to a negative pattern or thoughts that pull you down. Or perhaps it's time to address a toxic relationship you're afraid to release.

God helps us learn and grow from the past, instead of carrying it around like a heavy burden. Your painful experiences have shaped who you are today, and you are now stronger and wiser because of them. Still, it's important to heed those hard-won lessons and release everything else from the past.

Dear one, God's plan always involves people like you who are willing to follow his lead, bringing his divine healing and teaching to all who need help. Just as Jesus's disciples were willing to set aside their jobs, homes, and families to follow him, what are *you* willing to release to follow God's guidance?

Certainly, you can exchange painful memories for creating new, lovely experiences of partnering with God.

### Good Morning, Lord

*Please guide me to know: What do I need to release*
*and set down to fully follow you?*

---

*"But forget all that—it is nothing compared to what I am going to*
*do. For I am about to do something new. See, I have already begun!*
*Do you not see it? I will make a pathway through the wilderness.*
*I will create rivers in the dry wasteland."*

ISAIAH 43:18–19

## MEET GOD IN THE CENTER

The very center of your being is the sacred space where Spirit dwells. Right *there* is where God tends to speak the loudest. Beyond your five senses, beyond your mental understanding, in the quiet and stillness, he manifests his great love for you, his beloved child.

We long for this type of intimacy—this mystical, profound connectedness with the glorious Lord. And it's this deep, inspired intimacy that our Father wants to share with us.

Yes, doing his will as we go about life here on Earth is important. Yes, sitting before God making requests for ourselves and on behalf of others is necessary. Stillness before the Lord in the innermost part of our being is the sacred space where a divine exchange can occur, deepening our love for our Father and satisfying that innate craving for spiritual intimacy.

This personal, intimate relationship is the kind of relationship God truly desires. Go ahead, dear one, and plunge into the heart of this sacred space throughout your day.

### Good Morning, Lord

*I want to share closeness with you, and I need your*
*help to know how to do so. Please pull me in closer, Lord,*
*and don't allow fears or distractions to block*
*my awareness of your healing love.*

---

*"The Lord is close to all who call on him, yes,*
*to all who call on him in truth."*

PSALM 145:18

## YOUR PRESENCE MAKES A DIFFERENCE

You may feel insignificant at times, wondering if your passion or presence is really making a difference in the world. Whatever your occupation—stay-at-home parent, student, entrepreneur, waiter—God needs youe to carry out his plan for peace.

If we could talk to saints of the past and ask why God chose them to show up in the world as they did, they'd probably say it was because they prayed for a divine assignment. They fully put their trust in him. They'd likely say it was God in them who was doing the work. They humbled themselves before God with an open heart. God often uses common folk to carry out his plans.

Keep your eyes on Jesus. Invite Holy Spirit to continually lead you. Maybe you don't notice a difference now. Perhaps you don't see any fruit manifest from the seeds you've been sowing. Take heart, dear one, and please keep the momentum going. Believe God when he says, "I am with you. I am preparing the way." Because he is!

Your presence on this planet does make a difference, child of God. You are having a huge positive impact.

### Good Morning, Lord

*I want to make a positive difference and help others.*
*Please guide my actions, and increase my faith and motivation*
*to keep going, even if I can't yet see the fruits of my labor.*

---

*"But as for you, be strong and courageous,*
*for your work will be rewarded."*

2 CHRONICLES 15:7

# In Times of Sorrow, God Is There

When we're troubled by circumstances often beyond our control, we may pull away from God and our loved ones. We may want to isolate at a time when we really need to turn *toward* our Source of love, comfort, and healing.

While it's true that the passage of time will ease our suffering, what do we do in the interim? In addition to allowing friends or a counselor to assist in our recovery from a wounded spirit, we need to recognize that God is always there. He knows our sorrow, and he will offer us comfort. Although he is not physically present to give us an encouraging embrace in the way our friends are, when we put our burdens in his hands, God provides the consolation we need. Imagine God gently cradling you in his arms like a crying baby, soothing your distress with his loving Spirit. He hasn't promised that we will never have a broken heart or a crushed spirit, but he *has* promised that when we do, he will be there with us.

The next time you experience a disheartening event in your life, pray for God's guidance and comfort and have faith that he will provide what you need.

## Good Morning, Lord

*I need a hug from you! Please help me feel your reassurances that I will overcome these hurt feelings and this fear. Thank you for being my best friend!*

*"The Lord is close to the brokenhearted; he rescues those whose spirits are crushed."*

**Psalm 34:18**

# PRESENT YOURSELF AS AN INSTRUMENT TO GOD

If you set the intention to mow your grass today, would your mower automatically start mowing? Assuming it's not a programmable robot, that mower wouldn't move. You must start it and push or drive it to get the job done. The mower is a tool, or an *instrument*. It's helpful and appreciated, but left to itself, it really just takes up space.

Likewise, in God's Kingdom, every soul is a tool or an instrument for God. Every soul is valuable and can be helpful for the building of God's loving Kingdom here on Earth. But on our own, without God, life can resemble a mower that's just sitting under a cover in the garage. It can feel dark and empty, maybe even meaningless.

But with God behind us, igniting us with the power of his Spirit, what an instrument we become! All of a sudden life takes on a new meaning. We have hope. We feel like our existence matters to God *and* others. We surrender to his will and allow him to do as he wishes.

My hope for you, dear one, is that you will allow the greatest power in the universe—*God*—to fire you up and make you an instrument for his divine energy to flow through you. That you will look to the One who has called you, even before you entered your mother's womb, to shine bright as the stars in a world that welcomes more light.

### Good Morning, Lord

*Please give me a divine assignment, utilizing me in
a wonderful way to bring blessings to this world.*

*"Do not let any part of your body become an instrument of evil to
serve sin. Instead, give yourselves completely to God, for you were
dead, but now you have new life. So use your whole body as
an instrument to do what is right for the glory of God."*

ROMANS 6:13

# Sing a New Song

God knew what he was doing when he created our minds to reap the powerful benefits of music! Almost every part of a person's brain is involved when they listen to uplifting music, play an instrument, or dance to a song. When we sing, we use additional parts of our brains, which creates a feeling of euphoria. Even if we sing off-key, it doesn't matter.

A beautiful melody can soothe a place in our soul that nothing else can touch. Gentle, positive music is effective in the treatment of emotional conditions, including depression and anxiety, and neurological conditions such as brain damage and stroke. Many with Alzheimer's disease seem to come alive when hearing a familiar tune. A lively song can raise our spirits, cause our toes to tap, and urge us to sing along or dance. A gentle lullaby will soothe a baby. Stories are told through ballads. Love songs remind us of sentimental memories. Spiritual songs praising God bring us to a place of comfort, where we can worship in a peaceful state of mind.

When we enter a place of worship, whether inside a church or on a mountaintop, music can enhance our experience. Listening to inspirational music and singing songs about God's love can draw us closer to him. It escorts our spirit to a place of acceptance and trust, where we are receptive to the truths God want us to receive. Sing a new song, whenever the urge strikes.

## Good Morning, Lord

*Please guide me to musical choices that uplift and soothe me,*
*and help me sing praises and worship from my heart.*

*"He has given me a new song to sing, a hymn of praise to our God.*
*Many will see what he has done and be amazed.*
*They will put their trust in the Lord."*

**Psalm 40:3**

# WATCH THOSE WORDS

You create your reality with your thoughts and words. In fact, words can cultivate or ruin relationships, attract or block health, and promote peace or create discord. Words can heal a broken heart, give hope to the hopeless, comfort the grief-stricken, and perform countless more good deeds.

Scripture backs this teaching as well. Proverbs 18:21 states that "the tongue can bring death or life." This means that the words you speak are either producing blessings or blocks. You can prophesy a positive or negative future.

The Word says you will essentially eat the fruit of your words. Therefore, how do you create a reality that you can enjoy? Sow good seeds. Soak in the Word so that your heart will be full of God's wisdom and grace. Then speak words that will bring blessings to you and others. Affirm that your health is great, your family is flourishing, your finances are secure, your faith is strong, and so on.

Dear one, may your words be a spring of life, showering edifications and blessings so that the reality you're creating is the same kind God has planned for you.

## Good Morning, Lord

*Please guide the words I choose
to say and write so that my vocabulary is
empowering and life affirming.*

*"The tongue can bring death or life; those who
love to talk will reap the consequences."*

**PROVERBS 18:21**

# THE BATTLE IS THE LORD'S

As inhabitants of this world, we may face battles as we journey through life. Some challenges are straightforward—for example, when a health challenge necessitates a lifestyle change. Those will be a matter of perseverance to the task. Other encounters may bring us to our knees in frustration, fear, sadness, and confusion. We might be tested to the limit of our sanity and our faith in God.

During intense conflicts, remember the apostle Paul's advice. He tells us to be strong in God, making sure to put on our armor each day. Paul wrote these words while in prison, being persecuted for following Jesus. Even in the midst of his own battle, he encouraged others to be faithful and to serve Jesus in harmony and love.

When faced with overwhelming challenges, we are compelled to fight for what is right, but we will never win a spiritual battle with physical strength. God strengthens and protects us with his Word, with Holy Spirit, and with his unconditional love for each of us.

It's important that we continue to pray during these struggles and not lose faith. Remember that God works in mysterious ways, so his answer might not be exactly what we want or expect. This is where faith in God is crucial. When you pray, ask God for strength to keep going, for reassurance that his guiding hand is leading you, and for forbearance to accept whatever happens in your life as his will.

## Good Morning, Lord

*Like you, I desire peace. I am leaning upon your wisdom, guidance, and protection to show me the way there.*

---

*"And everyone assembled here will know that the Lord rescues his people, but not with sword and spear. This is the Lord's battle, and he will give you to us!"*

1 SAMUEL 17:47

## SEEK A RIGHTEOUS TEACHER

The Bible instructs us to become students of the Word. It's wonderful that we have scriptures in written form that we can read as often as we'd like.

The Word also says it's wise to be taught the meaning of scripture by a teacher. In Ephesians, Paul explains that God has gifted some people to be teachers in order to encourage and equip believers to do the work of Christ. It's not that we can't learn truth on our own; we certainly can. But as we all know, a good teacher can help us understand things we may not have understood had we tried to learn it by ourselves.

Assuming you want to become more like Jesus, scripture says to seek reputable teachers that will lead you in the right direction. In the second book of Peter, it says that there are false prophets and teachers out there who do not serve God—that there are some who will twist scriptures for their own convenience. This is why you need godly teachers who teach the truth of the Word of God.

Dear one, as you continue your study of scriptures, ask God to bring you the teachers he has ordained for you to learn from.

### ⤛ Good Morning, Lord ⤜

*Thank you for guiding me to the right*
*teachers who can accelerate and deepen*
*my understanding of God's Word and will.*

---

*"Students are not greater than their teacher.*
*But the student who is fully trained will*
*become like the teacher."*

LUKE 6:40

# FOLLOW JESUS'S FOOTSTEPS

Picture yourself living back in the first century with Jesus. He's the talk of the town, considering the way his words and actions upset the religious leaders; gathers large crowds; and performs many miracles. Walking down the street, the two of you make eye contact. Lovingly, he says, "Follow me."

You may wonder: *Did he mean follow him just for the day?* Or must you leave your family and follow him from town to town? The Word says that some men and women did leave behind everything to follow him. They became his disciples, eager to learn all that he had to teach.

Jesus still asks us to follow his footsteps. He desires that his disciples receive his Words with gladness, and allow them to lift us all up into a higher spiritual state. In addition, he gives us his Spirit for guidance so we can show up as beacons of light and love in the world.

God's will is that we follow the footsteps of Jesus. How can we do this? Start by learning about him in the Word of God. Resist the temptation to try to navigate your journey on your own. Pay close attention to his teachings, and do your best to emulate them as you go about your day. Ask Holy Spirit to draw you closer to Jesus and *listen*, dear one. Jesus is always speaking.

## Good Morning, Lord

*You are my teacher, role model, and guide,*
*and I will follow your lead and example*
*today and every day.*

---

*"Jesus called out to them,*
*'Come, follow me, and I will show you*
*how to fish for people!'"*

**MATTHEW 4:19**

# BE AN INSPIRATION

Yesterday, we discussed Jesus's instruction to follow his footsteps. The topic of following Jesus is a central theme in the New Testament. Today, let's look at the apostle Paul's message in a letter he wrote the church in Corinth.

He tells believers to imitate him because he is of Jesus. He feels confident enough about himself as a follower of Christ to tell others that they should follow him. This is a rather bold statement, for sure, but Paul understood that to follow in Jesus's footsteps wasn't about his own nature. After all, resurrected Jesus appeared to Paul and forever changed his life. He understood that to live each day abiding in Jesus, living out God's will, he had to allow Spirit to help him put his fleshly nature aside.

Paul stated in Galatians 2:20, "My old self has been crucified with Christ." He now had a new nature, born of faith in Jesus. His new, Christ-conscious nature allowed him to walk in obedience to him and by faith in God.

As a follower of Jesus, could you confidently say to others, "You should imitate me, just as I imitate Christ"? It is my prayer that through the power of Spirit, each day we *can* live the kind of life that will inspire others to follow the ways of Jesus.

## Good Morning, Lord

*I would love to inspire others to be
open to your love and guidance, and I pray for
your help in modeling myself after you.*

*"Be imitators of me, even as I also am of Christ."*

1 CORINTHIANS 11:1

# GO ABOUT DOING GOOD

Jesus and the disciples went about the world doing good—feeding the hungry, healing the sick, giving hope to the hopeless, teaching the public, and other services. This is certainly what the world needs now, as it did then—and as followers of Jesus, we are certainly fit for the task.

Giving can occur in many ways. Practically speaking, you could extend love to whomever you meet, donate to those in need, offer upliftment to anyone hurting, give sincere compliments and praise, teach others something valuable, spend time with the lonely, pray for the sick, and so much more.

Now, you may find it more challenging to give if you're anxious, sad, or ill. You may even believe that you *have* nothing to give. But when people who feel this way do get out and do something for others, it oftentimes makes *them* feel better. They give from the heart, and that just *feels good*. I'm sure you can relate to feeling cheered after spending time encouraging another.

Additionally, if you want to be out there doing good, it's necessary to keep your eyes wide-open, looking for opportunities to serve others and spread light and love. Dear one, there are many earthly callings, but what *really* makes the world a better place is to go about doing good consistently. This pleases our Father, who is continually doing good for his children.

Do good today, darling. Shine your heart light brightly!

## Good Morning, Lord

*Please lead me to those who are in need and*
*help me help them with a joyful heart.*

*"And you know that God anointed Jesus of Nazareth with the Holy Spirit and with power. Then Jesus went around doing good and healing all who were oppressed by the devil, for God was with him."*

ACTS 10:38

# EXTEND COMPASSION AND COURTESY

To be courteous means to show kindness to another. It's being a gentleman or gentlewoman, even when others are being less than kind. Peter tells us in the Word that as Christ followers, we should aim to be compassionate and courteous.

Granted, when someone lashes out at us rudely, it doesn't feel very good. Our first reaction may be to lash back, but if we are really imitating Jesus Christ of Nazareth, then we will not take rudeness personally. We will return rudeness with kindness.

Now, this doesn't mean that you must put up with continued rudeness or any form of abuse. There are certainly boundaries that you can set. One thing to remember is that when someone is rude, there is some upset going on in their life. They're frustrated or confused, and their desire is not getting fulfilled. Not everyone knows how to handle overwhelming feelings.

But when you can tap into Holy Spirit, you're more willing to empathize with and feel compassion for them. You're able to turn the other cheek in a sense, and repay them with the love of Christ. And, who knows, this may even draw them to want to know more about the Christ who lives in you, dear one.

Think about this as you go about your day. If you happen to encounter rudeness, remember the words of Peter and ask Holy Spirit to help you respond with courtesy. In this way, you are a spiritual healer like Jesus.

## Good Morning, Lord

*You know how sensitive and emotional I am, so I need your strength, please, in offering kindness and compassion to those who are rudely expressing their hurt.*

*"Finally, be all like-minded, compassionate, loving as brothers, tender hearted, courteous."*

1 PETER 3:8 (WEB)

## COUNT THE COST

If you were building a house, wouldn't you go over the plans and the cost before you began? In the Gospel of Luke, Jesus poses this scenario to the crowd, asking them to really sit and think about the cost of following him and his ways. He specifically said it *would* cost them some things.

Is there a cost associated with following Jesus? I think we'd be naïve to say no. After all, the ways of Jesus are not typically the ways of this world. There's a wide path and a narrow path, and Jesus invites his followers down that narrow path, which isn't always easy-breezy.

Jesus holds the bar rather high. He does not expect perfection, but he does ask for our best effort. Those who model the ways of Jesus may tell you of the cost in doing so. They may say it's not always easy to show love to others or to make time to commune with God. When someone judges you, it's not always easy to turn the other cheek and stay compassionate. It's not fun being ridiculed for your faith.

As Jesus's followers, we're called to give up acting out of the ego. We're to walk in the Spirit rather than walking in the fleshly desires like greed, pride, lust, selfishness, and so on. However, the rewards of following Jesus are well worth the cost. May we rejoice in counting the cost of following Jesus, becoming more attuned with our Heavenly Father each day.

### *Good Morning, Lord*

*I gladly follow you, and I appreciate your giving me protection and insulation from worldly energies.*

---

*"But don't begin until you count the cost. For who would begin construction of a building without first calculating the cost to see if there is enough money to finish it?"*

LUKE 14:28

## BEFRIEND GOD'S FAITHFULNESS

We tend to trust a lot of things in life without question. We trust that the sun will rise every morning and shine bright so we can see God's glorious creation. We trust that the medicine the doctor prescribes will heal. We trust that the chairs we sit in won't break. There are plenty of things that we trust in, but when it comes to God's promises, sometimes we're just not sure.

Psalm 37:3 reads: "Trust in the Lord and do good. Then you will live safely in the land and prosper." This means that when we can fully put our trust in the Lord, we are doing good. We will do good because we are fully putting our trust in our loving Father. And when we're trusting, it says we will be safe and prosperous. This means that if we're trusting God, we won't be worried or discouraged. We won't allow pity to pin us down or disappointments to block us.

We will befriend faithfulness, knowing that God is faithful to do what he promises. This pure trust in God above all circumstances helps us recognize God's presence within us.

God has proven himself worthy. He shows up for us, so no matter what's going on in your life or what obstacles you're facing, trust in the Lord and do good. Invite faithfulness to be your friend, as the Lord is faithful. Surely, he is directing your path, dear one. Rejoice in this truth today!

### Good Morning, Lord

*Why do I ever doubt you? Please help me purify*
*and uplift my thoughts and emotions, so that*
*I have a steady foundation of faith.*

*"Trust in the Lord and do good. Then you*
*will live safely in the land and prosper."*

PSALM 37:3

## SOMETIMES IT'S A LIFE LESSON

The disciple Peter says that we shouldn't be surprised when we face adversity, because sometimes it comes as a test. The things we come up against aren't necessarily a result of anything we've done. Rather, they arise to test our faith.

When God helps us through a challenge—particularly if it's a recurring pattern—his Spirit sheds light on some aspect of our ego that may need healing. Did we take an action that was ego based instead of God guided? Did we defy the will of God, knowing that it wasn't the right path but forging ahead anyway?

Regardless of what type of adversity you face, God can use it to compassionately teach you valuable lessons and draw you closer to him. You can probably look back on a trial in your life and realize how much you learned about yourself, others, and God through it. Perhaps it became a life lesson about following God's guidance instead of the ego's impulsiveness.

Dear one, if you are facing adversity today, do not be surprised. Know that in and through it all, God is with you. This may very well be a test of your faith, so choose to be steadfast, relying on Holy Spirit every step of the way.

### *Good Morning, Lord*

*Thank you for holding my hand through challenges
and helping me learn whatever lessons they contain.*

*"Dear friends, don't be surprised at the
fiery trials you are going through, as if something
strange were happening to you."*

**1 PETER 4:12**

# My God, My God

According to the Gospels, when Jesus was suffering on the cross, he cried out, "My God, my God, why have you abandoned me?" Surely, he knew his Father's ultimate plan to save mankind from separation from him. Surely, he knew that in three days he would be resurrected from the dead.

Sometimes we may feel as if God abandoned us. A loss we perceive as too cruel to be part of God's plan may befall us, and seemingly senseless tragedies occur on the broader scale, like natural disasters or wars. We wonder where God is in all these things. We want him to speak comforting words, letting us know that all will be well—that whatever is going on, there's some sort of grand plan and the "aha" moment will definitely come.

Note that when Jesus cried out to his Father, he was quoting the first verse of Psalm 22, which King David wrote when he was facing distress. If you keep reading the psalm, David goes on to say that God did not hide his face from him in his distress. Rather, God heard him loud and clear.

Jesus expressed his anguish, and his Father heard. But Jesus also affirmed God's ultimate plan of redemption by going to the cross. Jesus knew his Father's plan and offered obedience for the greater good.

Maybe you or a loved one is experiencing anguish right now. God hears you, dear one. And especially during moments of suffering, he's right there with you.

## Good Morning, Lord

*I'm coming to you with my arms and heart wide-open,
asking for you to hold me steady through this situation.
I trust you to be there for me. Thank you.*

*"My God, my God, why have you abandoned me?
Why are you so far away when I groan for help?"*

Psalm 22:1

# ANGELS ABOUND

All throughout scripture, we find the presence of angels. From the book of Genesis to the book of Revelation, and in the noncanonical Dead Sea Scrolls, angels have been recorded as protectors, warriors, comforters, and more. The highest-ranking and best-known is Archangel Michael, whose primary mission is to eliminate fear or ego. Other well-known angels are Gabriel, Raphael, and Uriel.

Can angels help us with our service to the Lord? Absolutely. The angels were created by God to assist him and his children. The Word describes angels as ministering spirits, available at any time to believers.

How can angels help us? They can offer protection; strengthen us; impart understanding, as they did for Daniel when he was trying to decipher visions from God; show us divine guidance; and accompany us wherever we go. You can deepen your relationship with the angels by simply talking to them.

Just like you talk to God, Jesus, or Holy Spirit, you can talk to your guardian angels and ask them for help. You may not always *hear* them reply back to you, but you may have a knowing, see a vision, or feel their presence. As long as you first pray for God and Jesus to guide your interactions with your guardian angels, you can enjoy a close relationship with these amazing beings, whom God has assigned to watch over you.

## Good Morning, Lord

*My heart is so filled with gratitude for the presence and love of God, Holy Spirit, Jesus, and my guardian angels!*

*"Praise the Lord, you angels, you mighty ones who carry out his plans, listening for each of his commands."*

PSALM 103:20

# JESUS WANTS US ALL CONNECTED

When I was 17, I had a profound spiritual experience. I'd just graduated from high school with no real plan for my future. Before long, I was struggling with finances and feeling discontent. I didn't know what to do, so I got quiet and prayed for answers.

I then had a vision of three people floating in my room. I recognized one as Jesus and another as Mother Mary, but I did not know the third. As you can imagine, this vision startled me. I thought they might have come to take me to heaven. I resisted and tried to get away, but they followed. At that point, something in me caused me to give up the fight and surrender. I figured that if they needed me to go with them, I would go. Then something amazing happened: they came up to me—and passed right through my body.

It was on that day that I believe I was born again and saw life differently. I became a student of the Bible and developed a personal relationship with God, Jesus, Mother Mary, and the angels, sharing what God and heaven taught me. Eventually, after I had another profound experience with Jesus, I began teaching more openly about him and the scriptures. Through my faith in God, I have found happiness and the most blissful unconditional love I've ever experienced.

Dear one, let's be careful not to judge others on a different path. Rather, let's pray that those who struggle will experience freedom and the unconditional love of God. Jesus wants all of us to be connected, regardless of our current religious background or beliefs.

## Good Morning, Lord

*I feel the most happiness and security when I keep my thoughts and focus upon you. Why would I allow myself to drift away from you?*

---

*"Jesus replied, 'I tell you the truth, unless you are born again, you cannot see the Kingdom of God.'"*

JOHN 3:3

# BE QUICK TO MAKE AMENDS

The second book of Samuel recounts the story of the relationship between King David and Bathsheba. Even though she was married, David desired her intimately. They had a one-night stand while her husband was away at war, and David pulled some shenanigans in an attempt to conceal the scandal. Unsuccessful with the cover-up, he arranged to have Bathsheba's husband killed in the war, and he went on to marry her.

Now this was the same David who had found favor in the eyes of the Lord many times. He loved God, yet he let his fleshly desires lead him to do something that God would not approve. David kept his secret until God sent the prophet Nathan to call him out. Some men might have denied the accusation, but David immediately felt the rebuke. He broke emotionally, weeping and refusing to eat. He humbled himself and was truly repentant.

I think this is a good reminder that God knows what's going on in our lives. We may endeavor to keep a secret from other people, but we cannot keep secrets from God. He sees our hearts. He knows when we've missed his mark, and if we do, we can choose to immediately humble ourselves, truly feel sorrow, and ask him to forgive us. As our loving Father, he will. It is this grace and mercy that should prompt *us* to keep the faith, extending the same unconditional love to others along the way.

## Good Morning, Lord

*Please help me drop my defenses and be more authentic, honest, and humble about the missteps that I've chosen to take.*

---

*"Jesus answered them, 'Healthy people don't need a doctor—sick people do. I have come to call not those who think they are righteous, but those who know they are sinners and need to repent.'"*

LUKE 5:31–32

## Jesus's Life as a Pattern

I understand that many turn away from Jesus due to pain or hypocrisy they experienced. Some just can't get on board with a religion. But studying the life of Jesus and modeling it can unite people in love and service. It doesn't have to be about joining a religion. As spiritual beings and the collective children of God, we can bring his Kingdom of love to the earth.

Jesus brought God's Kingdom to Earth. He was one with God, born of God, and reached enlightenment, or what some may call Christ-consciousness. His teachings expressed the idea that we can create God's kind of Kingdom now, here on Earth, if we wake up and unite as spiritual children of the most high God. It's quite extraordinary. This divine nature of Jesus is the same divine nature we can walk in as we allow Holy Spirit to dwell within. And as we do, dear one, we can also bring God's Kingdom to Earth.

What does the splendor of God's Kingdom look like here? It looks a lot like imitators of Jesus waking up each day with a deep knowing of who they are in Christ. It's you and me showing up for others, motivated by a heart committed to honoring God first. It's recognizing that God can heal what needs to be healed in us, so we can go out and help *others* heal. It's forgiving, extending compassion, offering selfless love, and radiating joy.

Again, it's bringing a kingdom like the heaven described in the Bible to Earth using Jesus's life and ministry as a blueprint. What a privilege, dear one. May you enjoy a beautiful day spreading the love of Jesus wherever you go.

### Good Morning, Lord

*I love when I can feel your presence, and I wish to help others experience your healing love as well.*

---

*"Again he said, 'Peace be with you.*
*As the Father has sent me, so I am sending you.'"*

JOHN 20:21

# TRUST IN GOD'S TIMING

It's wonderful to have intentions and dreams in life. At the same time, it can be frustrating when you work for so long and feel as if you're not getting far. You may even be tempted to give up. I remember feeling this way many years ago when I set a goal to write my first book. I was so excited for the opportunity to touch others through my writing. I wrote up my proposal and sent it to a publisher—and got rejected.

I was disappointed, but I knew that I had God in my corner. The Word says that "faith shows the reality of what we hope for; it is the evidence of things we cannot see" (Hebrews 11:1). I had faith that I was called to reach many people as an author, and this helped me not to stay down in discouragement. My guardian angels prompted me to send out more book proposals, so I did—to 44 publishers. I received 40 rejections, but also received 4 offers. I was so excited!

There's something about persistence and relying on the favor of God while pursuing your dreams. Do you feel called to write a book? Start a business? Invent something? Set your sights upon your intentions, because as children of God, we have his favor. If God has called you to it, he'll back you every step of the way and open doors in his perfect timing.

## Good Morning, Lord

*Thank you for your encouragement and for*
*believing in me, even when I'm struggling with*
*self-doubts. I now intend to see myself as you see me.*

---

*"If it seems slow in coming, wait patiently,*
*for it will surely take place."*

HABAKKUK 2:3

# SPEAK WORDS THAT BUILD UP OTHERS

Words are so powerful. Words can either build up or tear down. I believe the first few seconds of a conversation are the most important, because the words spoken and the tone used set the stage for how the communication will go. If you start off with harsh words or an angry tone, that other person will automatically go into defensive mode. They will sense accusation or insult immediately and put up walls for protection.

However, if you start off with constructive words spoken in a peaceful manner, that conversation will proceed differently. Beginning with positive words such as "I know you mean well and I appreciate the effort, but . . ." will go over much better than "What the heck were you thinking?"

God's Word instructs us to speak words that will help build others up, not tear them down. Even if someone has offended you or made a mistake, you can still dialogue with them in a way that is respectful, kind, and courteous. If they've hurt you, approach them sincerely with the truth, but from a space of unconditional love rather than rejection or anger. Granted, this may take some practice and help from God. You may slip occasionally, and hopefully learn from it.

Please be mindful of how you approach your conversations today, dear one. Ask God to help you speak words that encourage and build up others, regardless of what mood you or they are in.

### Good Morning, Lord

*Please guide my words and tone in my spoken and written communications. May everything that I speak and write be both kind and true.*

*"Don't use foul or abusive language. Let everything you say be good and helpful, so that your words will be an encouragement to those who hear them."*

EPHESIANS 4:29

# GIVE YOURSELF PERMISSION TO LAUGH

I see the phrase "Live, Love, Laugh," which is a great sentiment, written on all sorts of home decor items. But when was the last time you truly had a good laugh, the kind that made you sigh and feel like a giddy child?

I love to watch children play. They giggle and simply delight in playing, wild and free. They're imaginative and silly, and don't take everything so seriously. I notice many adults who get caught up in the busyness of life or the things that weigh them down. They rarely smile and almost never laugh. Sure, life can become mundane and humdrum at times, but that doesn't mean there can be no joy!

While there may be times of sadness, there is still room for regular smiling and a good belly laugh. Laughter can relieve stress, turn your "sad" into "glad," and help decrease pain. And it's contagious, having a positive impact on those around you. You'll find ample medical research indicating that those who laugh regularly are happier and healthier.

Darling, God wants us to be joyful. God wants us to laugh often, because laughter, according to the Word, is powerful medicine. As such, be mindful to smile and laugh a whole lot more. Ask God to help you experience his joy in wondrous ways, and no matter what's going on, give yourself permission to giggle and see the lighter side of life each day.

## Good Morning, Lord

*Please help me notice the humor within
my day, and relax with heartfelt laughter.*

*"A cheerful heart is good medicine, but a broken
spirit saps a person's strength."*

PROVERBS 17:22

## TAKE YOUR SCHEDULE TO GOD

One reason why some find it challenging to feel joyful is because their schedules are swamped with things that don't bring them joy. This can make for an exhausted, grumpy person. It's tempting to think that we don't have enough time to do things we say we want to do, but perhaps we forget how many hours there are available. With 24 hours in a day and 168 hours in a week, I think if we take an honest look at our schedules, we can rearrange them to spend more time doing that which is joyful.

Though God doesn't operate on our timetable, he does understand that we are working with a certain number of hours in a day. But God doesn't want us to be so busy running around taking care of things, or worrying about the past or the future, that we don't enjoy life.

God wants you to go to him with your schedule and solicit his thoughts on it. He may ask you to cut some things out. He may ask you to add some things that bring you joy, because when you laugh and are joyful, you're more likely to feel fulfilled. You may need to ask for help more often or refuse new commitments.

You can waste your time, or you can spend it wisely. Please choose to spend it in a way that honors God and brings you joy. Take your schedule to God and rework it so that joy becomes your best friend.

### ⌘ Good Morning, Lord ⌘

*I am giving you my schedule because I can't do this on my own any longer. Please give me the strength to make the necessary changes so that my schedule is healthier for me and more efficiently serves my priorities.*

*"You will show me the way of life, granting me the joy of your presence and the pleasures of living with you forever."*

PSALM 16:11

# BE DOERS OF THE WORD

It's uncomfortable to realize that we may be fooling ourselves if we think that identifying as a Christ follower and learning God's Word is enough. Some who proclaim themselves to be followers of the ways of Jesus have been accused of hypocrisy—acting pious on Sunday and neglecting their beliefs the rest of the week. The Epistle of James is reminding us that this is not acceptable in the eyes of our Lord.

The entire first chapter of James is devoted to understanding that, as followers of the ways of Jesus, we will have various temptations. James gives us direction and encouragement to persevere. He says we must be doers of God's Word. He makes the blunt observation that if we only "hear" the message without acting upon it, we are deluding ourselves.

The good news, dear one, is that it's not that challenging to be a doer! Simply watch throughout your daily life for ways in which you can be a representative of God. Treat others as you know Jesus would treat them, and how *you* want to be treated. Offer help to a neighbor, donate to a charitable cause, babysit for a single parent . . . The possibilities are virtually endless.

Christ followers don't perform acts of kindness for acknowledgment or reward, but because that's what is expected by God. However, remember that James assures us that when we are doers of God's work, we *will* be blessed as a by-product. And that, darling, is icing on the cake.

## Good Morning, Lord

*I want to help others, and I ask for your guidance, support, and encouragement in doing so. Please give me divine assignments showcasing how I can best be of service.*

---

*"But don't just listen to God's word. You must do what it says. Otherwise, you are only fooling yourselves."*

JAMES 1:22

## LISTEN TO YOUR CONSCIENCE

Have you ever been ready to do something and suddenly get a gut feeling that you shouldn't do it? Maybe a red flag is raised, a sense of danger comes over you, or you simply *know* that what you're about to do would not be pleasing to God.

We all have a conscience, which acts somewhat like an alarm, letting us know to pause and pay attention to what's going on. Resist the urge to rush into a decision and instead take a moment to pray. Behind our conscience is God, and he will use it to guide us in a good way.

It's important to be sensitive to your conscience and respect it. If the siren is going off within you, pause briefly and pray. Ask God to show you clearly what to do. This will ultimately save you from making choices that can harm you or others.

God may be warning you to stay away from certain people who will cause you grief, such as someone you're dating or new friends at the office. Pay attention to those red flags, or you may end up in a toxic relationship or an environment that you really dislike. Learn to hear your internal alarm, and when it sounds, stop and ask God what he's trying to show you. This makes for a lot fewer headaches, heartaches, and bad days.

### Good Morning, Lord

*Please help me heed the red-flag warnings to change directions. I pray that I will notice and follow these important signals.*

*"Cling to your faith in Christ, and keep your conscience clear. For some people have deliberately violated their consciences; as a result, their faith has been shipwrecked."*

1 TIMOTHY 1:19

# JESUS CAME TO BRING THE KINGDOM

If you can imagine living back in the days of Jesus, you may better understand the role that he came to earth to fulfill. Your family would be having an ordinary day, when this prophet comes along and turns whole cities upside down with his special message, miracles, and unconventional methodologies. But Jesus didn't come to create mayhem. He came to bring *freedom*.

In the book of Luke, we find Jesus saying that he came to bring Good News to everyone. He came to set free those who were in bondage—spiritually speaking. He came to teach people there was a new kingdom, or level of consciousness, available that they could partake in: namely, God's Kingdom that is full of light, love, forgiveness, compassion, joy, and so much more. It says he came to proclaim God's favor on mankind.

Think about this. You're there sitting among the masses, listening to Jesus speak and teach. You're watching as he lays hands on the sick and they are healed. You're hearing how he transformed lives and equipped people through his teachings to live better. What would be going through your mind?

Reading the Gospels, we can see so much about this man who came to liberate those who would heed his words and follow his example. What a gift! What a gift to be able to have a relationship with the Lord Jesus! May we continue to follow his ways, walking in his light and enjoying the freedom that is ours in him.

## Good Morning, Lord

*I am opening my arms and my heart to loving you and receiving your love for me. Please take me into your arms, and support and strengthen me.*

*"The Spirit of the Lord is upon me, for he has anointed me to bring Good News to the poor. He has sent me to proclaim that captives will be released, that the blind will see, that the oppressed will be set free, and that the time of the Lord's favor has come."*

LUKE 4:18–19

# ALWAYS CONNECTED WITH OUR FATHER

We've never separated from our Creator God. Being formed in his image and Spirit, the connection has always been there.

Have you ever felt like you're separated from God? Have you felt *abandoned* by God? Have you felt alone in this world, trying to navigate and make sense of things that sometimes just *don't* make any sense?

One thing I really love about Jesus is that he was so connected with his Father that he was willing to do whatever God asked, whether he understood it or not. Whether he had to suffer or not. I think we can all agree that Jesus was a highly evolved, spiritual man in the flesh. He knew that not everyone would understand his messages or purpose for coming to the earth.

He proclaimed to the masses (my paraphrase), "I come from a different place. A higher, heavenly place. As such, I am not of this world, but I have come to this world to show you profound truths. To open the eyes of the spiritually blind and help you realize that you are always connected to your Heavenly Father."

Dear one, God sent Jesus for the greater good of humankind. We are indeed spiritual beings having a human experience.

## Good Morning, Lord

*Please help me open wide my eyes to see and attune my ears to hear the Truth of your Gospels. Though I may feel weighted down with this fleshly body at times, please allow Holy Spirit to bring me the remembrance that I am in this world, but I am most certainly not of it.*

*"Jesus answered, 'My Kingdom is not an earthly kingdom. If it were, my followers would fight to keep me from being handed over to the Jewish leaders. But my Kingdom is not of this world.'"*

JOHN 18:36

# Prepare to Birth Your Dream

I think dreams are important, both the kind you have while sleeping, and your positive intentions for the future. To go through life courageously dreaming and going after your desires just feels good. I remember when I was pregnant with my children, I started making preparations for their arrival well before they were born. I understood the importance of planning ahead.

Yes, we dream up good things, and I also believe God lays upon our hearts his dreams for our lives. He knows what we will enjoy, and he also uses his children to accomplish his will on the planet, so he sows dream seeds in the heart. If we're careful to listen and pay attention, we can decipher what those dreams are.

Maybe *you* have some dreams that have penetrated your heart. Whatever they might be, start preparing for them now, instead of saying, "Well, when this happens or that happens, *then* I will get that dream off the shelf." If you wait until the conditions are perfect, you'll never get going. If you start preparing now, you create momentum that will help that dream become a reality faster. When you prepare, you're *believing* that you're going to fulfill that dream. You have faith that it will come to pass. With God's help, Spirit's guidance, and the angels' assistance, there is no reason why you *can't* fulfill the dreams God has placed in your heart.

Dear one, ask God how you can begin preparing for the birth of your dream. Then be diligent to follow his lead, because he is more than willing to show you the way.

## Good Morning, Lord

*You know what my dreams are, and I thank you for ensuring that my intentions are God based instead of ego based, so that I'm truly walking upon the path where I can bring the most blessings.*

---

*"Good planning and hard work lead to prosperity, but hasty shortcuts lead to poverty."*

**Proverbs 21:5**

# WATER YOUR DREAM SEED WITH THE WORD

Yesterday we talked about preparing for your dreams to come to fruition by acting in faith. For the next few days, we're going to look at several ways you can get that momentum going. Today, let's concentrate on how we can take the Word of God, which is like a seed, and cultivate it to take root in our hearts.

A while back, we discussed the parable of the sower, and the four types of soil that seeds may fall on when they are scattered. Remember that the seed that was sown in the fertile, good soil took root and grew nicely. Proverbs 12 says that "the godly are well rooted and bear their own fruit." When we have right standing with God, we have cultivated deep roots that allow us to thrive. They're the kind of roots that keep us steady, continuing the journey to which we've been called.

Now, bear in mind that it takes time for roots to develop. They require adequate water and sunshine for optimal growth. That dream in your heart is the seed of God, and you can grow that seed by nourishing it with his Word regularly. Time in the Word and communing with Jesus is the "water and sunshine" that will help you accomplish your dreams.

Today, please keep this in mind, dear one. Let God's Word penetrate your heart as you spend time with it, knowing that you're cultivating deep roots and bringing your dreams into reality.

## Good Morning, Lord

*Thank you for helping me root myself in the Word
to increase the depth of my connection with you.*

*"Blessed are those who trust in the Lord. . . . They are like trees planted along a riverbank, with roots that reach deep into the water. Such trees are not bothered by the heat or worried by long months of drought. Their leaves stay green, and they never stop producing fruit."*

JEREMIAH 17:7-8

# WEED YOUR DREAM GARDEN

Yesterday we talked about using God's Word to grow strong roots into your heart soil. You really cannot go wrong spending time learning and thinking about applicable wisdom found in the Bible. As we continue today, we're going to talk about weeds. Now, it's not that weeds are bad; they're just not welcome to overtake a garden.

To fulfill your dreams, it's necessary to cultivate secure roots and weed out things in your life that will come in to crowd or choke out your momentum. Practically, you may wonder what these "weeds" may look like. What kinds of things suck the life or the dreams out of people? Well, weeds can be the ego, more concerned about building its own kingdom than God's Kingdom. It could be some sort of addiction. It could be wasting time on things that don't really matter, certain people who bring a lot of drama into your life or drain the energy out of you, and so on. Weeds show up randomly, and if you don't take the time to tend your garden regularly, before you know it they're everywhere.

Dear one, if you want to pursue the dreams in your heart and feel as if you're not making much progress, check to see if you have some weeds growing. Assess your motives, gauge the time you're spending with God and in his Word, look at your plan of action, and do an honest inventory. The fewer weeds, the more likely that your dream garden will flourish.

## ⌇ *Good Morning, Lord* ⌇

*Thank you for showing me any weeds in my garden and giving me the strength to release them.*

*"Other seed fell among thorns that grew up and choked out the tender plants so they produced no grain."*

MARK 4:7

## STAY BALANCED

Today, let's discuss a verse in James concerning dreams. While there are many success-oriented people out there, there are some who are so focused on the manifestation of their dream that they don't enjoy the present. In other words, they take it to the extreme.

It's likely that you know someone out of balance in this area. Yes, they can be doing a world of good, but if they're leaning toward preoccupation, they're liable to lose out on some things. They may become exhausted and burned-out. Some people lose sight of God while they're chasing after their dreams, no longer looking to bring glory to their Father, but to themselves. Learning how to stay balanced in any and every area will help you live a happier life.

Planning and preparation is helpful. However, the book of James reminds us that we don't even know what next month or next year holds. We can't see into the future. Why overly concern ourselves with the distant horizon down the road at the risk of losing the good things we have right now?

Dream up good dreams and create wise plans, sweetheart. Allow God to be in the midst of it all. But don't forget about today. Don't forget to invite God into your plans so that you can enjoy the journey instead of just focusing on a certain destination. It's good to set goals and pursue your dreams, but avoid the extreme. The Word says when we put God first, he'll work out the details. You can trust in that.

### Good Morning, Lord

*Please show me how to balance my life so that
I am taking care of my priorities in all areas.*

*"How do you know what your life will be like tomorrow? Your life is like the morning fog—it's here a little while, then it's gone."*

JAMES 4:14

# WAIT WITH PATIENCE

Imagine wanting a beautiful flower garden, so you till the soil and plant the seeds. Then your child comes along two days later and digs it all up, leaving the seeds exposed to the hot sun. You ask why, and he says, "They weren't growing, so I thought something was wrong with them. I wanted to check."

It's an honest misunderstanding. He didn't realize that the seeds *were* growing; it just takes time for them to push their way out of the soil.

In the same way, it takes time for good things to come to fruition, but people can get in a hurry and forget about the transformation going on in the growth process. Perhaps you have felt frustrated or think that God just isn't working on your behalf as you wait for your goals and dreams to manifest.

Dear one, it will help you so much if you simply do your best and trust God for the rest. God is at work whether you see signs or not. His timing is not ours. However, if you've done your part and you're still not making headway, check if there are any weeds to pull in your life. It's so easy to point fingers at others, but sometimes the breakthrough may be stalled because we're not being honest with ourselves.

God wants you to remain steadfast in faith regardless of what you see. He wants you to walk in patience, believing that in due time you will reap a harvest. Allow patience to do its work, as you're learning valuable lessons along the way. Continue dreaming up good dreams and going after them in the power of God.

## Good Morning, Lord

*Please fill my mind and heart with patience*
*and faith. I trust that as I follow my divine guidance,*
*everything is growing for the greater good.*

*"But if we look forward to something we don't yet have, we must wait patiently and confidently."*

ROMANS 8:25

## CALLED TO LOVE EVERYONE

There's no doubt that God wants us to love and take care of each other. In John 13:34, Jesus says, "So now I am giving you a new commandment: Love each other. Just as I have loved you, you should love each other."

Perhaps you noticed that there are no exceptions given to the commandment. It's easy to love people when they're nice, but what about when they are filled with hate? As challenging as it may be, we're called to love *all* as brothers and sisters of Christ. We may not agree with their behavior, but the higher road is always love.

In Matthew 5:46, Jesus asks, "If you love only those who love you, what reward is there for that?"—essentially saying that if we only love good people, we are not fully following God's commandment to love all. Nobody says loving your enemies and blessing those who curse you will be easy. It's quite difficult to invite positive feelings in for those who hate, mistreat, or persecute. It goes against feelings we might have about "bad" people, whom we think deserve to suffer. But when you rise to the challenge of loving the unlovable, you have God on your side, and receive peace knowing that you have done what he expects of you.

Pray for your enemy, for those who curse you and mistreat you, for strength to love them despite the wrongs they commit. Pray that your love is a direct reflection of God's love for them, and pray that their hearts turn to him. In so doing, you are praying for true peace.

### ⟶ *Good Morning, Lord* ⟵

*I want to be like you and forgive those whose actions*
*I find hurtful. Please take my hand and teach*
*me about the true meaning of forgiveness.*

*"But I say, love your enemies! Pray for those who persecute you!"*

MATTHEW 5:44

# COLLECT TREASURES FOR HEAVEN

There is nothing wrong with having and spending money. However, God's Word does state that the love of money can be the downfall of many (1 Timothy 6:9–10). With that said, it's not money itself that's the issue; it's the *love* of money, or greed. Focusing too much on material wants distracts us from focusing on God.

I believe God wants us to enjoy life, and this will mean different things to different people. Think about a family who wants to have an enormous home and can afford all that is required to furnish and maintain it. Perhaps another family with the same income has made the decision to live a modest lifestyle in a small house, and give their excess to charity. Who are *we* to judge which people are following God's direction? Perhaps both families are living in a way that pleases God too, so it is important that we not judge others.

The main concept of this scripture is not that we shouldn't enjoy "treasures" while we are here on Earth. We just need to remember that the material things we possess are fleeting, and can't go with us when our days are up. Whatever we own now will eventually get old and decay. The real treasures that will follow our spirits onward don't cost a cent. All we need to do to collect these real treasures is to follow God's ways the best we can.

 *Good Morning, Lord*

*I need your help, please, to keep my focus upon what really matters in the depths of my soul. Please help me walk the path of Spirit instead of the path of material distractions.*

*"Store your treasures in heaven, where moths and rust cannot destroy, and thieves do not break in and steal."*

MATTHEW 6:20

# SAFE IN GOD'S SHELTER

As Christians we might know in our hearts that God is present in our daily lives, but during times of need we tend to feel insecure and wonder whether he is truly aware of our problems—and if he is, why isn't he fixing them? We have his promise that he listens to our supplications, although we might not always get an answer right away. We should remain faithful, continue in prayer, and ask God for his Spirit to be with us until his will is done in our lives.

Imagining will help you create positive reinforcements of God's presence and provide encouragement. When you think of God, picture in your mind a huge, sturdy structure, such as a stone castle; a dependable lighthouse; or, as this scripture says, "a strong fortress." These are all safe places relied upon to give shelter during sieges or storms. An army might be attacking the castle or fortress, or a hurricane pounding the lighthouse, just like challenges at your door. Imagine that God is standing at the entrance, beckoning you to run to him and be safe. He will enfold you in his arms and protect you while you weather whatever trials are going on outside.

We all experience periods of doubt, feeling like we are alone and allowing ourselves to become anxious or depressed. Always remember that God is our refuge we can run to. Rest assured, God's strong tower is always there, waiting for you. He will see you through every storm.

## Good Morning, Lord

*Thank you for your steady protection and for being my shelter and tower of strength.*

*"The name of the Lord is a strong fortress; the godly run to him and are safe."*

PROVERBS 18:10

# SPEAK WORDS THAT PLEASE GOD

I find social media to be a wonderful tool for teaching and connecting with loved ones. However, it can also become a time waster and a space for people to spread judgment and hate. You may have been on the receiving end of a rude comment before or seen threads where people really go at it, trading barbs. We don't have to engage or respond in a similar manner, although it may be tempting to mirror back to a person their rudeness. Remember that Jesus also faced insults, threats, and accusations. What did *he* do?

David captured the essence of what Jesus would do in Psalm 19. He affirms that he is committed to speaking words that will be acceptable in God's eyes. Had Jesus received a rude message through e-mail or social media, I imagine he would have taken the high road, like David. He may have even smiled, thinking, *They know not what they are doing.* Instead of seeing their anger or character defects, he would probably see their pain and their need for the unconditional love of a Father who could heal that pain.

Should you be the recipient of a rude comment, before reacting, think about what Jesus might do in the same situation. Recognize that this is your opportunity to wait and let God direct the words from your mouth. Pray for the person. Or simply ignore the comment or delete it and move on, knowing that God is your Source of worth.

### Good Morning, Lord

*Please insulate me from people who act, speak,*
*or write in unkind ways. Let me have compassion for*
*them in their suffering, which is triggering their behavior.*

---

*"May the words of my mouth and the meditation of my*
*heart be pleasing to you, O Lord, my rock and my redeemer."*

PSALM 19:14

# WHAT ABOUT THE GRAY AREAS?

Wouldn't it be nice if life was black and white, with definitive answers to all the questions? If we knew without a shadow of a doubt where God stood on every issue? The reality is that there are a lot of gray areas in life, and the Bible doesn't always touch on such areas in depth. Take alcohol, for example. Those in favor of consumption argue that Jesus turned water into wine, so obviously he didn't disapprove of it. Yet others can point to scripture that deems it unhealthy.

No matter what the gray area is, studying the ways of Jesus can lead us down the path for the greatest good. If God's kind of love is our motivating factor for everyday living, and we're following our holy conscience, then gray areas aren't so much of an issue.

God's Word can shine light on areas we just aren't positive about. Be sure to look throughout the Bible for the bigger picture rather than focusing on a single verse to back your position. For example, the beginning of 1 Corinthians 10:23 says, "I am allowed to do anything." By this phrase alone, you might feel entitled to do whatever you feel like, regardless of the consequences. However, the last part of that verse is "but not everything is good for you." The full context makes a big difference.

There is such wisdom in the Word of God. When you're seeking answers, turn to the scripture and prayer. Ask God to show you the best path, dear one, and he'll guide you with love.

## Good Morning, Lord

*I wish to utilize my time so as to bring*
*maximum blessings to my life and benefit humankind.*
*Please guide my actions, and show me the way.*

---

*"You say, 'I am allowed to do anything'—but not everything*
*is good for you. You say, 'I am allowed to do anything'*
*—but not everything is beneficial."*

1 CORINTHIANS 10:23

## ASK AND RECEIVE

Sometimes we grumble when things don't seem to be going well. How much healthier and more effective it is to ask for help, though, rather than complain!

Complaining is an affirmation of powerlessness. Yet the ego tries to convince us that asking for help is a sign of weakness. It's not! The most successful and healthiest people in the world have learned that teamwork, cooperation, and delegation are essential. We can't do everything alone.

Prayer is one of the most powerful ways to ask for—and receive—help. Again and again in the Gospels, Jesus reminds us of this essential spiritual principle. We probably *need* to be reminded to ask for help.

After we pray for help, the answer usually comes as an idea to take positive action steps. This inner knowingness guides us to shift our behavior in an empowering way. If we dismiss this inner guidance, or if we don't act on it, we may mistakenly believe that our prayers aren't answered.

Prayers are *always* answered in the highest and best way, for everyone who asks, without exception. Be sure to ask from your heart with whatever words are sincere.

### Good Morning, Lord

*Sometimes I feel shy or worried about asking you for too much, or asking for the wrong thing. So please, Lord, help me know what to ask for, remind me to ask, and help me understand and follow the guidance you send me.*

*"Yet you don't have what you want because you don't ask God for it."*

JAMES 4:2

# EARLY WILL I PRAISE YOU

When you open your eyes in the morning, does your mind instantly start racing with thoughts, or do you offer God a "Good morning"? Do you dread getting out of bed, or kiss the morning with a "Thank you"? Do you run out the door, or pause for a few minutes before your Heavenly Father?

Throughout scripture, we find King David consistently spending time with the Lord every morning. He took those moments to make requests and give praise, and then went about his day in expectation mode. He had faith that God heard him and would answer his prayers.

Many people will tell you that their moods are better on days when they spend time with God bright and early, whether it's a few minutes or an hour. It could be time sitting in silence, in meditation, making requests, or singing songs of worship to the Lord. It can be whatever you feel led to do.

If you wake up and rush off without spending time with the Lord, it doesn't mean you're doing something wrong. Perhaps your quality time with the Lord is in the afternoon or evening. However, scripture backs up the claim that putting God at the very beginning of the day can help it head in a positive direction.

Perhaps this is something you could try for a while and see if you notice any changes in how your day goes or how your mood fares. You may find that your days go better when you begin them in communion with the Lord.

## Good Morning, Lord

*As I grow deeper in my communion with you, and you fill my heart with the most beautiful love I've ever known, I gladly make the time to consciously connect with you in the morning and all throughout the day.*

*"Listen to my voice in the morning, Lord. Each morning I bring my requests to you and wait expectantly."*

PSALM 5:3

# MAKE YOUR LIFE A PRAYER

As you deepen your relationship with God, he becomes even more important to you. He is your best friend, your beloved, and the One whom you talk to about everything. Just as you cannot wait to spend time with your favorite human companions, the deep relationship with God motivates you to want to enjoy his company all the time. To "never stop praying," as the apostle Paul instructs, involves your having a continual silent dialogue with God. In your mind, you're talking with your best friend about how are you are doing and what you are experiencing right now.

As you know, the mind can race with so many thoughts throughout the day, but we can cultivate a spirit of prayer where our thoughts automatically gravitate toward God. Like developing any new healthy habit, turning to God becomes a way of life through practice and persistence.

Prayer isn't always about speaking words. Sometimes it's about sitting and listening, letting the thoughts rest, enjoying the present moment. Sometimes it's singing a song to the Lord or meditating on God's Word. You'll find that when you meditate on the Word, you're more apt to memorize it. When faced with some challenge, God's Word automatically comes up as a prayer. As you deal with frustration, your spirit suddenly interjects, *"I can do all things through Jesus Christ, who gives me strength."*

So, dear one, make your life a prayer, directing your thoughts toward God often, communing with him continually.

## Good Morning, Lord

*I love waking up with you on my mind and in my heart.*
*Let nothing distract me from focusing upon you today and every day.*

---

*"Always be joyful. Never stop praying."*

1 THESSALONIANS 5:16–17

## BOLDNESS BEFORE THE LORD

Do you feel as if you can boldly approach God, asking him for what you want? When you envision God, do you picture him as warm and inviting, like a loving Father? Or do you see him as an authority figure, stern in his demeanor?

Your conception of God will have a bearing upon the way in which you approach him. The Word says that God wants his children to go to him boldly with their petitions. He's eager to hear your desires, dear one! Because when you have such confidence in yourself and him, asking according to his will, he's more than willing to approve your requests.

Now, keep in mind that God is not a magic genie who grants wishes. God is paying attention and deducing whether the things you desire will be good for you in a spiritual sense or if they will hinder you spiritually. If the request is contrary to God's will, he will lead you in a better direction.

Dear one, align yourself with God's will and go boldly before him, confident that he hears you and will bring to fruition what is best for you spiritually.

### *Good Morning, Lord*

*My prayer is that God's will be done,
as I know that is what brings me everything I need,
including love, happiness, security, and peace.*

*"And we are confident that he hears us
whenever we ask for anything that pleases him."*

**1 JOHN 5:14**

# GRATITUDE LETS GOD KNOW HE'S ENOUGH

Good morning, dear one. I hope that over the last couple of days, you have been enjoying a spirit of prayer more often and feeling more centered in God's presence. Maybe you've felt the presence of the Holy Spirit or your guardian angels, letting you know that you are surrounded by *so* much love.

This morning, I'd like to bring to your attention one key that can really unlock power in our prayer life. The key is gratitude or thankfulness. Yes, God wants us to go to him with our requests. He hears them and faithfully honors those requests when they line up with his will. But add a good dose of *gratitude* and watch how it opens the floodgates of heaven, raining down grace and favor upon your life.

See, gratitude is turning your attention from yourself to God, thanking *him* for his faithfulness and grace. Have you ever had someone come up to you in deep appreciation for who you are? Not for something you've done for them, but for your character and integrity? If so, then you know what it feels like to be appreciated just for being the good soul that you are.

This is how God is honored when you go to him with gratitude in your heart, thanking him, even if life is full of struggles or things just aren't going as planned. Gratitude is an affirmation of your loving connection to your Creator. Cultivating a heart of gratitude honors God, and extending thanks just feels amazing.

Have you expressed gratitude to God lately? How about to others? And while we're on the topic, I'm in highest appreciation for *you*, dear one. Grateful, indeed!

## ⟅ *Good Morning, Lord* ⟆

*I love you so much! Thank you for loving me
and for teaching me about true love.*

---

*"Devote yourselves to prayer with an
alert mind and a thankful heart."*

COLOSSIANS 4:2

# THE POWER OF FAITH

Scripture says that faith (our belief) is the means by which we can manifest our desires. In other words, what we ask for (if it accords with God's will), we should expect to receive. We are to *believe* ahead of time that God is faithful to his Word and will bring our requests to fruition.

For example, Jesus teaches that to move a mountain into the sea, we must speak to it and tell it to move. Granted, this was a metaphor, but essentially, he's saying we have power through our words, and because we have a direct line to our Father in prayer (because we are united), we can co-create the desires that are in our hearts.

It's mountain-moving faith! It's the kind of faith that God wants us to have individually and collectively. Why? So that everyone worldwide has their human needs met, and also feels love, happiness, and fulfillment.

## Good Morning, Lord

*Thank you for helping me to have complete faith that [describe situation] is already resolved. Please help me graciously receive your divine solution and guidance with a mind and heart filled with trust and gratitude.*

*"I tell you, you can pray for anything, and if you believe that you've received it, it will be yours."*

MARK 11:24

# YOU ARE MORE THAN ENOUGH

Over the years, I've had people come to me frustrated because they've tried various self-help techniques, religions, and spiritual paths in their attempt to feel happy and healthy.

Some feel that this life is a constant struggle. They've prayed, meditated, retreated in silence, sought to be counseled, journaled, and so on. They've healed layer after layer, only to discover *more* layers, leaving them feeling exhausted and disillusioned.

This is not uncommon. What do you do when you've walked the path toward self- and God-discovery and don't like the results? When you love God with your whole heart but still don't like yourself very much?

It's led many to wander on their path lonely and afraid, but Jesus is here to remind us that the road to feeling God's love never need be traveled alone. Dear one, Jesus wants you to know that *you are enough*. Right here, right now. There is absolutely nothing "wrong" with you. He's asking that you give yourself permission to rest. No more striving, wondering if this way or that way will be the answer. Just be authentically *you*, no matter how many more layers you feel you have left to shed. Let go and know that in Christ, you are *more* than enough.

## Good Morning, Lord

*Thank you for healing the way in which I see myself, and helping me love and value myself as you do.*

*"By his divine power, God has given us everything we need for living a godly life. We have received all of this by coming to know him, the one who called us to himself by means of his marvelous glory and excellence."*

2 PETER 1:3

## Jesus Came to Bring Life

Jesus said that he came to give abundant life. Is struggling with depression, as so many do, living an abundant life? It certainly doesn't feel like it, but keep in mind that Jesus wants everyone to experience his joy despite the challenges that arise.

Jesus said that he came to give new life, or a new perspective. Spiritually speaking, he saw humanity walking in darkness and was sent by his Father that we may be set free from that darkness. That we may begin walking in the light.

What happens when you're in a dark room and someone turns on the light? Don't you squint? Doesn't it take a little bit of time for your eyes to get used to that brightness? In the same way, if you've gone from living in a kingdom of darkness before you connected with Jesus to living in his Kingdom of light, it takes time for your spiritual eyes to adjust.

God knows that there are times in life when it seems dark. Dear one, if you're going through a season like this now, know that God is with you. He asks you to go within, to him. Let him know how you feel. In that darkness, he sits with you, comforting your soul. He will show you the way out, which sometimes includes guiding you to a good counselor or support group. Just as it takes time for your eyes to adjust to light, so may it take some time for that depression to lift. Put your hope in the Lord, dear one.

### Good Morning, Lord

*Thank you for shining your light to banish the darkness within and around me, and to show me the way.*

*"My purpose is to give them a rich and satisfying life."*

John 10:10

# God's Natural Therapy

A single mother I will call Emma went through a terribly dark season several years ago. Her grown children had recently moved away, and she felt abandoned and depressed. Emma didn't want to hear about a loving Father God. She was resistant to prayer. She didn't know what to believe anymore.

Eventually, Emma's best friend told her that she was exactly where she needed to be. She'd lost herself caring for others and had no idea how to live contentedly on her own. Her friend told her to make a list of a few things that she still liked doing and do them as often as she could. The problem was that Emma didn't even *know* what she liked doing. She primarily identified with the role of mother and felt worthless without someone to parent. But there is one thing she knew she enjoyed: walking in nature. So, she did.

During her walks, Emma felt lighter, happier, and more at peace. Eventually, she found herself thinking about God as she strolled. She began thanking him for the beautiful things she saw. She would pause to sit in silence, and the sacredness of the moment allowed her to transcend her worries. She was reminded of her prior relationship with Jesus and invited him into her life once again.

Slowly, over time, her heart began healing. Emma resumed trusting God and allowed him to show her who she was in him. Today, she's no longer feeling alone and depressed. In fact, today Emma reaches out and provides hope to those who struggle the same way she did. God never left her, even when she chose to ignore him . . . And, honey, he'll never leave you either.

### ∽ Good Morning, Lord ∼

*Please help me deepen my relationship with you.*
*I pray to feel, hear, and know your presence in my heart.*

---

*"I will meditate on your majestic,*
*glorious splendor and your wonderful miracles."*

Psalm 145:5

## TELL ME ABOUT YOURSELF

*You* are not your job title. Your role doesn't define you, yet it may sometimes feel like it does. I understand, as work is fundamental to many people's sense of identity. But is that *all* you are? What happens to your self-identity if you get laid off? Retire? Get burned-out and need a season to rest? Some lose their sense of purpose and feel anxious and depressed.

God knows who you are inside and out. He knows your identity because he created you. Your "self" isn't based on what you "do" with your time. It's who you *are* at every moment. It's who you've always been. Scripture says that we are sons and daughters of the Most High God. Those who choose to walk in the light of God's ways can center their identity around him and the relationship that unfolds from there.

So, when you're asked "Tell me about yourself," go ahead and define yourself in terms of your roles, because they are valuable. But as God's child, with an understanding of the biblical framework for identity, feel free to share that you are also the Heavenly Father's beloved son or daughter showing up in the world as a representative of God's love.

This, my dear, will clear up any confusion about identity issues you may be struggling with, especially when an external role, like a career, changes or ends. You can show up rooted in Christ, with your identity that stems from a spiritual perspective.

### Good Morning, Lord

*My heart is so filled with gratitude and love for your presence in my life, and for helping me to find my identity and purpose with you.*

---

*"Even before he made the world, God loved us and chose us in Christ to be holy and without fault in his eyes. God decided in advance to adopt us into his own family by bringing us to himself through Jesus Christ. This is what he wanted to do, and it gave him great pleasure."*

EPHESIANS 1:4–5

# HEALING THE HURTING HEART

A woman I'll call Donna grew up in a dysfunctional home where she suffered emotional and physical abuse from both parents. Experts say that we primarily form our identity in childhood, so as you can imagine, Donna's sense of herself and her worth didn't fare well. She grew up guarded, angry, depressed, and controlling.

Fast-forward through a toxic marriage to an abusive alcoholic, and Donna was ready to do whatever it took to feel happy. She was desperate and called on God to save her from her misery. Ever faithful, her Father swooped in and gave her comfort. For the first time in her life, she felt hopeful. She started growing in God, doing all the things she thought he wanted her to do—and still ended up in another toxic relationship.

This drove her to study God's Word diligently, with a desire to understand his abundant love for her. Eventually, she saw that she had a tough time receiving the kind of love she deserved because she harbored such anger toward her parents. Her epiphany helped her realize that her identity in God was enough and that his love was the kind that could heal those old wounds. Over time, that's exactly what occurred.

Donna, seeking God's Kingdom within, received emotional healing and was able to forgive her parents, stop choosing inappropriate partners, and let go of her past. She received the gift of love from her Heavenly Father, loving and accepting herself as he did.

## Good Morning, Lord

*Please help me learn about true love and trust that I am lovable.*
*Please guide my choices in relationships so that I am with*
*like-minded people who share my love for you.*

*"Create in me a clean heart, O God.*
*Renew a loyal spirit within me."*

PSALM 51:10

# No Masks Necessary

Don't judge a book by its cover. This is a familiar admonishment we get while growing up. Rightly so, because it's great advice! It reminds us that even if the "cover" of something looks a certain way, the reality may be entirely different. When it comes to your assumptions about people, how many times have you later found out you were mistaken in your first impressions?

God forms his perception of people entirely differently from most. The Word of God says he looks at the heart, not outer appearances. God sees right past the externals with x-ray vision, zeroing in on the heart of the matter with laser precision. Even when we put on masks to the world, portraying a life of happiness and contentment, God sees behind the facade. He sees if we're hurting or caught up in an addiction. God knows if we're following the ways of Jesus for real, or if we just want others to think we are. God looks at the heart.

Paul prayed consistently that the church in Ephesus would be strengthened with God's spirit in their "inner man," or the inner self. So, too, do I pray that we will be strengthened by God's Spirit to resist the temptation to wear masks or make false assumptions based on the outer appearance of others. I pray that we can embrace vulnerability and authenticity, allowing God to work out that which is not of him, so no masks will be necessary.

May you and everyone feel safe to be your beautiful true self.

 *Good Morning, Lord*

*I need your help, please, to figure out who I really am and have the courage and inner security to be my authentic self publicly.*

*"But the Lord said to Samuel, 'Don't judge by his appearance or height, for I have rejected him. The Lord doesn't see things the way you see them. People judge by outward appearance, but the Lord looks at the heart.'"*

1 SAMUEL 16:7

# POWER TO FORGIVE ALL

I love the story in the second chapter of Mark when Jesus went to Capernaum to share the Good News. Word traveled that Jesus was teaching at a house, and a crowd showed up. There were those curious to learn more about him, those eager to learn how they could take part in this Kingdom that he was talking about, and those who were sick and asking that he heal them.

Specifically, a paralyzed man and four of his friends showed up in the hopes that Jesus would heal the man. However, the crowd was overwhelming, and they could not reach the door to take the man in. Cleverly, they hoisted themselves up on the roof and removed a portion of it so they could lower their friend down to Jesus.

I love the faith of this group of friends because they didn't let anything stop them from reaching Jesus, and they were inventive in their problem-solving. Jesus, of course, saw their great faith and did exactly what they'd hoped, healing that man so he could walk.

This great story affirms that Jesus sees the inner man clearly, as he knows each heart. It also encourages us to act in faith when we're seeking something. Last, it reminds us that there are some who are emotionally paralyzed by things like unbelief, guilt, depression, anger, and the like, and we can befriend and help them, just as the paralyzed man's friends did.

## Good Morning, Lord

*I want to be with you all throughout each day in my thoughts, feelings, and actions. I need your help, please, to creatively manage my time and develop the focus to do so.*

---

*"'Stand up, pick up your mat, and go home!' And the man jumped up, grabbed his mat, and walked out through the stunned onlookers. They were all amazed and praised God, exclaiming, 'We've never seen anything like this before!'"*

MARK 2:11–12

# EQUALLY IMPORTANT IN THE BODY OF CHRIST

Scripture talks about each believer being part of the body of Christ. You may wonder what this means. How can we be part of Jesus's body? Well, the phrase is essentially a figure of speech that refers to the church. Not a denomination, but "church" in the sense of all believers or followers of Jesus.

Think of your body. It's made up of individual parts that all work toward the function of the whole. Each part is important. Just like the physical body is made up of individual parts, the body of Christ is composed of individual believers, with each one having a function that benefits the whole.

Now, at times you may feel that you're not doing enough for God or that your function isn't as important as someone else's. The truth is that no one's function is more or less important. Each part of the "body" is equally important, and God is not into measuring one against the other.

Dear one, you are just as important to the whole body, or God's church, as everyone else. Yes, *just* as important.

Rest easy, knowing that we're all in this together. We're all contributing to the "health" of the body of Christ, so to speak. Stay faithful to your part, darling, and know that God loves you no matter what your function is.

## Good Morning, Lord

*I want to do my part in helping, and I need your help, dear Lord,
to know what to do. Please give me clear guidance, courage,
and motivation to take positive and beneficial action.*

*"All of you together are Christ's body,
and each of you is a part of it."*

1 CORINTHIANS 12:27

# You Are God's Temple

Your life purpose involves bringing peace, healing, upliftment, and love to the world—and that starts with bringing this to yourself. In fact, the best way to teach about peace is to be at peace yourself. By treating yourself as God's temple, you *glow* and inspire others to do the same.

Most likely, you already know this. However, making the time for your spiritual and self-care practices may be challenging if you're juggling multiple responsibilities, or if you feel tired and unmotivated.

Fortunately, there are divine solutions. Praying for more motivation and energy really works! So does praying for more time. In fact, any "excuse" that the ego tries to give you can be banished by tapping into God's ingenious solutions.

### Good Morning, Lord

*Please help me find balance in my life, learning how to take care of myself and fulfill my desire to help others. Thank you for helping me lose guilt and embarrassment associated with spending time or money on my self-care.*

*"Don't you realize that all of you together are the temple of God and that the Spirit of God lives in you?"*

1 Corinthians 3:16

## PAY NO ATTENTION TO CRITICISM

Most of us have run into someone who has unkind things to say about us. I learned a long time ago that I cannot please everyone. In my heart, I aim to help people and am genuine in my endeavors. But not everyone agrees with me, and some have no qualms about telling me why. Others are quick to judge without getting to know me. I don't waste time or energy worrying about what others think. I sow seeds of love and allow God to work through me. I give up all control to him.

There's never been a person whom everyone liked. Even beloved saints and wonderful artists have their critics. *Jesus* was criticized many times. In fact, entire political parties despised him.

Likewise, dear one, don't waste your time or energy battling accusations or criticism from others. Bless them, as God would. If you tie yourself up in knots, consumed with what others are thinking about you, you may lose out on opportunities to be a blessing to others. Instead, keep your eyes on God's path before you. Focus on the truth of who you are in Christ. Because when you know your own worth in Christ, and concern yourself with only God's approval, things that other people say will have no power over you.

I'll let you in on another secret: very often, those critics will turn into your greatest supporters if you just give them some space, prayers, and time.

### ⟿ Good Morning, Lord ⟿

*Thank you for giving me the grace to deal with criticism in a healthy way, according to God's will. Please help me turn the other cheek and transform battlegrounds into blessings.*

---

*"Don't speak evil against each other, dear brothers and sisters. If you criticize and judge each other, then you are criticizing and judging God's law. But your job is to obey the law, not to judge whether it applies to you."*

JAMES 4:11

# KNOWING JESUS PERSONALLY

There is a difference between believing in Jesus and knowing him on a more personal level. Though many people use the words *believe* and *know* interchangeably, they don't necessarily mean the same thing.

I'm reminded of the story of Paul and Silas in Acts 16. They'd been beaten and thrown into jail. As the two men were singing praise to God, an earthquake ripped open the foundation and loosed their chains. Thinking the men had escaped, the prison keeper nearly committed suicide, but Paul and Silas called out to the jailer, letting him know they had not left.

The prison keeper was surprised. What if God had allowed that earthquake to happen so they could break free? The jailer ended up going to Paul and Silas, asking how he could be saved. I think he saw how those men loved Jesus with all their hearts and carried the presence of the Spirit, and so he wanted to know Jesus personally. While the jailer may have believed Jesus existed before this, that evening he came to *know* Jesus personally. The Word says he and his household were baptized that very night, rejoicing greatly.

There are many who believe in Jesus, but they may not *know* him in the intimate way he desires. To simply agree with head knowledge about Jesus isn't the same as having a deep-rooted knowing of the heart. Just as the jailer went home rejoicing in his newfound faith in Jesus, so we can be transformed as we get to know Jesus personally.

## Good Morning, Lord

*I greatly want to have a personal relationship with you, and I'm asking for your guidance to feel closer to you. I pray that you will help me sense your loving presence and hear your wise teachings.*

*"He brought them into his house and set a meal before them, and he and his entire household rejoiced because they all believed in God."*

ACTS 16:34

## MOVE TOWARD GOD

There are many things that influence us in life. Some will benefit us, and some won't. Some will move us toward God, and some won't. Some will cause us to become more like Jesus, and some won't.

When Jesus showed up in the first century, he shared how he came to save people from the darkness they were in. He proclaimed a new way, a new perspective, telling people that he was the light that would lead them to eternal peace.

That same message holds today, with Jesus calling those in the darkness to discover the light within. But for those of us who imitate Jesus, there will be things that will try to lead us astray. Paul urges believers to "turn from godless living and sinful pleasures." In other words, avoid people, places, or conditions that will move you away from the awareness of God.

It doesn't take a scholar to identify what types of things constitute "ungodliness." We have a conscience backed by the Holy Spirit, so we can tune in as we go about our day, with the intent of being the light that Jesus asks us to be. When influences come that you know aren't pleasing to God, renounce or resist them. If you need help, ask Holy Spirit, always willing to grace us with the power we need.

### Good Morning, Lord

*Thank you for guiding my actions today, moving me toward God, and keeping me away from that which would darken my world.*

---

*"For the grace of God has been revealed, bringing salvation to all people. And we are instructed to turn from godless living and sinful pleasures. We should live in this evil world with wisdom, righteousness, and devotion to God."*

TITUS 2:11–12

## WALK IN THE SPIRIT

We come to this planet as a precious baby in a fleshly body. As we grow, we hear our parents tell us to take care of this body: "Eat your vegetables," "Brush your teeth," "Take a bath," "Get outside and exercise," and so on. Rightly so, as health experts tell us that we should feed the body nourishing food, practice good hygiene, and exercise regularly for optimal well-being.

Nonphysically speaking, we also come here with a spiritual body, and as we grow, we acquire an ego, or personality, which the Bible calls "old nature." This old nature tends to gravitate toward things that do not serve our spiritual path: "a craving for physical pleasure, a craving for everything we see, and pride in our achievements and possessions" (1 John 2:16). These are distractions from our life purpose.

Now, at times some may give in to the cravings of the old nature. Yet God wants us to walk in his Spirit, instead of obsessing about material items.

Holy Spirit can empower us to choose what will nourish our spiritual body, or new nature in Jesus Christ, and keep our eyes on the good things that bring us closer to God and glorify him. So, dear one, allow God's Spirit to help you deny lusts of the flesh and instead walk in the gifts of his Spirit.

### ≪⸺ *Good Morning, Lord* ⸺≫

*Thank you for lovingly steering me away from that which would distract me or pull me off my path. Please help me stay true to you and my life purpose.*

*"So I say, let the Holy Spirit guide your lives. Then you won't be doing what your sinful nature craves."*

**GALATIANS 5:16**

## SHINING UNDER PRESSURE

Every stressful situation you've experienced has made you the strong person you are today. Each stressful event is an opportunity to notice the patterns in your life, and learn about the choices you've made. Just as pressure creates diamonds and irritants form pearls, so too do upsetting situations bring us valuable opportunities to evolve spiritually.

When our hearts are breaking, they're also more open to love. When we're worried about tomorrow, we're also reminded that the only thing we can control is this present moment. When situations are so overwhelming that we feel backed into a corner, we learn to rely upon faith in God.

What are your favorite ways to manage stress? Know that part of your purpose is to take good care of yourself so that you can enjoy, and withstand the long haul of, a life of service. Remember that Jesus would often go into the wilderness to pray and fast.

### Good Morning, Lord

*Please help me see this situation in a new way, through your eyes of love and wisdom. Please help me have the faith and confidence to deal with stress as you clearly guide me.*

*"Don't let your hearts be troubled.*
*Trust in God, and trust also in me."*

JOHN 14:1

# Family Healing

Focusing upon family may involve your reconnecting via a phone call, a visit, or a gathering. It might be that you pray for a family member, including praying for a healing of any misunderstandings.

One powerful method to help with healing is to write a letter to a family member and pour your heart out about your true feelings. Don't send the letter, but release it in a ceremonial way.

If you miss a family member, reach out to them. Whether they are on Earth or in heaven, you could stir love in their heart (and your own) by initiating a conversation.

If there's an abusive family situation, you certainly don't want to put yourself in harm's way. However, you can still initiate a healing through prayer, counseling, and other support so that your heart can be at peace.

## Good Morning, Lord

*Please guide my words and actions and help me love my family in a way that's healthy, honest, and respectful of everyone. If I need to forgive anyone in my family, please give me the strength to do so.*

*"Go and be reconciled to that person.
Then come and offer your gift to God."*

Matthew 5:24

## BELIEVE IN GOD WORKING THROUGH YOU

You are so lovable, and you are deeply loved. Be assured of your worth and your deservingness. Know that you merit being treated with respect, and take time for your self-care.

Believe in yourself because God believes in you. All the power of God—the same energy that holds every one of the planets in the sky in orbit—is supporting and strengthening you.

Have confidence in God working through you, and you will enjoy self-confidence. When you work in unison with your Creator, loving ideas and messages flow through you.

### Good Morning, Lord

*Please help me feel good about myself—to like, love, and care for myself as you do. Please help me trust and follow through with the ideas that you send to me.*

*"This is my command—be strong and courageous! Do not be afraid or discouraged. For the Lord your God is with you wherever you go."*

JOSHUA 1:9

# BE TRANSFORMED BY GOD'S LOVE

Change is only stressful when we resist flowing in the direction we are evolving. Everything is continuously growing and evolving, and we can either fight against change or surrender and enjoy the adventure.

When you pray for a change, very often your old life must first be dismantled. People may leave or situations may cease to be, or you may no longer feel attracted to them. Your tastes and interests shift. This is part of the transformational process.

Apostle Paul's transformation from Christian-persecutor to Christian-promoter was so drastic that his name even changed from Saul to Paul. Every part of his life was different once he allowed God to use him for a higher purpose.

Making room for the new is a part of change. The river can't hang on to the old without getting stagnant. Life is short, and we are here to learn, remember, grow, help, and love.

## ∽ Good Morning, Lord ∽

*Please help me flow along the path as you are guiding me.*
*I wish to learn, gain new insights, and release any*
*heavy weights that could pull me down.*

*"Don't copy the behavior and customs of this world,*
*but let God transform you into a new person by changing*
*the way you think. Then you will learn to know God's*
*will for you, which is good and pleasing and perfect."*

ROMANS 12:2

# HIS MERCIES ARE NEW EVERY MORNING

Every morning is a fresh opportunity for God's grace to bless your day. No matter what yesterday held, what obstacles it presented, or even how blessed it was, today is brand new, with a clean slate and fresh canvas to paint the kind of life you desire.

Each morning, dear one, is an opportunity for us to set our minds on the Lord to whom we belong, even if it's just a few moments taken to attune to his perspective and offer gratitude for his faithfulness. The Word says that God's mercies are new every morning, that the steadfast love of the Father never ceases. Therefore, we can wake up daily with renewed hope in God, who made a way to bring those lost in darkness into the light.

Are you struggling this morning? Are you anxious about the coming day? Cast your cares on Jesus, for God promises to be with you in the power of his Spirit today. Be aware of his loving presence as you go about your day, fully trusting that he will impart peace, joy, and so much love.

## Good Morning, Lord

*Please help me release these cares and worries,
and trust that you are attending to the details
and guiding my actions on the right path.*

*"The faithful love of the Lord never ends!
His mercies never cease. Great is his faithfulness;
his mercies begin afresh each morning."*

LAMENTATIONS 3:22–23

# UTTER GOD'S WORD EACH DAY

We've talked a lot about the importance of learning God's Word and how powerful it is. God's Word can enlighten, guide, equip, encourage, instruct, heal, and more. In the book of Joshua, we're told to meditate on God's Word night and day.

Now, meditation is an ancient technique practiced throughout the world, usually for the benefit of quieting the mind and becoming more enlightened or conscious. In the Bible, the word *meditate* means "to utter," essentially contemplating and repeating something over and over, like a mantra.

So, with this understanding, you're encouraged to meditate on verses in the Bible. The more you do so, the more beneficial this practice will be. You can also say a prayer for help, and then open the Bible randomly; the first verse you see will usually provide the answer you seek.

Now, dear one, please make it a habit to take God's Word and meditate on it. As you do, I think you'll find that your faith will really soar!

## Good Morning, Lord

*Thank you for guiding me to scriptural passages that are supportive of my situation, and for helping me understand their meaning in my heart.*

*"Oh, how I love your instructions!
I think about them all day long."*

PSALM 119:97

## You Are God's Masterpiece

Have you felt pressure to conform to other people's ideas of who you should be? Have you ever succumbed to this pressure and *tried* to conform? Trying to be someone other than who you are doesn't work very well, does it?

God has created all of us to be different. Each person has an individual life purpose. As long as you're following your divine guidance and doing your best to be kind, you can confidently celebrate your uniqueness—even if other people don't understand. God understands!

Isn't it a wonderful feeling to know that God personally hand-selected and crafted you for a divinely specific reason? Be yourself, as God created you, and you will inspire others to live authentically as well.

### Good Morning, Lord

*Thank you for helping me love myself
as you love me. As I value myself, I am
appreciating your amazing handiwork.*

---

*"Thank you for making me so wonderfully complex! Your
workmanship is marvelous—how well I know it."*

**Psalm 139:14**

# CAST YOUR ANXIETIES ON GOD

Anxiety is a real concern for many people. Is there any hope for those whose nervous systems are constantly on high alert? The Word of God says that we don't have to be anxious; we can cast our cares on the Lord and trust in him solely. But what about those who do this and still find themselves ridden with anxiety?

The reality is that some people pray about their anxiety, yet it remains, causing them to think that they aren't praying hard enough or don't have enough faith. But this isn't true. Feeling anxiety even after you pray doesn't mean you're doing something wrong. God hears your prayers and can bring you to a state of peace, but the truth is that it can take time and practice to let go of anxious thoughts and trust that no matter what, everything will be all right.

Maybe you struggle with a habit of worrying. Ask God for guidance. He may lead you to make lifestyle changes that can help reduce stress and anxiety, or perhaps he'll lead you to a wise therapist. It may take some time, during which you can draw near to God, knowing that you're not doing anything wrong. Anxiety can prompt you to put your trust in God, depending on him to help you learn how to contend with your cares.

God is for you. With the eyes of faith, see the hope that you have in him.

## Good Morning, Lord

*Please help me release these fears and anxious feelings that I've lived with for far too long. Show me the answers and what I need to do, please, as I deeply desire to feel peaceful and calm.*

*"Give your burdens to the Lord, and he will take care of you.
He will not permit the godly to slip and fall."*

PSALM 55:22

# Conforming to Christ's Image

*Why can't I just be like Jesus already?*

Have you ever thought this? As a Christ follower, you make it your aim to become more like Jesus. But what if you find yourself wondering why you're still doing things that don't fit who you want to be? If you're this "new creation in Christ," shouldn't you resemble him already? Why is it taking so long? *Why do I still get angry, judge others, or get distracted by trivia?*

Dear one, the desire to become more like Jesus is wonderful, but the truth is that transformation takes time. Just like the weeks-long metamorphosis of the caterpillar into a beautiful butterfly, so does it take time to walk in this world as Jesus did. It takes effort, discipline, faith, and practice to become more like Jesus. It takes consistent study of the Word, learning how to navigate life with eyes of faith. It takes trial and error, self-love, and a sense of humor. And it often takes support of a loving church congregation or your pastor.

When you put pressure on yourself to be just like Jesus *now*, you'll end up frustrated. Accept where you are on this transformation journey. Rejoice at every milestone, knowing that as you keep your eyes on Jesus, Holy Spirit is at work within you, conforming you to the image of Christ.

## ⤙ *Good Morning, Lord* ⤚

*I love you so much and desire to be like you, but I can also see that I am at times perfectionistic, with unrealistic expectations. I feel that you must have had high self-esteem during your earthly life, and I ask for you to help me find my way as well.*

*"So all of us who have had that veil removed can see and reflect the glory of the Lord. And the Lord—who is the Spirit—makes us more and more like him as we are changed into his glorious image."*

2 Corinthians 3:18

# God Is Clearing Your Path

God can use anyone to fulfill his plans. Take King Cyrus, for example. In the book of Isaiah, God called upon Cyrus, even though he wasn't Jewish, to be his instrument and complete a task that ultimately helped release the children of Israel from exile. God promised Cyrus that he would go before him, clearing a path and removing any obstacles. It's a firm reminder that God's plans will be done, and he'll tap anyone he wants to execute them.

God's will for humanity is that all walk in his divine light, and he uses anyone with a willing heart to accomplish this. We will likely face obstacles, but God promises to go before us, clearing the path so we can move forward. Does this mean it will always be easy? No, but it may be a lot easier than we anticipate.

Whatever obstacles lie in wait, trust that God is well ahead of you, clearing a path to victory as you trust him. He may grant you favor or the courage you need to reach out for help. He may show up unexpectedly in the middle of your day and "wow" you!

As you read through his Word, notice how many times God went before his people, preparing the way to their Promised Land. Listen to victory testimonies from those who have had breakthroughs. Increase your faith and know that God goes before you, dear one, even during your challenges, doing what you cannot do. Trust in your faithful Father.

## Good Morning, Lord

*I am following you. Please show me the way in a manner that I can easily notice and clearly understand.*

*"I will go before you, and make the rough places smooth. I will break the doors of brass in pieces, and cut apart the bars of iron."*

**Isaiah 45:2 (WEB)**

# ENTER INTO REST

I'm a strong woman. However, there are things I simply can't do all by myself, such as moving a heavy object or tending the hundreds of rescue animals that I care for. To attempt to do such things alone would cause me distress and even injury.

Self-sufficiency feels good, but leaning solely on "self" for everything can lead to burnout, frustration, bitterness, and more. Yes, God wants his children to have the ability to do many things, but he doesn't want us to leave him out in the cold because of pride.

"I can do it myself," "I'll figure it out," and "I don't need anyone": These types of statements are usually made by those who have a tough time asking for and receiving help from people and God. While they may be self-sufficient in many ways, they're usually struggling with exhaustion and negative emotions under the surface.

God wants us to be responsible and practice self-care. He also wants us to be able to rest in him. *Rest.* The word just sounds good, doesn't it? How many of us spend every day pushing, striving, doing, and so forth and are desperate for *rest*?

Life happens, and there will always be things to do, but resist the temptation to do it all on your own. Ask for help. Delegate. Take a break from your obsessive-compulsiveness for a while. Enjoy communion with God, resting in his glorious light.

## Good Morning, Lord

*I need your help, please, to know how to balance my life so that I can fulfill my responsibilities, take care of priorities, and also get enough rest and self-care.*

*"For all who have entered into God's rest have rested from their labors, just as God did after creating the world. So let us do our best to enter that rest. But if we disobey God, as the people of Israel did, we will fall."*

HEBREWS 4:10–11

# GOD DESIRES HIS CHILDREN TO BE WELL

God wants you well, dear one—mind, body, and spirit. The Word says "Jesus went around doing good and healing all who were oppressed by the devil" (Acts 10:38). His disciples are recorded as having healed people, too. But does God still heal today?

Just as a parent desires that a child walk in a state of health, so does our Heavenly Father. Why, then, are so many people suffering mentally, emotionally, and spiritually? There are some things we may never fully understand while we're in the flesh.

*Can God heal me?* This may be your question. Yes, it is possible. If you read through scripture, you'll see that faith is key to receiving God's promises. A great way to increase faith is to turn to the Bible and get to know God's Word on the topic. Ask Spirit to reveal your path to healing. You may be instructed to adopt a healthier lifestyle, take a certain supplement, or choose a different healing modality.

God may send a healing angel to you as well. Archangel Raphael has been instrumental in many healings. Spend time in silence, listening to what your body is telling you. Maybe you've been stressed lately, and your body is tired. It may be telling you to take a rest.

If you or a loved one is suffering with illness, my heart goes out to you. I know it can be quite challenging. My prayer is that you can find hope and comfort in God, and receive your healing soon.

### Good Morning, Lord

*I am asking for your healing help again. Just as you've healed so many, please help me increase my faith and receive your healing blessings.*

*"He sent out his word and healed them, snatching them from the door of death."*

**PSALM 107:20**

# RELEASE GUILT AND SHAME

Some people are afraid of love. They're unable to receive it from others, as their hearts are closed off for fear of getting hurt. This can lead them to carry guilt and shame.

Now, there is a difference between *guilt* and *shame*. If you're feeling guilt, you feel bad about your behavior, but if you feel shame, you feel bad about *yourself*. Positivity is very important, but it's not enough. To simply recite positive affirmations with a heart that is filled with guilt and shame is like putting Band-Aids over a deep, gaping wound.

So how do we contend with guilt and shame? First, dear one, recognize that there are lower energies that can create doubt, anxiety, depression, shame, and guilt that will keep you from progressing on your path. It takes confidence to move forward and fulfill God's purpose for your life.

Do you carry guilt or shame? Have you turned to an addiction to such as work or social media to dodge such feelings? Dear one, partner with God and let him help you dig deep down to reconcile those feelings. Allow his living presence to begin healing at the core level, so you can walk fully in his light. Run to Jesus, who has paved the way for you to walk this life in his Kingdom. As you do, you'll be able to not only receive extravagant love but also lavish the same kind of love on others.

## Good Morning, Lord

*Please help me face my feelings so that I can discover the "true me" whom you see and whom you unconditionally love.*

*"Those who look to him for help will be radiant with joy; no shadow of shame will darken their faces."*

PSALM 34:5

## WAIT PATIENTLY FOR GOD

King David wrote many psalms, penning expressions of his deepest emotions to his Lord. He unashamedly voiced his fears, proclaimed great praises, and cried out with all his heart in prayer. Psalm 40 is no exception, as David begins, "I waited patiently for the Lord to help me, and he turned to me and heard my cry."

How could Davis wait so patiently before God? After all, he was in very frightening circumstances at times. As you keep reading through the psalm, David answers this question.

First, David knows that God hears him when he prays. He's got a solid connection with his Lord. Second, David can look back at all the times God has helped him before. They've got history together, and God had delivered and blessed him over and over. God had pulled him out of a pit, set him on firm ground, and put a new song in his mouth.

Dear one, he will do the same for you. Whatever your "pit" is, do as David did and turn to the Lord. Make your requests, remind God of his promises, remember what he's brought you through before, and sing a new song of praise. Wait patiently, darling, trusting that God hears every prayer.

### Good Morning, Lord

*I need your help. Please hear my urgent plea,*
*and if I must wait for your answered prayer,*
*please help me trust and have patience.*

*"I waited patiently for the Lord to help me,*
*and he turned to me and heard my cry."*

PSALM 40:1

## BECOME AS LITTLE CHILDREN

Jesus's disciples were curious. They asked Jesus what kind of person would be greatest in his Kingdom. Who would get to sit near him in heaven?

I imagine the disciples on the edge of their seat, eager to hear "keys to being the best in the Kingdom." Jesus tells them that unless you're just like a little child, you won't have a chance at even getting *into* the Kingdom.

Jesus's answer may have confused them. They may have been thinking, *What do children know? Why should they be great?*

Jesus says that the most important in the Kingdom will be those who are as children, largely because of the innocence and humility intrinsic to small children. It's not about your status or how powerful you are. The man who preaches to millions is no more powerful or greater in God's Kingdom than the eight-year-old who shovels his neighbor's driveway just to bless her. It's a heart issue. The way to become great in God's Kingdom is to humble yourself, as a child, recognizing your dependence on Father God.

Become as a child, dear one, in humility before the God of the universe. Surrender to him, acknowledging your dependence, and trust in his mighty redeeming power.

### *Good Morning, Lord*

*I deeply wish to be more humble, and I can feel my ego resisting this call and wanting to stay in control. Please help me regain that part of me that is a trusting child, dear Lord.*

*"Then he said, 'I tell you the truth, unless you turn from your sins and become like little children, you will never get into the Kingdom of Heaven.'"*

MATTHEW 18:3

# THE WORD IS ALIVE

I have a deep love for the Word of God. It's a necessary and helpful guide for this life journey. But more than that, the Word is living and powerful. The words in the Bible are animate forces that can produce mystical and long-lasting transformation in those who receive them. I've certainly found that reading the Bible daily enhanced my life.

Have you ever read or heard something in the Word that caused you to render a "conviction" over something you said or did that didn't honor God? Or were you moved to do something that blessed another? That's the power of the living Word.

Scripture says we should meditate on the Word daily and become students of the Word, allowing it to increase our faith and transform us. Remember Jesus likening the Word to a seed in the parable of the sower. Just as a seed is alive and grows, the Word is alive and grows in our hearts as we spend time cultivating it.

The results can be astounding. Psalm 1 says we'll become like a fruitful tree by the stream, producing nourishment for all creation. We'll be refreshed and revived, and enter God's rest with a heart of gladness.

Dear one, spend time in God's glorious Word treasure daily. Let it take root deep in your heart and nourish you. Watch how the living seed transforms you, and share the Good News with others.

### Good Morning, Lord

*I love spending time with you, both your words written in scripture and your living words received in prayer and meditation. Thank you for being here for all of us!*

*"For the word of God is alive and powerful. It is sharper than the sharpest two-edged sword, cutting between soul and spirit, between joint and marrow. It exposes our innermost thoughts and desires."*

HEBREWS 4:12

# BE FILLED WITH HOLY SPIRIT

You are one with All That Is. You are light. You, as spirit, are joined with God's Spirit. Dear one, when you really get revelation of this, you won't be the same. When you realize that God really has given us his Holy Spirit, you feel blessed, loved, and safe. Once you know without a shadow of a doubt that God himself dwells within you, your perspective changes. Your thoughts and actions shift. Your faith incalculably increases.

As a branch is nourished from the root and cannot produce fruit without it, so are we completely dependent upon God's Spirit to produce fruit in our lives. Walking as children of God, moving and having our being in him . . . How blessed are we!

There's so much we can learn from sitting in nature observing God's magnificent creation. Look at the tall trees and their massive root systems producing life in the branches, growing fruit with which everyone can nourish their bodies. It's magical!

In and of myself, I can accomplish some things. But in and of God's Spirit, life takes on new meaning, and I accomplish God-inspired things. It is no longer *I* who live, but God's Holy Spirit lives in me!

Dear one, I ask that you really take some time this week and contemplate the reality that Jesus has sent Holy Spirit as our teacher, guide, comforter, and partner. Allow Holy Spirit to give you what you need at every moment, whether that's grace, courage, strength, unconditional love, forgiveness, wisdom, patience, or whatever the case may be. Be filled with God's Spirit, darling. Be joy filled.

## Good Morning, Lord

*Thank you for sending Holy Spirit to abide within me and everyone. I appreciate this help to overcome my fears and control issues.*

---

*"Don't be drunk with wine, because that will ruin your life. Instead, be filled with the Holy Spirit."*

EPHESIANS 5:18

# TALK TO HOLY SPIRIT THROUGHOUT THE DAY

Yesterday we talked about how we are encouraged to walk in the power of the Holy Spirit every day. But what exactly does this look like? Practically, how do we abide in Christ?

The first thing is to ask to receive God's Spirit, opening your heart to his presence. Trust that as you ask, he fills you. He comes to partner with you, leading you as you allow.

Next, a practical way to abide in his presence is to pray. Communicate with God at moments throughout your day. Don't just give God your prayers in the morning and then forget about him. That's depending on yourself, for the most part.

Talk with God during the day. Ask him questions, such as whom you should make the time to talk to. Pause before reaching decisions, asking Spirit for guidance. It's about consciously making the effort to feel as if you really are partnered with another person and always in his presence.

Dear one, as you go about your day talking to Holy Spirit, you are abiding in his presence. He will become more real to you, and he will teach you many things. The result will be beneficial to you and God, because when you abide in Holy Spirit's presence, you are not concerned about your will or your fleshly desires. You're concerned with God's desires for you and for humankind, with faith, hope, and love being the most important things in your life. Indeed, Holy Spirit's presence is powerful. Call on him now, and let him abide with you today.

## ∽ Good Morning, Lord ∽

*I now commit to praying, speaking, and listening to the loving wisdom of your Holy Spirit throughout today and every day.*

*"No one can know a person's thoughts except that person's own spirit, and no one can know God's thoughts except God's own Spirit. And we have received God's Spirit (not the world's spirit), so we can know the wonderful things God has freely given us."*

1 CORINTHIANS 2:11–12

# GIVE THANKS FOR EVERYTHING

God is joyful, and in spiritual truth, so are you. I'm not saying everything will be easy or that you won't face obstacles. But you can learn to fly above those issues, above the clouds, so to speak, where the sun is always shining!

First Epistle to the Thessalonians tells us to give thanks in all circumstances. Often, we give thanks only when things are going well. When something fortunate happens, someone will say, "Isn't God good?" But the reality is that God is good all the time, even when things aren't going the way we'd prefer.

Cultivating joy takes wisdom and practice. Without God, Jesus, and his presence, mustering up joy isn't always an easy task. Now, gratitude is a force that will help you cultivate joy. A heart bubbling with thanks tells God that you are grateful for his presence in your life and love him unconditionally, no matter what temporary struggles you're going through. This is the kind of love that God loves *us* with, which is something to rejoice about.

This week, to cultivate even more joy in your life, begin saying "Thank you" to God for everything—the good things and the unpleasant things that happen. It's not that you are praising God for that set of circumstances, but thanking him for who he is. It's gratitude that lives by faith, trusting that all is ordained by God, that your life is in his hands, and that all is well. Sweetheart, give thanks to God in all things, for he is good and faithful, and he loves you more than you can even fathom.

### ⌒⌒ *Good Morning, Lord* ⌒⌒

*Thank you for your presence in my life and in this world.*
*Thank you for watching over me, for loving me, for supporting*
*me, and for guiding me. Thank you for everything!*

*"Be thankful in all circumstances, for this is God's*
*will for you who belong to Christ Jesus."*

1 THESSALONIANS 5:18

# GETTING UNSTUCK

Why do we feel stuck in unhealthy situations and seem unable to leave them behind? It's often because we fear that change will lead us to a worse situation. Sometimes it takes an intense wake-up experience (like an illness, breakup, or job loss) to push us out of the nest and allow us to fly on our own.

However, you needn't wait to hit bottom to be convinced that it's time to leave, because you've already heard this inner calling. As you become increasingly sensitive, you increasingly dislike harsh energy. You need to protect your physical and emotional health by being in gentler situations.

Leaving behind a stressful situation can refer to releasing the past, especially if recurring memories are triggering you. It can also mean healing the situation so that you can stay in peace.

If you feel stuck, reach out to draw from God's strength for support and courage. God can clear the way miraculously for a much-needed life change, ensuring that everyone involved is taken care of.

## Good Morning, Lord

*I feel stuck and afraid to make a change, yet I know I need to stay away from that which is unhealthful for me. I need your help, dear Lord, your strength, your support, and your guidance to show me the way. Please protect my heart as I make this change, and protect the hearts of my loved ones as well.*

*"Then, turning to his disciples, Jesus said, 'That is why I tell you not to worry about everyday life—whether you have enough food to eat or enough clothes to wear.'"*

LUKE 12:22

## SIT AT THE FEET OF JESUS

I love the story about sisters Mary and Martha, as told in Luke 10. One day, they invited Jesus to their house for fellowship. Martha got upset with her sister because she wasn't helping her prepare a meal for their guest. Instead, Mary was sitting down with Jesus, having a conversation with him. Martha asked Jesus to tell Mary to help her, but he said Mary had chosen wisely by sitting with him. He told Martha that she was worried about too many things.

I think this story can speak to those who feel they have so many things to do. We may become frustrated, feeling like we must do everything, and end up complaining about how it takes time away from Jesus.

Now, Martha's heart was in a good place, wanting to serve food to Jesus, but her frustration toward Mary didn't become her. This is a firm reminder that there will always be things to do, but making quality time to sit with Jesus is priceless.

Don't be so busy with "things" that you miss opportunities to sit with Jesus or spread his love to others. There are numerous activities that could rob us of our time or peace, and if we're not being mindful, we may choose as Martha did. This story encourages readers to commune with Jesus regularly, spending quality time together, forgetting about the list of things that need to be done. Choose as Mary did, dear one. Choose to sit at the feet of Jesus to listen to him and enjoy his presence.

### ∽ Good Morning, Lord ∽

*I love you and want to spend more time consciously in your presence, feeling your love and receiving your wisdom.*

---

*"There is only one thing worth being concerned about. Mary has discovered it, and it will not be taken away from her."*

LUKE 10:42

## RELY ON SPIRIT TO HELP YOU EXERCISE SELF-CONTROL

Not everyone embraces self-control when tempted. Even those who follow Jesus admit that earthly desires get to them every now and then. James 1:14 says, "Temptation comes from our own desires." Self-control is having the ability to not act on impulses that go against what God desires, whether that's saying no to that alcoholic drink or the married man flirting with you.

The reality is that we're going to come up against cravings or desires that are ungodly. This makes me think about addiction, a major problem in the world. Whether someone is addicted to alcohol, drugs, food, gambling, television, social media, or toxic love, lack of self-control can bring great harm upon that individual, loved ones, and society.

I understand it's challenging to take an honest inventory, but God desires his people to live in freedom. And the first step to freedom is admitting if you have a problem. If you're letting addiction control you, can you own up to it? Are you ready to tackle it, knowing that God is on your side?

Honey, God asks that you reach out to him for help. Ask him to deliver you from addiction or acting out on impulses that are not pleasing to him. One of the fruits of the Spirit is self-control, so call on Holy Spirit to accompany you every moment, depending on him to help you walk strong. This way, you'll feel less of a pull into earthly desires, and more of a pull toward God.

### ⤙ *Good Morning, Lord* ⤚

*Please help me walk the straight and narrow path of Holy Spirit, which I know is the true path of happiness and everlasting peace.*

*"Temptation comes from our own desires, which entice us and drag us away."*

JAMES 1:14

# BE AT PEACE WITH EVERYONE

I see a lot of people get into relationships hoping that the other person will make them feel whole. The truth is that only God can bring us to wholeness. The apostle Paul says that God "brought us back to himself through Christ. And God has given us this task of reconciling people to him" (2 Corinthians 5:18).

Sooner or later, conflict will arise in any relationship. Learning how to contend with it in a healthy manner will help you and your relationship endure. Conflict is an opportunity for you to spiritually grow. Conflict resolution is making a commitment not to run or act out, but to sit down and discuss the matter in a way that would honor God—as if Jesus were sitting right there with you. It's sincerely apologizing when appropriate, listening intently without defensiveness, and not yielding to the temptation to let your emotions take over and control the conversation. It's going within and asking Holy Spirit to help you and your partner find resolution. It's taking seriously God's desire to resolve the conflict in a peaceful and loving way, resisting pride or ego.

It's not a matter of who's right or who's wrong. It's about committing to honor God and God's Word no matter what. Romans 12:18 says, "Do all that you can to live in peace with everyone." Dear one, if you're struggling in resolving conflicts with loved ones, take a season to pray and work on this. If you find you need additional help, reach out. May your relationships be blessed with the love and peace that can only come from Jesus Christ.

## Good Morning, Lord

*Please help me face relationship conflicts with
honesty and openness, staying strong and centered
in faith in the process of negotiating resolutions.*

*"The Lord gives his people strength.
The Lord blesses them with peace."*

PSALM 29:11

# YOUR STORY MATTERS

Your story matters. Regardless of where you've been or what you've done, the lessons you've learned are valuable. Maybe you don't believe you have much to share with others, you struggle with depression or lack, or you don't feel as if your life is any big deal. Dear one, I'm telling you that it matters. *You* matter.

Every life has instances of pain, struggle, and mistakes. There are things you want to kick yourself for doing, but there are also victories, lessons learned, and amazing memories that can help others.

How many times have you read a story that gave you hope? How many times have you looked to others' example for guidance on what you're going through? In Mark 5 there's a story of a man possessed by unclean spirits. He was out of his right mind, living as a savage in the caves. Jesus delivered that man from those spirits, setting him completely free. The man begged to go with Jesus as he ministered, but Jesus encouraged him to go home and tell of the wonderful miracle he received from God.

We are encouraged and empowered to teach what we've learned. We're to share our stories with others, to empower and give them hope in the Lord. Write down some of the lessons that you have learned in life. See how God worked behind the scenes of situations, and share the nuggets of truth he taught you. Whether you blog or contribute to another online forum, write a book, or sit with family to share, please own and voice your story. What a way to encourage others!

## ∾ *Good Morning, Lord* ∾

*I so appreciate and admire your teachings,*
*and I also feel guided to teach others as you lead me.*

---

*"But Jesus said, 'No, go home to your family,*
*and tell them everything the Lord has done for you*
*and how merciful he has been.'"*

MARK 5:19

# GOD IS MY SHEPHERD

When I look at the sheep on my rescue ranch, I often envision what the shepherds of biblical times would have looked like among this herd. The Bible mentions sheep more than 500 times. There are beautiful metaphors of Jesus as a shepherd, gently tending his flock of humans who need his guidance. It's comforting to think of God watching over us in the same loving way that a shepherd is devoted to his sheep.

To say that a shepherd simply takes care of sheep is an understatement. Although sheep were frequently tended by families, it was a job that most often fell to an adult male. He had to be strong to protect the flock, and wise to guide them through their day. A good shepherd supplies all the needs of the sheep so that they lack nothing.

The symbolism is unmistakable. God takes care of our every need. He is with us 24-7 to watch over and guide us. He will protect us from dangers outside the fold. If we wander, he will seek us and lead us to still waters and green pastures that restore our soul.

Psalm 23 of David has just six verses, yet it is one of the most powerful scriptures in the Bible, memorized by children and spoken as a mantra of comfort by adults. It's a mighty promise: Goodness and loving-kindness shall follow you all the days of your life, and you will dwell in the Lord's house forever. Use this blessing and know that God is your shepherd, and you lack nothing.

### Good Morning, Lord

*My shepherd, my guide, my protector, my teacher,*
*my love, bless you for keeping me and the rest of*
*your flock safe. I promise to listen to your call.*

*"The Lord is my shepherd; I have all that I need."*

PSALM 23:1

# WALK IN THE SPIRIT AND ENJOY GOOD FRUIT

When you think about a tree or vine, the fruit you find is straightforward. You won't see apples growing on an orange tree, or strawberries on a tomato vine. Everything produces what it was meant to. As we see in Matthew 12:33: "A tree is identified by its fruit. If a tree is good, its fruit will be good. If a tree is bad, its fruit will be bad."

The fruit of God's Spirit is good, and he is known by this goodness. The fruit of the flesh is corrupt, and it can lead to temptations—lustfulness, idolatry, hatred, strife, jealousies, divisions, and drunkenness, just to name a few. We are warned that indulging will inhibit our ability to enjoy God's Kingdom.

I believe that people are inherently good, but even good people can be enticed by the temptations of daily life. Nobody's humanly perfect, despite our commitment to trying to follow God's Word. When we recognize an undesirable situation has arisen, we should ask for forgiveness and try to use the experience to avoid future temptation.

When you commit to live by the Holy Spirit, you learn to walk in the Holy Spirit and enjoy the good fruit. If you allow your life to be led by God, nothing will keep you from the blessings he promises. Learn to practice virtuous attributes and to seek the fruits of God's Spirit, that you may walk confidently on the path of peace and love, straight toward God's Kingdom.

 *Good Morning, Lord*

*Thank you for reminding me that true happiness comes from the spiritual, not the material.*

*"But the Holy Spirit produces this kind of fruit in our lives:
love, joy, peace, patience, kindness, goodness,
faithfulness, gentleness, and self-control."*

GALATIANS 5:22–23

# THE RIGHT PATH FOR A CHILD

As parents, guardians, ministers, friends, relatives, or teachers, we have a solemn duty to teach children everything we can to ensure they grow into confident, functioning adults. It is our duty to provide love and guidance throughout their lives. Patterns and habits formed early on and reinforced through adolescence likely will be retained and practiced throughout life. A child will mimic what they see, even if they don't understand it yet. If a family prays together over their meals, even an infant will mirror their actions as they bow their heads. As a child matures, they will comprehend what's happening and understand what it means to speak blessings over food.

When we direct our children, we are teaching them the moral and spiritual lessons they must master to become strong and faithful as they follow their own paths in life. Sharing Bible stories, singing songs, providing instruction in ethics, modeling healthy boundaries, and guiding children to follow God's commandments will instill core values and bring them comfort, true happiness, and reassurance. This translates to confidence and dependability in their belief system, creating a firm foundation for living the kind of life God wants for each of us.

Anyone who has had children knows that there are periods of uncertainty, particularly as teenagers go through "low" times of selfishness and rebellion. When they occur, pray that God will guide the child through their valley and help *you* remain strong, faithful to his Word. Remember, he's in control.

### Good Morning, Lord

*Please give me the strength to be lovingly strong
and consistent in guiding my child in the best way.*

*"Direct your children onto the right path, and
when they are older, they will not leave it."*

PROVERBS 22:6

# BE PATIENT WITH ONE ANOTHER, IN LOVE

Sometimes Christians are viewed as holier-than-thou and judgmental. Tragically, this perception pushes some people away from Jesus or keeps them from joining a church. Such people don't need a scolding lecture from a Christian; they need a gentle, from-the-heart conversation with someone who can share Jesus with them.

Apostle Paul issues a reminder in Ephesians 4:1 to "lead a life worthy of your calling." Our calling is to follow God, and it is unworthy of him to be impatient toward, or intolerant of, our brothers and sisters in Christ. We don't need to be bossy, preachy, or pushy to share God's message of love. When we view each other through God's eyes, we accept the good *and* the bad. We forgive the wrongs that occur even between believers and work together toward a unified goal.

More people will be receptive to following Jesus when we act and speak with a gentle heart—with love, forgiveness, and understanding. Instead of calling someone a sinner, take his hand and have a loving conversation with him.

Remember, the greatest man who ever walked the earth was born in a humble manger and died on a cross saying, "Father, forgive them." We need to walk humbly in our teaching ministry as well.

## Good Morning, Lord

*Please guide my words and actions to reflect your true message. Help me mirror your love to everyone I meet.*

---

*"Always be humble and gentle. Be patient with each other, making allowance for each other's faults because of your love."*

EPHESIANS 4:2

# A NEW HEART

The word *heart* appears hundreds of times in the Bible. At numerous points, the Word says we are to love God with all our heart. In Acts 13:22, David is described as a man after God's own heart. We see in Romans 10:10 that it is with the heart that we are "made right with God."

Jesus also talks about the human heart. He knew what people were thinking in their hearts. He also knew when hearts were far from him or when people were pretending to love him with all their hearts, yet were faking—like the scribes and Pharisees in Matthew 23:25–26.

Biblically speaking, the heart is the essence of our being—the center of our spiritual life. Before Jesus came on the scene, the Old Testament prophets referred to the heart as wicked and deceitful. But Jesus came to give us a new heart, or a new spirit. When we accepted Jesus's liberation from the darkness, our hearts were born anew, clean and pure.

This means the new heart will have new desires and embrace a new way of life in the Kingdom of light. It will have the power of the Holy Spirit to help guard it against the ego and the lower energies. When we study the Word of God and sow its seed into our hearts, blessings are sure to come our way. Matthew 5:8 says, "God blesses those whose hearts are pure, for they will see God."

Darling, rejoice in a new heart that is passionate for the Lord God! Guard it "above all else, for it determines the course of your life" (Proverbs 4:23).

### Good Morning, Lord

*Thank you for purifying my heart and
helping me keep it open to true spiritual love.*

*"And I will give them singleness of heart and put a new spirit
within them. I will take away their stony, stubborn heart
and give them a tender, responsive heart."*

EZEKIEL 11:19

# WHO WILL YOU SERVE?

Choices come at us every day, from which foods to eat and what clothes to wear to what kinds of friends to associate with, and more. What about spiritually? Are there choices we have to make as followers of Jesus?

Absolutely. God desires *all* our hearts, so there's a choice right there. Will we give God all or just part of our lives? For example, will we lean on God when times are rough but forget about him when things are going well? Or act "good" in front of others but indulge ego-based desires in secret?

In the Old Testament, Joshua makes a bold statement that he and his house will serve the Lord. He chose to follow God's will, and as head of his household, he declared that faith in God would be their way of life.

But shouldn't partners, spouses, and kids be allowed to navigate their own spiritual path? Within reason, yes, but the gist of the message is that if you choose to commit to living by biblical principles, then don't go looking for a relationship with someone who has no desire to do the same. If you're committed to following Jesus, do it with your whole heart.

There are plenty of causes to serve in the world, but whose will *you* serve?

## Good Morning, Lord

*Please help me be a role model to my family and friends, demonstrating what it's like to be completely devoted to you. I also ask that you help me be discerning in my choices.*

"But as for me and my family, we will serve the Lord."

JOSHUA 24:15

# MAGNIFY THE LORD

Jesus's mother, Mary, was an incredible woman, to say the least. God used her as a vessel to carry his Son, as he knew she was a humble woman with a heart disposed to serve him. Imagine being Mary, told that you're going to have a baby you didn't plan on. Raising a child, God's Son or not, is a huge responsibility. Certainly, Mary could have chosen to be upset or resentful, but instead she rejoiced! She received the Word of the Lord unto her and felt immense honor to be able to be such a servant.

It says in Luke 1 that Mary sang a song of praise to God, elated and grateful. She begins: "My soul magnifies the Lord!" As a magnifying glass makes things larger, her soul enlarged God significantly! Mary goes on to proclaim the mighty acts God has done for his people and for her. She says that he fills the hungry with good things. I love that.

Mother Mary remains an inspiration to many all over the world. If you read through Luke 1 entirely, you'll also see how God used her cousin Elizabeth for his holy purposes. Both of these women were humble and faithful, and graciously served God.

God loves everyone, but he's on the lookout for those who walk with a humble heart. Dear one, clothe yourself in humility and faith as you serve the Lord. "Clothe yourself" is a biblical phrase that means to adopt positive attributes. After all, "clothing yourself" with these virtuous characteristics seals them into your consciousness, guiding your actions and thoughts from love.

### Good Morning, Lord

*Please help me humble myself, and detach from the ego.*
*I am truly honored and grateful for your support.*

---

*"Mary said, 'My soul magnifies the Lord. My spirit has rejoiced in God my Savior, for he has looked at the humble state of his servant.'"*

LUKE 1:46–47 (WEB)

# THE POWER OF WITNESSING

If you've ever seen a loved one suffer, you know what it's like to long to take their suffering away or "fix" what's going on. This is when the power of witnessing can be powerful. By *witnessing*, I mean standing alongside your loved one patiently, extending unconditional love. It means surrendering to the Lord, asking him to intervene on your behalf.

God calls us to extend kindness, patience, and compassion to the suffering. This means consciously standing alongside them to love them through their process.

Is it easy? Not necessarily. Just ask the mom whose daughter is addicted to drugs. Or the son caretaking his chronically ill father. Or how about Mother Mary, who had to watch her Son suffer at the hands of men. No, it may not be easy, but offering empathy and God's kind of love is required.

My hope is that if we are confronted with such suffering in a loved one, we'll rely upon God to help us witness with compassion and patience. That we'll stay balanced and neither think we have to "fix" them nor turn a blind eye to them. That we'll be Christlike to them. I think of Mother Teresa and how she so humbly served the sick and dying, witnessing their suffering and bringing Jesus to each and every one.

May we do the same.

## Good Morning, Lord

*I intend and commit to be fully present in love and strength for those who are suffering. Let me be helpful to them as you guide me, and be both truthful and kind, supportive without enabling, and resolute without being judgmental.*

---

*"Since God chose you to be the holy people he loves, you must clothe yourselves with tenderhearted mercy, kindness, humility, gentleness, and patience."*

COLOSSIANS 3:12

# JESUS AS MIRACLE WORKER

In Jesus's short three-year ministry, the Word tells us that he performed many miracles. There are dozens described in the Gospels, and I imagine many were performed that were not recorded. Jesus healed the sick, cast out spirits, raised the dead, and more. He didn't exclude anyone based on ethnicity, sex, or religion; he included the outcasts and Gentiles (non-Jews).

What strikes me as I read through the Gospels is Jesus's compassion for the sick. When he saw people suffering, whether emotionally or physically, he did something about it. He acted on his faith.

Chapters 5 through 7 of the Gospel of Matthew discuss Jesus's Sermon on the Mount, with Jesus teaching golden nuggets of truth about his Kingdom and guidelines for living. In chapter 8, it's recorded that Jesus comes down from the mountain and immediately heals a man suffering with leprosy. In those days, lepers were considered unclean and were banished from the community! But Jesus was all about a "new way." He healed the man and went on to heal many more. Jesus didn't look at the outer appearance of man, but the inner—at the soul.

For the next few days, we're going to look at some of the miracles Jesus performed, as recorded in the Gospels. I believe it helps us gain a clearer picture of Jesus and the Kingdom he wanted to open believers' eyes to.

As you go about your day, dear one, keep your eyes open for miracles and miracle-working opportunities in the power of God's Spirit!

## Good Morning, Lord

*I believe in you, and I believe in miracles.*
*I would love to see and experience you and miracles.*

---

*"Jesus reached out and touched him. 'I am willing,' he said.*
*'Be healed!' And instantly the leprosy disappeared."*

MATTHEW 8:3

# Let It Be Done as You Believe

Luke tells the story of a centurion (Roman officer) who went to Jesus. He told Jesus of his servant at home, paralyzed and suffering terribly, and said, "I am not worthy of you coming to my house. If you just pray for him right now, I know my servant will be healed."

Jesus marveled at the man's great faith. Just as the man asked, Jesus prayed and said, "Let it be done for you as you have believed." Miraculously, his servant was healed that same hour.

With this miraculous healing, Jesus was teaching that in this new Kingdom of his, those suffering did not have to continue to suffer. Perhaps at the time people thought that Jesus had to lay hands on a person to heal, but here he demonstrates the power of his words. To this day, praying in the power and authority of Jesus Christ of Nazareth can bring healing to people.

Does everyone have this power to heal? According to the Bible, yes. We cannot ignore the many instances in the Word that recorded Jesus healing emotions and physical bodies. I'll be the first to admit that I don't understand why everyone does not receive healing, but this doesn't keep me from using my authority in Jesus's name in the power of Holy Spirit to pray for those who are suffering, just as Jesus did.

My hope for you, dear one, is that as you study the biblical accounts of Jesus's healing and miraculous ministry, your faith increases and you go about *your* life ministry as a servant of Jesus.

### ❧ Good Morning, Lord ❧

*Please guide me to heal myself and others.*
*I would love to be in the service of healing.*

---

*"Then Jesus said to the Roman officer, 'Go back home.*
*Because you believed, it has happened.' And the*
*young servant was healed that same hour."*

**Matthew 8:13**

# EVERYONE IS WORTHY IN GOD'S KINGDOM

Persistence can oftentimes get you what you want. We've all witnessed a child whose persistence in asking a parent for something paid off. When it comes to prayer, this quality is even more valuable.

Matthew 15 tells the story of a Canaanite woman going to Jesus because her daughter was sick. At first Jesus did not pay attention to her. Then, when she persisted, he told her that he had been sent only to the Jewish nation, and she was a Gentile. Yet again she kneeled before Jesus, pleading for mercy.

Jesus's initial reaction is interesting because he'd just healed the centurion's servant, a Gentile. Perhaps he used this as a teaching opportunity for the disciples, who thought that Jesus came only to save Israel. Jesus knew that he was sent to all people—the Jewish and the Gentile communities alike. Jesus might also have responded the way he did in order to test the woman's faith. Ultimately, Jesus did commend her for her incredible faith and healed her daughter.

I feel that this story is a wonderful lesson on the value of persistence in prayer and holding on to faith that God is able to do mighty things. I believe the reason why it works to pray repeatedly is that the more we pray, the more faith we have. We don't repeat our prayers to appease God but to increase our own belief in the power of God.

Whatever you're seeking for, continue to take it to God in prayer, in the mighty name of Jesus Christ and the power of his Spirit. Hold fast to your faith, darling. Persist!

### Good Morning, Lord

*Thank you for helping me build and strengthen
my faith by hearing my repeated prayers.*

---

*"'Dear woman,' Jesus said to her, 'your faith is great.
Your request is granted.' And her daughter was instantly healed."*

MATTHEW 15:28

# Enjoy a New Season of Growth

Throughout life's journey, there are ebbs and flows. We have seasons where we grow tremendously spiritually, and seasons where growth seems to come slowly or not at all. Over the years, I've learned that when I want to experience growth in a particular area, it helps if I make a firm commitment. By this, I mean taking time regularly to research the area in which I wish to grow.

As adults, we are free to grow and develop as we wish. We can give ourselves the opportunity to tap into the many resources available for personal and spiritual growth. This could mean investigating a new career, hobby, or place to visit. Or perhaps you might get yourself a spiritual mentor and commit to a season of growing spiritually. Maybe your kids are out of the house, and now you'd like to go on a spiritual walkabout, traveling the world!

Yes, it will take some effort and time, but we just feel better when we're cultivating growth in our lives. I'm reminded of the Serenity Prayer, which is popular in recovery circles but is applicable to everyone: *"God, grant me the serenity to accept the things I cannot change, courage to change the things I can, and wisdom to know the difference."*

Make this your prayer today, dear one. Give yourself permission to move those still waters that you've been sitting in. Enjoy new insights, lessons, and experiences that cultivate much fulfillment and joy in your life.

## ᕦ Good Morning, Lord ᕤ

*Thank you for being with me through my various experiences and moments of growth and stagnation. Thank you for showing me that it is a valuable pursuit as I reach out now to learn and grow again.*

*"Let the wise listen to these proverbs and become even wiser. Let those with understanding receive guidance by exploring the meaning in these proverbs and parables, the words of the wise and their riddles."*

Proverbs 1:5–6

# ESTHER KIND OF FAITH

The story of Esther in the Old Testament captures the essence of a woman clothed with beauty, humility, strength, and faith. It also allows us to see God's divine timing and immense love.

Haman, a jealous adviser to King Xerxes (Esther's husband), was plotting to wipe out the Jewish people. Queen Esther had kept her Jewish heritage a secret, but the Jewish people went to her, pleading for help. She knew she had to find the courage to face the treachery of Haman, so she asked her people to fast and pray with her for three days before she went to her husband.

Even knowing that approaching the king without permission could mean death, Esther did so, and her courage saved the Jewish nation. Her bravery and faith in God speaks loud and clear lessons to those who face what may seem like insurmountable obstacles today. Even if she had to die for speaking out, she was willing to take that risk to save her people.

Esther's story shows us how bravery, faith, sacrifice, and patience are all qualities we can embody as we travel through life. Dear one, no matter what your struggles are, apply an Esther kind of faith and courage, knowing that God will back you and show you the way to victory. You may not have to save a nation or speak with kings, but you *will* benefit when you stand on the Word of God, with faith and courage as your companions.

## Good Morning, Lord

*Thank you for giving me the courage to do what I know is right.*
*Even if I can't see how it will work out, you endow me*
*with the faith and the strength to do so.*

---

*"And then, though it is against the law,*
*I will go in to see the king."*

ESTHER 4:16

# For Just Such a Time as This

There's a verse that really speaks to me regarding the story of Esther: "Who knows if perhaps you were made queen for just such a time as this?" It is said by Mordecai, Queen Esther's cousin, who knows God will deliver the Jews one way or another. It's what God does. But, just maybe, God has orchestrated this whole thing—making Esther an extraordinarily beautiful woman and giving her favor in King Xerxes's sight—so that she could be in a position of power to save the nation of Israel! It would be just like God to choreograph such a scenario. For it to work, though, Queen Esther had to be on board.

Even when we know what God's will is (that people be saved from darkness, that the helpless be provided for, and so on), it can still be frightening to take the action we are guided to. Esther knew what to do, and she was brave enough to do it. She prayed and fasted, and invited others to join her. The power of prayer should not be minimized. Esther said essentially, "Yes! God *did* put me here for such a time as this!"

Dear one, may you have the courage and faith to say the same. Maybe you are right where you are for such a time as this! Maybe God's been orchestrating things behind your back, and now is the moment for you to pray and fast for favor, courage, and the kind of faith that will rescue others from peril. God's purposeful choreography is amazing, darling, for just such a time as this!

### ∽ *Good Morning, Lord* ∽

*You are a testament to supreme courage, and I aim to be like you: taking action in God's power, with faith and confidence.*

*"If you keep quiet at a time like this, deliverance and relief for the Jews will arise from some other place, but you and your relatives will die. Who knows if perhaps you were made queen for just such a time as this?"*

Esther 4:14

# The Value of a Good Name

Is it better to have favor instead of gold and silver? Proverbs 22 says, yes, it is.

The truth is that many people, including Christians, opt to pursue wealth and fame at the expense of their good name. Remember the story of Satan tempting Jesus in the desert, telling him that if he'd only bow down before him, he'd have all the riches in the world? This is a firm reminder that such temptation has been alive and well for centuries.

But what exactly is the proverb saying? What does it mean to have a good name?

It's not about your name given at birth, per se, but about integrity. You're given a name, but your reputation and character are earned. Are you honest, trustworthy, patient, dependable, faithful, and a good steward? Or are you the opposite?

Granted, money is a valuable resource. But refrain from tarnishing your character by using dishonest means to obtain it or boasting about it. Being a person of integrity is far better than being the richest person in the world. It's about maintaining good morals and ethics and using what God has given you as a faithful servant.

Loving others is so much better than lusting after "things." Check your heart, dear one. Are your affections captured by money or "things" at the expense of others? Has any dishonesty crept in? Take it to God, and ask him to reveal anything that may be displeasing to him. Aim for a good name, full of integrity and love, as you serve God.

## ∽ Good Morning, Lord ∾

*Please guide me to know the right thing, to do the right thing, and to trust that doing the right thing is its own reward.*

---

*"A good name is more desirable than great riches, and loving favor is better than silver and gold."*

Proverbs 22:1 (WEB)

## SOAR AS AN EAGLE

When eagles are approaching a storm, they don't fly into it. They could; their agility and sheer strength would probably get them through all right. But instead of being battered around by fierce winds and rain, do you know what they do? They rise above the storm.

In fact, eagles can soar at high altitudes that other birds cannot. They are amazing creatures, sometimes used metaphorically in the Word of God to depict things like strength and protection.

I love the majestic splendor of eagles. The way they fly vigorously against the wind, soaring far above all other birds, taking ownership of the sky. When I recognize that I'm in a metaphorical storm, I remember the eagle. I square my shoulders, take a deep breath, extend my faith wings as far as they can go, catch a big gust of Spirit, and soar with the angels. I gaze at the heavens with the eyes of faith, above all the things swirling around in that storm. We can all do this!

Dear one, don't stay down in the midst of all that lower energy. Catch a big gust of Holy Spirit's wind and soar like an eagle above it all.

### Good Morning, Lord

*Please help me soar, with my eyes fixed on God's Kingdom,
full of light and the kind of peace that surpasses understanding.
May Holy Spirit's wind carry me and lift me high.*

*"But those who trust in the Lord will find new strength.
They will soar high on wings like eagles. They will run
and not grow weary. They will walk and not faint."*

ISAIAH 40:31

# BLESSED ARE THE MERCIFUL

The Lord blesses those who show others mercy and compassion, and Jesus exemplified such a life. Mercy is a necessary attribute for building the Kingdom of God. Tenderhearted Jesus bestowed mercy wherever he went, extending grace to outcasts, the poor, the tax collectors, sinners, and religious leaders who thought they had it all together.

God is merciful to all who come to him. Without God's mercy, all would be separated from him because no one can stand before God without fault. When the scribes and Pharisees brought the adulterous woman to Jesus and asked whether she should be stoned to death, Jesus said, "All right, but let the one who has never sinned throw the first stone!" (John 8:7). The men could not, as none were blameless. His words were a reminder that we've all bent the rules, made a mistake, and fallen short of God's mark.

Dear one, Jesus knows every heart and chooses to extend mercy to all, regardless of what they've done or who they are. Does this give people permission to go against what God desires? Not at all. God sees the motives of the heart, but for those who do miss his mark and are truly sorry, he extends mercy—and we are called to do the same.

Have you experienced mercy when you've missed the mark? Have you extended mercy toward others, forgiving them? Kept your tongue quiet instead of passing judgment? Look to Jesus as your role model, dear one. The Word says that the merciful will be blessed, so accept and give mercy freely.

## Good Morning, Lord

*Please help me be like you, offering myself and others genuine compassion and mercy.*

*"God blesses those who are merciful, for they will be shown mercy."*

MATTHEW 5:7

# YOUR WORTHINESS COMES FROM GOD

Do you ever wonder if you're doing a good job with your life or measuring up to God's standards? Many people find themselves thinking a lot about trying to get his approval. In our society, we tend to hold ourselves up for comparison with others. Churchgoers size up their relative contributions, coworkers compare their projects, kids yearn for approval of their peers.

If you have been questioning yourself lately, take some quiet time with the Lord. Understand that you are already worthy just being who you are in Christ. You are a part of God, as he created you in his own image.

Are you striving? Are you grasping for meaning? If you are, ask Holy Spirit to guide you each day and look for opportunities to be of service to others. This could be as simple as consciously being present for your immediate family. Sometimes just getting your eyes off yourself and onto others is a way to make life more meaningful.

There may always be room for improvement when it comes to being a servant of the Lord, but there is also something to be said for the ability to enjoy the journey, content with who and where you are right now. Dear one, ask God to remind you where your true worth comes from. Remember that being saved comes from grace, not from your actions. I'm certain God will remind you that it arises from your unconditionally loving relationship with him.

### Good Morning, Lord

*Thank you for reminding me that I am loved and valued,
and for guiding me to be of true service—motivated by
my heart, not by my ego trying to get accolades.
I want to walk upon the path as you lead me.*

*"And this is the way to have eternal life—to know you,
the only true God, and Jesus Christ, the one you sent to earth."*

JOHN 17:3

# GRIEVING IN PRAYER

God hears the grieving heart. In fact, he's right there helping the griever bear it. The story of Hannah paints another picture of how he moves on behalf of those who cry out to him.

Hannah, wife to Elkanah, wanted a child desperately and grieved that she hadn't been able to bear one. She made a promise to the Lord that if he blessed her with a male child, she would entrust his care to Eli, the high priest. Eli saw her sincerity and prayed that she would conceive, and she did. Samuel was born to Hannah and grew up in the temple under Eli. As you can imagine, Hannah was thrilled, offering prayers and praise to the Lord. She played an important role in Israel's history, bringing a great prophet into the world, and God further blessed her with more children!

Hannah was persistent in her prayer and faith. Her story reminds us to be the same. It also reminds us that God extends mercy to those who are grieving. Hannah deeply desired to be a mother and was willing to entrust her son's care to the high priest, seeing him only once a year. God could have chosen someone else to birth the prophet, but he chose sweet-spirited Hannah. God takes note of the pure of heart.

Is there something you desire with your whole heart? Take your prayer to God continually. Be fervent in making your request known. In divine timing, God will find a way to optimally fulfill it.

## Good Morning, Lord

*This is me, asking for your help and needing your help. Please hear my prayer. Please answer my prayer. Please give me the faith and the trust to know that you will answer my prayer in the best way, at the best time.*

---

*"And in due time she gave birth to a son. She named him Samuel, for she said, 'I asked the Lord for him.'"*

1 SAMUEL 1:20

## JESUS IS THE LEADER

Power can lead to an ego trip, as some go from genuinely interested in serving others to serving themselves. Promotions into leadership have caused plenty of people to exchange service for selfishness and an unquenchable thirst for power.

But Jesus was different. Serving God and people was what he aspired to in his heart. In fact, Philippians 2:7 says that Jesus "gave up his divine privileges; he took the humble position of a slave," yet he was oftentimes opposed by political and religious leaders. They did not want Jesus spreading his Gospel of love and grace. *They* created the patriarchal religious system, and that's the way they wanted it.

The world needs leaders who will imitate the selfless and humble servanthood of Jesus Christ in order to create lasting, positive change. Using a position to wield power over others, ultimately harming the masses, is not God's will. God's will is that all his children be led by those who are motivated by righteousness, peace, and a servant's heart.

Today, acknowledge Jesus as your true leader, making a fresh commitment to model your life after him. If you do lead others, please serve them with a humble and compassionate heart. Also, pray for your national and local leaders, that they too will adopt a servant's heart, embrace godly character, and serve people as unto the Lord.

### Good Morning, Lord

*Instead of worrying about news stories, I choose to pray for divine intervention. I trust that God is the true world leader.*

*"Some nations boast of their chariots and horses, but we boast in the name of the Lord our God."*

PSALM 20:7

# BLESS ALL YOU MEET

Most likely, you pray to make a positive difference in the world, and you are already doing so. One way to help others is by consciously sending them blessings. It's a shifting of the energy. It's not people-pleasing or trying to fix anyone. The Word says God did not give us a spirit of fear, but a spirit of love.

Today, please bless everyone you meet: your partner, friends, coworkers, and strangers. Take a moment and think, say under your breath, or mouth the words "Blessings to you." Or pray something specific for them as you are led. Ask God to reveal his love to them, request that angels surround and protect them, thank God for their presence in your life, and so on. Simply extend loving vibrations toward them.

As you do, you'll notice a difference in the way you view your relationship with others. You won't be on guard so much, afraid of giving your power away. You won't be giving to get something in return, either. You're simply blessing each person as an ambassador for Christ and staying within your own internal boundaries. Dear one, enjoy this beautiful day the Lord has made, blessing others along the way, and giving glory to your Heavenly Father.

### Good Morning, Lord

*Please fill me up with your blessings, so that I may pass these blessings along to everyone I meet. I trust that you will send people who need blessings my way.*

---

*"I urge you, first of all, to pray for all people. Ask God to help them; intercede on their behalf, and give thanks for them."*

1 TIMOTHY 2:1

# LOVE NEVER FAILS

Is your life a testament to unconditional and unstoppable love? Are you giving and receiving more of it as you continue to get to know Jesus on a more personal level? Do you take the time to show love to more people in more ways, even when it's challenging?

Everyone has the capacity to love. There is a love born of God that goes beyond the kind of love that the self can provide. It's that *agape* or unconditional, extravagant love that can transform lives in an instant. It's that word of comfort lovingly spoken to a hurting person that can start mending their heart. It's holding the tongue when someone lashes out because of their own frustration, extending them compassion instead.

As a Christ follower, I believe our lives ought to be marked by a certain kind of love that can only come from Jesus. This love can grow exponentially as we surrender fully to our Lord.

Dear one, it is my hope that individually and collectively, we will allow the love of Jesus to flow in and through us in an unstoppable way. That we will indeed walk in this Kingdom of light and shine that light to a world that needs it. Love indeed never fails. And, darling, I unconditionally love you with a divine love that never fails.

## *Good Morning, Lord*

*I love you so much! I can feel your love for me. Please guide me as to how to share this love with those who need uplifting.*

*"Love never fails."*

1 CORINTHIANS 13:8 (WEB)

# Practice the Presence of God

Though Jesus knew he was going to depart his earthly ministry, he would never leave his disciples alone. He prepared them for his leaving, telling them that he needed to go so he could send Holy Spirit to indwell all believers. Through the Spirit, he would be able to teach many things that they were not yet ready to learn.

Tuning in to the presence of God, Jesus, and Holy Spirit makes us more conscious. For example, practice cultivating an awareness of Jesus being with you everywhere. When you're cleaning the house, feel the presence of Jesus beside you. When you're driving to work, sense Jesus with you. When you're with your family, Jesus is, too!

Begin consciously feeling God's presence with you, beside you, and living life with you. Talk with Holy Spirit when you're at work, going for a walk, or while conversing with a friend. Your relationship with God is a continual one, always connected. Open up to the reality of that connection. The more conscious you are of the Holy Trinity's presence, the more peace and joy you experience each day.

## Good Morning, Lord

*I pray that my focus is upon you today.*
*May I be aware of you all throughout the day,*
*having continual conversations with you.*

*"I can never escape from your Spirit!*
*I can never get away from your presence!"*

Psalm 139:7

# ENTER BY THE NARROW GATE

The kingdom of God is in divine perfection. It's orderly and harmonious, offering peace and an abundance of joy. There's no darkness or violence in God's Kingdom, no feelings of unworthiness, greed, competitiveness, or dishonesty. This Kingdom that Jesus talked about is without flaw.

When there's struggle in life, sometimes people blame God, as if God isn't upholding his end of the deal. Blaming God, yourself, or another person is *never* helpful. Instead, take a personal inventory to see if you've veered away from his holy guidance.

Jesus talked about entering his Kingdom through the lightly treaded narrow path, as opposed to the crowded wide path. Jesus is saying that to fully enjoy the Kingdom of God, which is full of light and love, you must be on guard against darkness that may slyly infiltrate—meaning ego or the lower-energy forces that blind hearts to truth.

Jesus is calling his people to a *higher* way of life. A higher consciousness. A Christ-consciousness, where there's a new Kingdom of light that we can abide in. It's about the heart and a sensitivity to God's Spirit, who shines light on areas of ego and darkness so we can transmute them.

Enter the Kingdom of God through the narrow path. Ask Spirit to shine light on anything you may be clinging to that is pulling you down. Ask him to assist you in opening the inward eyes of your soul, leading you along that narrow path toward our great and magnificent Father.

## Good Morning, Lord

*If I have any blind spots, please heal this blindness
and let me clearly see what I need to release.*

*"You can enter God's Kingdom only through the narrow gate.
The highway to hell is broad, and its gate is wide for
the many who choose that way."*

MATTHEW 7:13

# MARY MAGDALENE'S FAITHFUL SERVICE

God welcomes women to participate in his divine plan of redemption. The biblical accounts of women are quite fascinating, and we can learn valuable lessons from their stories.

Take Mary Magdalene, for example. She was a faithful disciple of Jesus, following him throughout his ministry all the way to his death. She was devoted to Jesus up to and even after the crucifixion. Once he'd been buried, she got up early in the morning to bring burial spices to his tomb. She was the first person Jesus showed himself to after his resurrection. I love how the Word records that she didn't recognize him until he said her name, to which she exclaimed, "Teacher!"

Her faithfulness and dedication to Jesus is an inspiration to us all today. She did not leave him when things became dangerous or looked hopeless. She stayed with him, even if that meant giving up her own life.

Embrace a devoted heart, just like Mary Magdalene did. Cling wholeheartedly to Jesus as you go about your day.

## Good Morning, Lord

*I pray to be completely devoted to you and to have
an even closer personal relationship with you.*

---

*"'Mary!' Jesus said. She turned to him and cried out,
'Rabboni!' (which is Hebrew for 'Teacher')."*

JOHN 20:16

# People Need Jesus

People need a lot of things as they navigate their life journey, but what they need *most* is Jesus. Yes, because when people receive Jesus and all that he represents, their way to freedom—from whatever they are struggling against—comes to light.

People need Jesus because, in and of themselves, they cannot produce the spiritual fruits of the Kingdom of God. A self-created life can be a good one, but a God-inspired life can be phenomenal and everlasting. It can be the kind of life that rests in peace, hope, and joy, bringing blessings to the world.

People need Jesus because they are fearful, suffering, and lost without God. He leads us back to our Creator's love, care, support, and protection. How many people do you know who are wandering out there, unsure of what life is all about, disillusioned, confused? As ambassadors for Jesus, we are called to spread the Good News of his love Gospel to these people in need.

Dear one, please keep this in mind. When you see people as you go about your week, acknowledge within yourself their need for Jesus. You may find yourself called to that melancholy clerk at the store or that self-consumed person at work who tries so hard to get others' approval. Consciously extend them love and hope. You might spend quality time gently sharing with someone who is seeking answers about faith. It's everyone, darling. Everyone needs more of Jesus.

## Good Morning, Lord

*I pray to be an ambassador for you. Please guide me as to how to teach about you in a way that is honoring and respectful.*

*"And all of this is a gift from God, who brought us back to himself through Christ. And God has given us this task of reconciling people to him. For God was in Christ, reconciling the world to himself, no longer counting people's sins against them. And he gave us this wonderful message of reconciliation."*

2 Corinthians 5:18–19

# CHILDREN, OBEY YOUR PARENTS

Colossians 3:20 states that children ought to obey their parents in all things, because this is what pleases the Lord. It's safe to say this pleases parents, too! Tell this to a child, though, and they may roll their eyes. After all, obedience can feel restrictive.

If you're a parent, explain to your child the significance of this verse. Let them know that obedience delights God and leads to righteousness (right standing before God) and blessings. At the same time, pay attention to what God says about parents being obedient to him, as he delights in your commitment to obey, too.

1 Peter 1:14 calls adult believers "obedient children," no longer adhering to the old earthly nature. As parents, we can model this obedience to our children, letting them see that their parents don't just talk the talk, but walk the walk.

A home that is truly loving and Christ centered can heal or forestall some of the problems that wreak havoc on families, like addictions or arguing. Raising children with Jesus as the ultimate leader of the family can certainly make a positive difference in the home atmosphere, as long as it's a love-based home. Jesus can also give parents the strength to confront unhealthy behaviors they see in their children.

Do your best to model Christlike behavior to your children, in your home and everywhere you go. As you do, your children will be more apt to follow suit.

### ∽ Good Morning, Lord ∾

*I am asking for your parenting help, guidance, and support to raise my children with you in our lives.*
*You are the head of our family, Lord.*

---

*"Children, always obey your parents, for this pleases the Lord."*

COLOSSIANS 3:20

# STEP OUT IN FAITH

Have you ever felt like doing something new but didn't feel qualified or ready for it? Much of the time, if God has put something in your heart, he has already prepared you to take that first step. Granted, there is value in polishing your talents, getting further education, and making other provisions. However, I've learned that when I set out to do something I believe I'm called to do, God always shows up in mighty ways.

I once heard someone say that God doesn't call the qualified; rather, he equips the called. In my experience, that's absolutely true! First we commit to walking in faith, and then everything we need is supplied to us.

Much of the time we want the whole plan revealed in detail before we'll take action. But if God did that, we wouldn't have to rely on him that much, would we? No, we'd rely more on the plans and ourselves. But there's something to be said for stepping out in faith, completely reliant on Holy Spirit instead of our own power.

It's fine to dream, and it's also important to do what you can to prepare yourself before setting out on the path of something new. At the same time, it's okay to step out in faith, trusting that the Lord has your back.

If you've been waiting for the perfect time to make a move, go to God. Ask him to give you the courage to take that first step, trusting that you are ready in Christ Jesus.

### Good Morning, Lord

*Is that you beckoning me to change and grow? If so, I need your help, please, in gaining confidence and clear direction for the path you would have me take.*

*"It was by faith that Abraham obeyed when God called him to leave home and go to another land that God would give him as his inheritance. He went without knowing where he was going."*

HEBREWS 11:8

## Early Will I Seek You

Psalm 63 was written by David while he was in the wilderness of Judah. Chances are, he was tired, hungry, and parched in that hot, arid desert. David describes how his soul thirsted for God and his flesh longed for him in a desolate land. Yes, he may have been physically in need of water, but the thirst in his soul was much deeper.

Chances are, dear one, you will find yourself in the spiritual desert sometime—and your soul will be parched for God. Your flesh, or ego, will want you to reach outward toward transitory pleasures, or "fixes," that will do nothing more than temporarily satisfy this deep longing. During such times, when you're feeling separated from God, allow your thirst to motivate you to cry out to him early with all your heart. Yearn for his presence, just as David did. Just as David did, bless the Lord and praise him continually.

Dear one, there are things that may seem to fill you up, but the Word tells us that only God will quench that deep thirst in the soul. My prayer for you is that you will rise every morning and bless the Lord. That you'll remain thirsty for his presence each day, allowing him to satiate you in the good times and the darkest times. Remain hopeful in the Lord Jesus Christ, for he cares for you.

### *Good Morning, Lord*

*Thank you for filling up my heart so much, helping me to stay focused upon what matters. With your love, I don't get distracted by meaningless detours or chase after shallow goals. If I ever feel empty, I know to turn to you.*

*"O God, you are my God; I earnestly search for you. My soul thirsts for you; my whole body longs for you in this parched and weary land where there is no water."*

Psalm 63:1

## GOD SEEKS THE LOST

For the days when you feel lost and far from God, there are several parables that may bring you comfort. In Luke 15, we find Jesus sitting with the Pharisees and scribes, who were known for criticizing the way Jesus associated with the outcasts.

Jesus begins with a question: "If you had 100 sheep and 1 was missing, wouldn't you leave the 99 and go find the 1? And when you found it, wouldn't you hug it tight, rejoice, and bring it home with you to the others? Or if you had 10 coins and lost 1, wouldn't you look high and low to find that lost coin and then rejoice like crazy once you did?" The religious leaders knew what Jesus was getting at.

Such parables are wonderful examples to those who are not yet connected with God or who just feel disconnected. If you have wandered and are lost, Jesus won't leave you out there on your own. He'll go after you, and when the two of you reunite, he will scoop you up, hug you tight, and rejoice! Yes, dear one, God rejoices over every single soul who gets reconnected to Jesus.

These parables illustrate God's desire that all come to know him. God delights in bringing every soul to his Kingdom—not just a particular crowd. If you, dear one, are feeling lost and separated from the Lord, know that he is right there, arms open wide, to reconnect and share life with you.

### ⟜ Good Morning, Lord ⟞

*Please scoop me up and hold me tightly. Please reconnect me with you if I've disconnected in any way.*

*"In the same way, there is joy in the presence of God's angels when even one sinner repents."*

LUKE 15:10

# BE SLOW TO ANGER

The Word of God helps us learn how to contend with anger. In James 1:19, it says, "You must all be quick to listen, slow to speak, and slow to get angry." Granted, when someone's screaming in your face, it may be challenging not to respond to anger in kind. But do you know what kind of people hurt other people? Those who are hurting. Beneath anger is pain or fear. Nevertheless, this doesn't justify anger that hurts other people, nor are you obliged to stay in an abusive situation.

When you're spoken to in anger, the Word says, "Listen." Really hear what the other person is saying and get a feel for the negative emotions under the surface. The Word says, "Be slow to speak." This means don't shout back as soon as you hear yelling. Pause. Perhaps take a moment to pray and call upon Jesus to guide you. Ask Jesus to keep you from becoming angry yourself. Now, it may not be easy, and it may take some practice, but when *we* can maintain a spirit of peace in the world, even when such negativity is coming at us, the *world* transforms.

Practice pausing and listening in conversation. As you do, you'll be able to approach reconciliation and resolving issues in a peaceful manner. This may have a positive impact on the other person, as you model the patience, love, and compassion of Jesus. It will also help *you* stay in a positive frame of mind. Peace be unto you today, my friend.

### Good Morning, Lord

*Thank you for helping me to be like a lighthouse
in the midst of angry storms, allowing others
to see the light and find their way.*

---

*"Understand this, my dear brothers and sisters:
You must all be quick to listen, slow to speak,
and slow to get angry."*

JAMES 1:19

# THE KINGDOM IS POWER

You are full of incredible power, a spiritual power that can move mountains and shake the heavens.

The Bible is full of helpful lessons, but it's also more than that. It has a living, breathing life-force energy that heals. The Word, coupled with the Holy Spirit, is power that helps us show up on this planet as powerful light beings with a message of love and peace.

The Word carries the power to change lives! The kind of power that can offer hope to those who are hopeless. The kind of power to change those who cannot change on their own. The kind of power to help people keep getting up after they've fallen. Yes, the Word of God is practical and helpful as we navigate life on Earth, but the Word of God is also *powerful* to those who believe.

The Word of God is alive and has strike-of-lightning power to open hearts and transform them. The Gospel is amazing news, but the Gospel is also living power. It's not just talk.

Today, dear one, I ask that you meditate on this. As Christ followers, with God's Spirit dwelling within, we are empowered to speak the words of Jesus Christ to those we meet. And we believe those words to be powerful enough to draw them closer to Jesus and radically change the world.

### Good Morning, Lord

*I am here to study your words, both those written in the Gospel and those you speak today, and emulate them.*

*"For the Kingdom of God is not just a lot of talk; it is living by God's power."*

1 CORINTHIANS 4:20

# Engage in the Present Moment

To be *mindful* means to be aware of the present moment. When the mind wanders to the past or future, we miss out on the here-and-now. Though mind-wandering isn't usually dangerous, it can cause you to forgo rich, meaningful experiences.

Is being mindful relevant to living as a follower of Jesus? Absolutely. God wants us to pay attention to what's going on in the present moment. At the same time, he wants us to be mindful of *his* presence. But God desires that rather than trying to *empty* the mind of thoughts, we concentrate on *filling* it with thoughts of him and his Word.

If you find yourself thinking a great deal about the past or the future, you may benefit from learning how to bring your thoughts back to the present moment. The more you can be present, the more peace you'll be able to enjoy, trusting that God has taken care of the past and is taking care of the future.

Dear one, as you go about your day, pay attention to your thoughts. Evaluate whether you're attentive to the present, past, or future. When you notice that your thoughts have drifted, gently bring them back to what you're doing at that moment. Ask God to help you become more mindful of engaging in the present moment, so you can experience more peace and be fully there for those you're fellowshipping with.

## Good Morning, Lord

*You know that my mind tends to wander, and I ask that you please help me be focused upon the moment at hand, and be presently aware of you and your guidance for me.*

*"You must have the same attitude that Christ Jesus had."*

Philippians 2:5

## Conquer Fear

Fear may sometimes appear to have a stranglehold on your life, but fortunately we all have access to the armor of God. Storms of lower energy may come your way, but God has given us protective tools to deflect blows from fear: with the Word-Sword!

The Word says that at our core, we are *not* fear. The Word says we are power. We are love. We are peace.

What helps me in times of fear is praying and meditating on scriptures that calm my mind. I am sharing three verses you can affirm when fear comes knocking at your door:

- "The Lord is for me, so I will have no fear. What can mere people do to me?" (Psalm 118:6)

- "See, God has come to save me. I will trust in him and not be afraid. The Lord God is my strength and my song; he has given me victory." (Isaiah 12:2)

- "I am leaving you with a gift—peace of mind and heart. And the peace I give is a gift the world cannot give. So don't be troubled or afraid." (John 14:27)

Friend, please use these scriptures as your sword and armor. Meditate on them. Speak them aloud. Know that the Word is powerful and can help replace anxiety with peace. It may take some practice. That's all right. Prepare yourself before fearful circumstances come your way, and then stand strong in the Lord, for God has given you a spirit of power and love.

### Good Morning, Lord

*When I focus upon you and stay consciously aware of divine love, I feel insulated and safe. I am in my God-bliss bubble.*

*"Since we are receiving a Kingdom that is unshakable, let us be thankful and please God by worshiping him with holy fear and awe. For our God is a devouring fire."*

HEBREWS 12:28–29

# Vulnerability Breeds Intimacy

Do you find it tough sometimes to be honest about your feelings? Afraid that if you share them, people will think you're weak? Yes, to be vulnerable, to allow others to see your authentic self, can be scary. It's the you behind the mask, being real and raw.

Why is this valuable? Because vulnerability makes way for a deeper connection and intimacy with yourself, God, and others. To be vulnerable is to be honest. Sometimes we feel like we must have it all together, especially being a follower of Jesus. After all, aren't we supposed to trust God for everything? But the reality is that we are not perfect. There are real struggles that we deal with emotionally, spiritually, and physically.

Vulnerability is sacred. Go to God first. He knows exactly where you are and what you're feeling at all times. Being honest and vulnerable with God can help you develop deeper intimacy with him. With others, ask God to show you who can hold that space for you to genuinely share, listening without judgment: a spouse or partner, family member, friend, pastor, or counselor.

The apostle Paul said that when he was weak, God made him strong. Dear one, the Word says that God's grace is sufficient for you. Even though there are times when we just feel that life is hard, we can be vulnerable with God and others, knowing that when we are feeling weak, God will strengthen and carry us.

 *Good Morning, Lord*

*I know that you can see my true feelings and help me feel
safe in sharing them. Thank you for healing the shame
I have carried, allowing me to trust that this
process is a part of the human condition.*

---

*"Each time he said, 'My grace is all you need.
My power works best in weakness.'"*

2 Corinthians 12:9

# Faith, Not Fear

Fear only thrives when we feed it. Whatever we nurture grows stronger, and fear has a way of consuming its creator. The ego habitually looks for things to worry about, so it will obsessively read the news, rehash anxieties, and imagine a scary future.

Fear is a terrible roommate and coworker, however, as it blocks us from our life purpose, inner peace, and the experience of love. There are two ways to deal with fear: (1) fight it, or (2) shine light upon it.

Fighting fear is the same as feeding it. Whatever you fight thrives upon the drama and relishes the struggle. Fortunately, shining light upon fear *does* work. As you're filled with the awareness of God's peace and love, fear has no effect. It's like a little gnat, flying in the background, barely creating a disturbance at all.

Inner peace and divine love teach us that there's nothing to fear. The love of the Lord puts us in a God bubble of bliss. It's not that we ignore problems, but rather that we deal with them from a place of wisdom instead of reactive fear.

## ✎ *Good Morning, Lord* ✎

*Please fill my heart with your strong presence, and pour so much love into my conscious awareness that I have no room for anything but peace.*

---

*"The Lord gives his people strength.*
*The Lord blesses them with peace."*

**Psalm 29:11**

# WHAT RIPPLE EFFECT WILL YOU HAVE?

As much light as there is in the world, there's also darkness. And there are people who are looking for beacons of light to help them rest in peace and safety.

Whether you're in a leadership position or not, you have a sphere of influence. Maybe it's your children, spouse, family members, or friends. Maybe it's in your neighborhood or work environment. Regardless of *where* your sphere extends, there are people around you whom you influence. What kind of ripple effect will you have? What kind of influence do you exert?

Living a Christ-centered life not only makes a difference for you, as a follower of Jesus, but can also influence your closest connections. You can offer hope and assistance when necessary, whether it's to a circle of 2 or 200. God wants to use you to be a part of a community of believers who serve.

It's easy to focus on *you*, and there's nothing wrong with that. Self-care along your walk with Christ is essential. But it's also important to be a beacon of light for your sphere of influence, because when each person does this, the ripple effect in a community reaches everyone.

Dear one, pray about how you can be that Christlike beacon of light no matter what size your circle is. Pray for your community, and if you are led, join with others who are making a difference. Your life will be richer and the world a healthier and happier place.

## Good Morning, Lord

*I pray to be like you, a light who helps others.*
*Please guide my teaching, healing, and other*
*supportive work so that I do the best for the most.*

*"For God is not unjust. He will not forget how hard you have worked for him and how you have shown your love to him by caring for other believers, as you still do."*

HEBREWS 6:10

# LEAN ON JESUS

"Christianity is nothing but a crutch!" said the man to the woman who had just spoken about how God transformed her life. The woman didn't flinch. Instead, she calmly asked the man two questions.

"If you had two broken legs, would you find a wheelchair valuable?" The man said yes.

"If you had one broken leg, would you find crutches valuable?" The man said yes again.

"Well, honey, I was broken and Jesus Christ has proven valuable to help me become *whole*!"

How many people do you think feel broken? *Are* they broken? Well, if they're feeling that way, they're not living the kind of life God desires, as God is known for restoration and redemption.

Many people have walked away from the teachings of Jesus because of hurts they experienced in the church. They're out there seeking truth, and some have successfully found other paths that still led to the peace and love of God. Others, like me, have come back to Jesus, recognizing the valuable truths he teaches and how he can bring us to God.

I embrace God, Jesus, and Holy Spirit, and they've certainly helped me heal and grow in my mind, body, and soul. Our connection has deepened, and I gladly share the love of Jesus with all I can. I may not lean on Jesus as a crutch, but I certainly do lean on him. Dear one, it is my prayer that you do the same.

## Good Morning, Lord

*Thank you for allowing me to lean upon your strength, your goodness, and your wisdom. Can you please remind me to lean upon you when I feel alone or believe I must do everything by myself?*

*"I restore the crushed spirit of the humble and revive the courage of those with repentant hearts."*

ISAIAH 57:15

# Nourish Your Soul

If you choose not to eat for a day, your body may become weary. Your mood may drop, and you may become grouchy. Just as the physical body requires nourishment for optimal energy and well-being, so does your spirit require nourishment to remain strong and vibrant.

When we neglect feeding our soul, our spirit flame may feel diminished. We may become apathetic or stuck. Even the smallest issues may look insurmountable.

The good news is that you can rekindle your flame as you invest time to regularly nourish your spirit. Even if you have a busy schedule, you can carve out valuable time to eat. Likewise, realize that nourishing your soul is an investment with extraordinary returns.

Therefore, make a commitment to feed your soul in whatever way works for you. Maybe that's getting in time each morning with the Word, spending a few minutes in prayer, sitting in silence listening to the Lord, or going on a spiritual retreat. Devote some time to being alone with God, taking a break from people and technology regularly. This will nourish your spirit and allow God to light the fire of your passion so you can burn for Jesus. As always, dear one, stay strong in the Lord.

## Good Morning, Lord

*My priority is connecting with you, and I intend to
follow through accordingly with actions focusing upon you.
Thank you for shepherding my schedule and guiding me
to make the time to nourish my soul.*

*"I am the living bread that came down from heaven. Anyone
who eats this bread will live forever; and this bread, which
I will offer so the world may live, is my flesh."*

**John 6:51**

# Learn How to Be Content

What is the key to contentment? How can we feel peaceful and satisfied, no matter what's going on? Everyone is on their own unique journey, contending with different things, so these are great questions!

If we turn to God's Word, we'll find his answer regarding contentment there. In Philippians 4:12, Paul says he's learned to be content regardless of what's going in his life. Notice that he *learned* to be content. How? In the next verse he says he can do all things through Jesus Christ. He learned to fully rely on Jesus for his peace of mind.

Ultimately, true contentment only comes from God. If we're discontented—beset by feelings of boredom, frustration, or incompleteness—that's a sign of being confused as to who we are in Christ Jesus.

Once we recognize that the only source of lasting happiness is loving God, we can be content in all matters by realizing that in Christ, peace is available. We can forgo striving and reaching out for things to compensate for that discontentment.

Dear one, when such feelings arise, take some time with the Lord. Know that all is well right now, and you don't have to do anything. Take a deep breath and relax. Bring your focus back to your faith in God. Open up and receive all that is inherently yours in Christ Jesus, contentment included.

## Good Morning, Lord

*Intellectually, I know that you can lead me to true and lasting happiness. Please help me stop looking for happiness where it does not exist, to surrender to God's will and find what I'm seeking through you.*

*"Yet true godliness with contentment is itself great wealth."*

1 Timothy 6:6

# THANK YOU, GOD!

One form of prayerful asking that I've always loved is called "affirmative prayer," where you give thanks to God for that which you've asked for while feeling deep gratitude before the prayer seems to be answered.

For example, you might say:

- *Thank you, God, for my wonderful health.*
- *Thank you, God, for my career path.*
- *Thank you, Father, for my safe, comfortable, and affordable home.*
- *Thank you, God, for my happy and healthy family life.*
- *Thank you, Heavenly Father, for bringing my romantic partner and me together for this wonderful relationship.*

And so forth, with your specific prayer . . .

You say these affirmative prayers, along with feeling genuine gratitude, peace, and love, *before* there's physical evidence that the prayer has been answered. Put no worry into how, when, or if the prayers will be answered, only gratitude and faith that they're already answered and will therefore show up physically in the best way at the best time.

### Good Morning, Lord

*Thank you for hearing and answering my prayer in your name. Thank you for your love, care, understanding, and support.*

---

*"Don't worry about anything; instead, pray about everything. Tell God what you need, and thank him for all he has done."*

PHILIPPIANS 4:6

# The Beautiful Experience of Faith

Faith is the beautiful experience of relaxing and trusting that everything will work out in the best way. It's the path of peace and health. People who are considered "lucky" are actually people who trust and follow the trail that God leads them on.

However, we can't sit in our living room all day long and expect God to do all the heavy lifting of our lives—that's not faith. We have to take the action that God guides us to take. We also can't hand God a script of how we expect our prayers to be answered—that's not faith. We have to trust that God knows the best way for our prayers to be answered.

In other words, faith means letting go of control. That's no easy task when you've had hard life experiences that taught you that you can't trust other people or when your past prayers haven't been answered as you expected.

Beautifully, God helps us resolve these internal struggles through prayer. In other words, we can pray to have more faith. We can pray that our control issues are healed. We can pray to meet people who are trustworthy. We can pray to regain our trust in God.

Anything that you need, you can pray for—and then let go of expectations of how the prayer will be answered.

## Good Morning, Lord

*My heart is open to you, and I appeal to you for help with [describe situation]. Please lift me up, Lord, and help me trust, have faith, and be at peace. Here are my control issues about the situation; here are my doubts and fears. Please take these burdens from me, Lord. Please show me what action steps to take, and then help me take them.*

*"The Lord leads with unfailing love and faithfulness all who keep his covenant and obey his demands."*

**Psalm 25:10**

# EMBRACE TOLERANCE

The world could use more tolerance. As followers of the ways of Jesus, we are to be tolerant of others. This means to respect them no matter what their beliefs are and be fair even if we don't agree with what they believe.

God made humanity diverse, with unique cultures and backgrounds. To be Christlike is to be accepting of others for who they are, not for what they believe. It's engaging with others not with the intent of converting them to your worldview, but with genuine concern about who they are and their well-being.

Being tolerant does not mean that we turn a blind eye to corruption or allow people to be deprived of their human rights. Being tolerant means that we *value* human rights and equality for all, regardless of what our fundamental beliefs are.

Jesus did not stand for corruption, dishonesty, or hypocrisy. He was known for being tolerant of the person, but *in*tolerant of the ungodly behavior. There is freedom in Jesus Christ, and this freedom allows each of us to value who we are in him and be welcoming to others regardless of their beliefs or faith. It's not always one way over another. If we can let go of wanting to be right or wanting others to be wrong, there will be less intolerance in the world and more peace and love. And, dear one, that's something we'd all enjoy!

### ⌒⌒ *Good Morning, Lord* ⌒⌒

*Can you please teach me the discernment to balance taking the right action for myself with being graceful and compassionate toward those who are on a different path?*

---

*"So let's stop condemning each other. Decide instead to live in such a way that you will not cause another believer to stumble and fall."*

ROMANS 14:13

# BE THE SALT OF THE EARTH

For thousands of years, salt was considered a precious commodity. It was used primarily to preserve food, before the era of refrigerators. If you had salt to trade, you had something of value!

Jesus used salt as a metaphor when teaching the crowds. He told them that they were the salt of the earth—essentially, that they were a distinctive people because of their relationship with him. He was saying they were valuable and would enhance the flavor of the world because of their Christlike attitude and behavior. They'd "season" and "rub off" on the world!

Basically, what Jesus was telling the crowd was that there should be something about them as Christ followers that sets them apart from those not following the ways of the Lord.

Dear one, do you feel as if you are salt of the earth? Do you feel that there's something distinctive about you? Scripture also mentions that we can become like salt that loses its flavor, meaning that our faith and focus may become diluted by pollutants. Just as Jesus talks about being the light in the world, we are to be the salt of the earth as well. We are to add a flavorful note to those around us, talking about the Good News of Jesus Christ and promoting harmony for humankind. And we stay this way, without losing our flavor, by keeping our thoughts sober and purely focused upon God.

You are a precious commodity, dear one, so go and spice up the world in Christ Jesus.

### Good Morning, Lord

*I am so honored that you see me as the salt of the world. Please guide me to live up to this distinction.*

---

*"You are the salt of the earth. But what good is salt if it has lost its flavor? Can you make it salty again? It will be thrown out and trampled underfoot as worthless."*

MATTHEW 5:13

# THE FORGIVING HEART

Conflict happens. People inevitably say and do offensive things from a place of ego. Can we find it in our hearts to continue to forgive them? (This pertains to emotional arguments when remorse is felt—not to abuse!)

"I'm sorry. Please forgive me." Those five words are so challenging for some, but as Christ followers, we ought to make this our goal: On the giving end, staying in tune with the heart of Jesus, and humbling ourselves to say those five words when we've hurt another. On the receiving end, genuinely forgiving someone when they come to us with pure intentions.

Forgiveness requires humility, a laying down of pride, and sincerely feeling remorse. In the heat of an argument, pride oftentimes will want you to stay in flesh mode and not spirit mode. It will have you turn a blind eye to the unhealed wound that you're operating from or have you return hurtful words. But Jesus encouraged asking for and extending forgiveness.

Many people think that repeated conflicts ruin relationships. But often, their demise is because of the lack of conflict-*resolution* skills. It's saying, "I value our relationship. I don't want it to be strained because of this issue. I'm sorry. Please forgive me." And when someone comes to you sincerely asking for forgiveness, it's you saying, "I appreciate your apology. Yes, I forgive you."

Dear one, may we aim for a heart that apologizes and forgives as Jesus did.

## Good Morning, Lord

*I trust you to guide me in my relationships, to heal and clear anger—including repressed anger. Please help me with overcoming pride and fear by apologizing or accepting apologies.*

---

*"Then Peter came to him and asked, 'Lord, how often should I forgive someone who sins against me? Seven times?' 'No, not seven times,' Jesus replied, 'but seventy times seven!'"*

MATTHEW 18:21–22

# BE THE LIGHT

As part of his Sermon on the Mount, Jesus says to "shine out for all to see." Go into the world and do things that brighten it, even if that's simply to lend an ear to those in distress. Good works are about the "doing," but also about "presence"—simply being present to reveal a well-lit path that will lead those wandering in the dark to God.

As Christ followers, we are to share the light and love of Jesus and, as the Word says, "do good works." In this, God is glorified and praised. People come to know God through our light that radiates from our connection with him.

Practically, shining your light means showing up in the world as someone who loves and follows the ways of Jesus. Jesus said, to paraphrase Matthew 5, "Don't hide your light. You don't light a candle and then cover it with something." So shall we keep our flames lit with passion for the Lord and shine brightly, allowing others to get a glimpse of the marvelous Kingdom of God.

When you shine your light, dear one, God uses you and creates a ripple effect of his love in the world. People around you are waiting for someone to show them what God's love is all about, and he's chosen *you* to be that beacon of light and love! Rejoice, and shine, darling! Shine bright!

## Good Morning, Lord

*I know that God's divine light is within me. I ask that you help me stay aware of the light within me and shine even brighter, especially to help other people navigate their way.*

*"In the same way, let your good deeds shine out for all to see, so that everyone will praise your heavenly Father."*

**MATTHEW 5:16**

# BURN FOR THE LORD

In the Old Testament, while the Jewish people were wandering in the desert, Moses received divine guidance to build a tabernacle. In that tabernacle, there was an altar that they had to keep burning, the Lord instructed Moses.

Today, there's no need for sacrificial altars with eternal flames, but we can keep our *hearts* continuously burning for the Lord! We can ask God to light the fire, and we can stoke it and keep it burning brightly for the Lord.

Granted, this is a metaphor, but it depicts passion and zealousness for living a life that is on fire for God. Society uses the terms *fire* and *hot* all the time to describe things: "You're on fire!" or "He's hot stuff!" Such expressions have a lot to say about people.

Dear one, what kind of passion burns in your heart? Is your flame for the Lord burning brightly in your heart-altar? Or do you feel so-so? There are certainly flickers and dimmings, and if you're in a season where you feel "lukewarm," ask Holy Spirit to come and stoke your coals and fan his flames to get your fire raging! Continue spending time with God and his Word, knowing that as you do, your passion will certainly grow. This is a foundation of loving your Lord God with all your heart!

## Good Morning, Lord

*Please help me melt away any layers of ice or protective barriers around my heart so that I can feel—really burn with—great love for you.*

*"Jesus replied, 'You must love the Lord your God with all your heart, all your soul, and all your mind.'"*

MATTHEW 22:37

# JUST KEEP GOING

Every person struggles with the fear of failure at times. The question is whether you allow your fears to become obstacles or motivators.

We can look in the Bible and see Jesus and his followers coming face-to-face with very real obstacles to their mission. But they didn't give up. They pressed forward, leaning upon God to help them, courageously rising above their fear of failure.

Dear one, regardless of what you're working on, no matter what your intentions or dreams are, you're going to be confronted with some inner resistance. And, you'll have the option to quit. There may even be times you *do* quit. But I'm encouraging you to just keep going, especially if you feel that God is encouraging you.

Don't allow the fear of failure or rejection to keep you where you are. Continue moving forward, pursuing what's in your heart and relying upon God's Spirit within you for help. God's Spirit is rooting for you. He's shouting, "Go for it, child of God! Day by day, month by month, year by year, allow me to help you navigate obstacles and resistance, because I will make a way."

Just as Paul said, "I can do all things through Christ, who strengthens me," so can you, dear one. So, go, in the power of God's Spirit. Just keep going, remembering to enjoy the journey, darling!

## Good Morning, Lord

*I have been feeling* [describe fears] *about* [describe situation], *and I need your help, please, in not allowing fear to distract or delay me from moving forward.*

---

*"I can do all things through Christ, who strengthens me."*

PHILIPPIANS 4:13 (WEB)

# EXCHANGE ANXIETY FOR PEACE

*Anxiety.* That feeling that springs up when we're unsure what might happen. That stream of emotions that seems to rise from nowhere and, sometimes, for no reason. Oh, how the world could do without so much anxiety!

Philippians 4:6–7 says we should not be anxious about anything. Instead, we should speak to God, and let him carry the load. When we do, the Bible says that the peace of God, which is beyond human understanding, will guard our hearts.

When you try to deal with anxiety on your own, you're limited. In our human understanding, we see and know only partially. God, on the other hand, is not limited by time, space, or knowledge. The issues that may worry us are as clear as day to God. He knows every situation's beginning and its end. He even knows what you ought to do, or not do.

You say you fully trust in God, but do you *really*? You see, when we hand our worries to God, he takes them. In exchange, he gives us back peace. The kind of peace that causes you to shake your head at God's awesomeness! Since God is in charge, *he* never worries. He has peace. This is the peace that he's willing to give us.

Darling, you have a choice. You have the option of dealing with your issues with limited human capacity, or letting God deal with them in exchange for his peace. Trust God. Regardless of what happens, rest in him.

## Good Morning, Lord

*I am so appreciative that I can hand all these worries*
*to you and that you are glad to take them. Thank*
*you so much for lifting these burdens from me!*

*"And the peace of God, which surpasses all understanding,*
*will guard your hearts and your thoughts in Christ Jesus."*

PHILIPPIANS 4:7 (WEB)

# GOD, THE COMFORTER

*Why me, God?* To cry out in pain, wondering why we must suffer, is common. Even those who aren't walking a religious path ask this question. How can a good and loving God allow his children to go through so much in life?

God is not indifferent to the pain that we experience. Throughout scripture, God is with those suffering. He hears their cries. He hides them under the shadow of his wings for safe shelter and provides a refuge. If you read many of the psalms, you will see those who suffer crying out to God and him comforting them, reminding them of his great love.

I understand the question "Why me, God?" There are really no words to describe the depth of suffering a human can experience. It's all right to cry out to God and ask such a question. You may never know the answer, but God hears your cry. He sees your pain and is willing to comfort you. He will send others to comfort you as well.

If you're battling some pain, my heart goes out to you. Know that you're not alone. I encourage you to read the psalms. Allow God to minister to you through his Word and through his people. Experiencing pain does not mean that you've done anything wrong, or that you're being punished. It's simply a part of life as a human on this planet, and God will help you through painful times in the power of his Spirit.

## Good Morning, Lord

*The suffering I've endured has opened my heart to humbly and gratefully receiving your loving care, your support, and your ministering. Thank you for hearing me.*

---

*"The righteous person faces many troubles, but the Lord comes to the rescue each time."*

**PSALM 34:19**

## Beauty Defined

*If only I were more attractive.* That thought goes through many people's minds at one time or another. They reason that if they were more attractive, life would be better.

I recently heard a story that packs a powerful message: A woman who was at a store noticed a female clerk working there. The clerk had an appearance that many might perceive as unattractive, but there was something about her. She radiated such light and love that the shopper observed her for a while, drawn to her genuineness. She recognized that this woman had the most beautiful soul. The love she radiated, even toward a new acquaintance, was undeniable, and she spoke in a way reflected in scripture: "a gentle and quiet spirit."

Take care not to judge others, forming a poor impression of them based upon their physical appearance. We never can know what their life circumstances are. Learn to look beyond, and see what's in their heart and soul. No matter what they look like, how they adorn or don't adorn themselves, they are beautiful!

There's nothing wrong with paying attention to our appearance, wearing makeup, or having nice clothes and jewelry. However, outward adornments don't define true beauty. On the flip side, know that it's your inner self and the enduring beauty of your soul that has the greatest worth in God's eyes. You are attractive, darling! So extraordinarily beautiful just as you are!

### Good Morning, Lord

*Please help me adorn myself with my love for you, with my inner peace, and with the glow of my grateful heart.*

*"Don't be concerned about the outward beauty of fancy hairstyles, expensive jewelry, or beautiful clothes. You should clothe yourselves instead with the beauty that comes from within, the unfading beauty of a gentle and quiet spirit, which is so precious to God."*

1 PETER 3:3–4

# THE PATH OF POSITIVE CHANGE

Big positive change is usually preceded by a painful experience, like the darkness before the dawn's light. Often, you'll receive signals that something's wrong with your current situation. If you ignore these signals, they intensify until they culminate in a painful experience that convinces you of the need for a change.

What signals have you received heralding the need for change? Have you perhaps ignored these signals and later wished that you'd listened? These experiences are life lessons, teaching you to heed the signs when they occur.

As you become increasingly sensitive to your feelings, and as you become more committed to your self-care, the need to make positive changes becomes more apparent.

Sometimes, this means moving on: leaving a job that no longer fits you, relocating to a better-suited home, or parting ways from someone in a relationship that has become toxic. In other instances, this is a signal to stay and do your best to heal the situation. Whether you leave or stay, there's a need to address what's not working. Ignoring the issues isn't healthful.

## Good Morning, Lord

*I am surrendering this to you, with full faith that you know the best way for me to proceed. Please guide and support me through these changes, and send your angels to comfort my heart.*

*"Light shines in the darkness for the godly.*
*They are generous, compassionate, and righteous."*

PSALM 112:4

# RESIST PRIDE

To many people, pride is a normal part of humanity. Even some who frown upon it consider it an innocent state of all men. So it may come as a surprise to many how strongly God dislikes pride. Throughout Proverbs, pride is said to lead to disgrace (11:2), spark conflict (13:10), and go before destruction (16:18).

One verse in particular may explain why God detests pride so. The words in this verse were addressed to the king of Tyre but were also prophetic about Lucifer's fall. Ezekiel 28:11–19 references how Lucifer was thrown out of heaven after he became prideful of his beauty. Lucifer's ego puffed up after he saw the splendor that he was arrayed with. Is it possible that God opposes the proud so much because he saw what it did to Lucifer?

When we boast of ourselves alone, we leave God out. Pride says, "I did it! I'm the best!" But this sort of attitude discounts God entirely.

Jesus committed to acting in humility. He came "not to be served but to serve others" (Matthew 20:28). He washed the feet of his disciples, offered forgiveness even for those who rejected him, and spent time with the outcasts.

Dear one, resist the temptation to allow pride to reign in your heart. If you fall prey to it sometimes, ask the Lord to help you and forgive you, and he surely will. Embody humility, giving all praise to God.

## Good Morning, Lord

*Please show me the way to true humility, loving and caring for myself as God created me, without seeing myself as better or worse than anyone else.*

*"The Lord detests the proud; they will surely be punished."*

**PROVERBS 16:5**

## Be Servants to One Another

If today was your last day on this planet, how would you want people to describe you once you were gone? Chances are, you'd want them to characterize you as someone who was loving, compassionate, kind, and giving. Not to say that you must be that way 24-7, but in general, isn't that how you'd like to be remembered?

It's very easy to get caught up in a busy life, going after all sorts of things. Busy is not bad—it's what you're doing during your busy time that matters. A God-centered life inspires you to honestly look at how you spend your time. Evaluate your intentions. Make time for your family and friends, and reach out to those in need.

Life can become complicated, but it doesn't have to be that way. There's a lot to be said for simplicity. Rest in contentment rather than chasing after more in order to feel better. Embody the fruits of the spirit, like generosity, kindness, love, and patience.

Take some time this morning and really think about your schedule throughout the week. Make changes where you feel led. Cut back on work hours if you're stressed. Don't take on anything new for now. Limit your technology time.

You may have to make a "not-to-do" list and cut out time wasters so you can have plenty of time for yourself, God, and others. Live your life, absolutely! But don't forget to include serving others, answering the call of the Lord.

### Good Morning, Lord

*Thank you for helping me sort through my day, devoting time and energy to what really matters. Please show me the way.*

*"For you have been called to live in freedom, my brothers and sisters. But don't use your freedom to satisfy your sinful nature. Instead, use your freedom to serve one another in love."*

Galatians 5:13

# You Are God-Powered!

Instead of feeling frustrated or upset, use your God-given power to help fix the situation.

You have the strength and power of God within you to heal, transmute, and uplift. You're called to be a conveyor of divine power in your healing, teaching, creative, and prayerful work.

There's nothing wimpy, whiny, or weak about God—nor you! The key is to pause and pray before taking action. Even a few seconds of discussing the situation with God will ensure that you're heading in the right direction. This will save you time in the long run.

To tap into your divine strength, allocate and spend quiet time talking and listening to God.

### Good Morning, Lord

*I'm concerned about* [describe situation]. *What would you have me do to bring about peace in this situation? Please help me quiet my mind so that I may hear and follow your answers.*

*"And he will stand to lead his flock with the Lord's strength, in the majesty of the name of the Lord his God. Then his people will live there undisturbed, for he will be highly honored around the world."*

MICAH 5:4

# GOD'S LOVE SHINES IN YOUR EYES

You can tell a lot by looking into someone's eyes. Matthew 6:22 says "the lamp of the body is the eye," which shines light out to the world.

What is it that gives light and life to a human being? The Breath of God, his Spirit. Romans 8:11 says that the same Spirit who resurrected Jesus lives in Christ followers and gives life to the mortal body. This is a gift freely given to each person who will receive. Yes, our bodies are made up of flesh, but it is the Spirit of God that gives us spiritual life. God's Spirit is what fires up the spiritual body!

For when flesh and bones break down and turn to dust, the spirit continues. This is the great hope that we have in Christ Jesus, knowing that this earthly life is temporary, but the spiritual is eternal. And it is the Spirit of God that can dwell within us now. That same Spirit that raised Jesus from the dead now dwells in *us*! Resurrection power that we can receive by faith!

Dear one, my prayer is that you become acquainted with God's Spirit that dwells within you. If you've never asked God's Spirit to come and dwell within you, do so now. Receive him by faith. Don't try to wrap your mind around it. Simply believe. He'll come and make his abode in you, giving you the godly kind of life that ignites your spirit and allows you to radiate light and love to the world.

## ❧ Good Morning, Lord ❧

*Each day, I feel even greater love from you.*
*I can feel your presence within me, watching over*
*and guiding me, and helping me shine divine light.*

---

*"The Spirit of God, who raised Jesus from the dead, lives in you.*
*And just as God raised Christ Jesus from the dead, he will give*
*life to your mortal bodies by this same Spirit living within you."*

ROMANS 8:11

# DIVINELY GUIDED WRITING

Have you ever thought about writing a book, an article, or a blog to help others through an experience that you have gone through? If you keep receiving the same thought or feeling to write as an avenue to help others, this could be a nudge about your life path.

God and Holy Spirit answer our prayers about our life purpose by giving us repeated messages to take positive action. You may be guided to use the written word to share with others what you've learned. Writing also helps you get in touch with often-hidden feelings and insights. It can be a cathartic way to release repressed emotions.

Do you journal about your feelings? This is a healing practice, and your journal entries could become blog articles, which in turn could become a book if you are so guided.

### Good Morning, Lord

*Please help me have the time, energy, motivation,
and courage to express my honest and deepest feelings in
writing, which could help others who are feeling the same way.*

*"This is what the Lord, the God of Israel, says: 'Write down
for the record everything I have said to you, Jeremiah.'"*

JEREMIAH 30:2

# I AM THE BREAD OF LIFE

People flocked to Jesus for his teachings and miraculous healings. In John 6, the scene begins with Jesus heading to the other side of Galilee, while a great multitude of people followed. No matter where he went, he was busy healing the sick and teaching. As a result, he always had a large following.

Jesus also fed the multitudes at times, miraculously multiplying bread and fish. It's interesting to note that later in chapter 6 the multitude followed Jesus again, but not necessarily to see more miracles and hear his teachings. Rather, they wanted more free food!

Jesus, all-knowing divinity that he is, discerned this and said, "I am the bread of life. Whoever comes to me will never be hungry again" (John 6:35). Just as bread is a staple in our diet, Jesus was saying he was the essential spiritual-food resource they needed to fill up on—the nourishment required to enjoy everlasting life.

Dear one, God is a God of miracles. Jesus—Healer, Provider, Sustainer, Comforter, and Protector—is the bread of life that can sustain our spiritual lives.

Nourish your soul in him. Believe that he is the most satisfying spiritual food available. He desires to be your essential resource, darling. Freely, he gives to you.

## Good Morning, Lord

*Thank you for feeding my heart, nourishing my soul,*
*and enriching my life. You are all that I need!*

*"I am the living bread that came down from heaven.*
*Anyone who eats this bread will live forever; and this bread,*
*which I will offer so the world may live, is my flesh."*

JOHN 6:51

# For the Joy Awaiting You

Hebrews 11 is known as the "faith" chapter. We're reminded of those who have gone before us in great faith: Noah, Abraham, Isaac, Jacob, and many more. We're told they may even be gathered together, watching us from the heavenly realm, cheering us on.

Now, it says in Hebrews 12:2 that Jesus was able to endure hardships and suffering because he was aware of the final result. He did it for "the joy awaiting him," meaning he knew he was the bridge to connect the lost with God. He trusted in God so much that he laid down his own life and endured terrible suffering. He had *that* kind of faith!

This is the kind of faith you and I can cultivate, my friend. This is the kind of faith that can help you endure struggles, suffering, doubts, frustrations, and so on. For the joy awaiting you! For the oneness you share with your Heavenly Father forever.

Dear one, if you find yourself faltering in faith, turn to Hebrews 11 and 12. Study them. Let the saints who went before you spur you on in faith, and keep your eyes fixed on Jesus.

## Good Morning, Lord

*I am in awe of the pure perfection of your faith.*
*Please guide me to such faith that I may surrender*
*all fears and completely trust in the Holy Trinity.*

"We do this by keeping our eyes on Jesus, the champion who initiates and perfects our faith. Because of the joy awaiting him, he endured the cross, disregarding its shame. Now he is seated in the place of honor beside God's throne."

HEBREWS 12:2

# LET HOLY SPIRIT LEAD

God is the ultimate planner who can guide us in the best way. No matter how much we humans try to plan ahead, it's always wise to check in with God before proceeding, because he has the ability to foresee every future possibility.

God already has the map of your route; all you have to do is tune in to his voice and follow. Yes, this means you may have to stop and ask for directions, but I think we can all agree that we don't always know what's best for us. The lightbulb going off in the brain isn't always powered up by God.

So, we have two choices: (1) God's way, or (2) the way of our flesh or ego. But how can we distinguish between the two? First, study the ways of Jesus. Get to know his guidelines. Second, learn to hear God's voice via his Spirit. Cultivate an intimacy with Holy Spirit, inviting him to be the teacher and guide of your life.

What do you want? Better health? Security? Peace? Joy? Enter those coordinates into your God Navigation System; then lean in and lend an ear to Spirit's promptings. You think you should turn right, but Spirit says turn left. Follow him. He won't lead you astray. He guarantees that you show up at the destination God has approved for you.

Press on doing what you feel is God's will for your life. Tune in to Spirit. After all, the journey is meant to be enjoyed.

## Good Morning, Lord

*Thank you for helping me clearly hear,
understand, trust, and follow my divine guidance.*

*"Since we are living by the Spirit, let us follow
the Spirit's leading in every part of our lives."*

**GALATIANS 5:25**

# RECOGNIZE HOLY SPIRIT'S VOICE

If you spend any amount of time with children, then you've probably had the experience of having to ask them to do something multiple times while they were engrossed in a movie, caught up in play, or choosing to have selective hearing.

I imagine the same thing happens to God's adult children, too. Holy Spirit may try to get our attention time and time again, but we're distracted or opt for selective hearing. Or perhaps some haven't yet learned to recognize God's voice. They're not acquainted with Holy Spirit. Learning to hear God's Spirit occurs the same way we learn most anything. We learn by setting an intention, moving forward, and keeping at it along the way.

Holy Spirit is the spiritual teacher Jesus sent to us all after his crucifixion to lead us on the path of love and faith. Holy Spirit is the inner voice that "convicts" us by correcting us when we have veered off the path of God's loving will. The Holy Spirit firmly and lovingly shows us the error of our ways and points us in a better direction.

Learning to hear Holy Spirit's voice can be a reality. Practice. Consciously focus on Holy Spirit within you. Ask him to lend insight, to show you things. Step out with little divinely guided actions. The more familiar you get with his leading, the more confident you will be. God's Spirit is speaking, friend. May you hear his voice today.

### ⤞ Good Morning, Lord ⤝

*Please help me recognize the voice of God's Holy Spirit, so that I may hear and follow divine guidance.*

---

*"Jesus, full of the Holy Spirit, returned from the Jordan River. He was led by the Spirit in the wilderness."*

LUKE 4:1

## WORSHIP IN SPIRIT AND TRUTH

Worship is not just something you do; it's who you are. You are a worshipper.

We worship God because a heart filled with gratitude is a happy and healthy one.

Worship is giving God thanks and glory with focused attention. It's loving gratitude felt deep in your heart. It's *that* kind of worship that glorifies God, recognizing him for the amazing Creator he is. At the same time, a heart of worship transforms the worshipper, bringing you closer to God.

The prophet Isaiah said that angels continually worship God by proclaiming that he is holy, holy, holy. Dear one, become a worshipper at heart, allowing your entire being to be a vessel of praise for and worship of the Lord.

Psalm 134:2 says to lift your hands to the holy place and praise the Lord. You can do this at home, at the office, in the car, in your backyard—anywhere! Music or no music, dear one, make it your aim to sing a hymn to the Lord continually in spirit and in truth.

### ∽ Good Morning, Lord ∽

*I love you so much, and I am eternally grateful for you! You are my savior and the one whom I trust to lead and teach me.*

*"For God is Spirit, so those who worship him must worship in spirit and in truth."*

JOHN 4:24

# The Lord Is Faithful

We all desire to have trustworthy, dependable, faithful people in our lives. Our hearts yearn for reliability. In Psalm 33:4, it says that the Lord is true in all that he does. God is a faithful God. He's reliable, consistent, and trustworthy. He is there for us in the good times, and he's there for us in the challenging times.

We can fully rely on God, which is wonderful news! Now, when it comes to others, if you don't have faithful people in your life, you can ask God to bring to you those who value faithfulness. Everyone ought to have at least one person they can rely on in times of need, even if it's just to sit in silence together.

At the same time, check your heart to gauge your own level of faithfulness. Are you a faithful friend? Can people depend upon you? Are you true to your word? To find faithful friends, you must *be* a faithful friend.

Faithfulness is one of the nine fruits of the Spirit: *love, joy, peace, patience, kindness, gentleness, goodness, faithfulness*, and *self-control*. As you continue to grow strong in the power of the Holy Spirit, you're sure to grow in faithfulness. This will certainly enhance your relationship with God and others because, as Proverbs 28:20 says, "The trustworthy person will get a rich reward."

## Good Morning, Lord

*Please hold my hand and walk me
through the process of being faithful in all my
relationships, especially to the Holy Trinity.*

*"For the word of the Lord holds true,
and we can trust everything he does."*

**Psalm 33:4**

# Follow Jesus's Footsteps

The word *Christian* means "little Christ." In other words, someone who emulates the character of Jesus Christ. The early Christ followers became well-known because they didn't act as everyone else. They didn't go with the ways of the world. They took a vow to walk the path of Jesus Christ, to follow in his footsteps and continue to be light and love in the world.

This is still the call of Christ believers today. Regardless of where you're located, or what kind of resources you have, you are called to follow the steps of Jesus.

Each day, make it a habit to offer your heart to the Lord and ask him to show you if there is something that you've done that could have been done better. Not to shame you, but to teach you. To check your motives to see why you are doing things as you are. To gauge your character and your values. To be accountable to God for your life even when no one else is around.

It can be challenging, showing up in the world as compassion, patience, and love. It's not always easy. We don't always *feel* like being an imitator of Jesus, but we're not led by feelings; we are led by our *commitment* to be God's children. This is my hope for you, dear one—that you will be able to commit to the long-haul following of Jesus's footsteps in this world. Together, we are making a positive difference!

## Good Morning, Lord

*I am open to hearing—really hearing—your teaching ministry, and following in your footsteps the best that I can.*

*"For God called you to do good, even if it means suffering, just as Christ suffered for you. He is your example, and you must follow in his steps."*

1 PETER 2:21

# God's Beautiful Garden

How beautiful to gaze upon a blossoming garden. The colors, shapes, and smells can transport you to a place of serenity! If you take time to create a bouquet, you'll notice differences between each flower. Some are tall, others short. Some have thick stems, some thin. Some bloom exquisitely, and some shy away from opening their petals fully . . . But all are lovely.

I imagine this is how God sees us, his children. He gazes upon all different types of beautiful flowers, taking in the signature aroma of each soul. Some tall, some short, some blossoming radiantly, and some holding back. Reds, oranges, yellows, pinks, and so on—all different, but equally beautiful! God created this variety for a reason, and he made you unique for your life purpose.

Dear one, whether you're a rose, poinsettia, lily, or sunflower, God sees you! You don't have to do a thing. Just *be* the pure flower that you are. Don't worry that you look different from the other flowers, as your uniqueness contributes to the beauty of the earth's bouquet. Stand tall, showcasing your true colors, blossoming unto the Lord God Almighty. Dear one, go ahead and glory in his creation and presence! He created you beautiful and whole, and he loves to gaze upon your sweet spirit!

### Good Morning, Lord

*Please be my gardener, pulling weeds and pruning away anything that's unhealthful, helping me blossom and thrive.*

---

*"Look at the lilies and how they grow. They don't work or make their clothing, yet Solomon in all his glory was not dressed as beautifully as they are."*

Luke 12:27

# GLORIFY GOD IN TIMES OF TROUBLE

We're not sure why natural disasters occur, and we grieve the losses that result from them. Yet even in the midst of disaster, we find glimmers of bright blessings as people come together to help. Despite their heartache and loss, they pull together and serve the community as best as they can. In fact, lifelong friendships are often formed and familial bonds strengthened during these crises.

God wants to show up during such times. Instead of our focusing on "Why, God?" he desires that we allow him to use us mightily during these trials. That could mean taking time to pray; offering a helping hand; providing a temporary shelter; or giving donations of money, clothing, food, and so forth. It may mean taking a week or two to help rebuild the affected area. There are many ways to assist those in need.

It is unfortunate when a natural disaster strikes, but, dear one, let's turn our attention to God during such times and ask, *What can I do, Lord? What work would you like to do through me?* God desires to utilize hearts that will extend his love and compassion, and perform acts of kindness for those who have need. This glorifies him and helps in restoring hope that may have been lost. May this be our aim!

## Good Morning, Lord

*How may I help? What would you have me do?*
*Where would you have me be? I will do as you guide me.*

---

*"[Jesus said], 'Should I pray, "Father, save me from this hour"?*
*But this is the very reason I came! Father, bring glory to your name.'*
*Then a voice spoke from heaven, saying, 'I have already brought*
*glory to my name, and I will do so again.'"*

JOHN 12:27–28

## CHASING AFTER THE WIND

King Solomon is known as one of the wisest men of the Bible, but all his wisdom did not spare him from temptations of the flesh and self-centeredness. Solomon went after all the worldly things that he thought would bring him lasting joy: wealth, multiple relationships, fame, and the like. Yet he ended up in despair, declaring, "All is vanity. All is meaningless!"

What did he mean by this? Solomon lusted after vain things that provided only brief flashes of happiness. In the end, he felt like he was grasping at nothing because none of it truly satisfied. This sometimes happens, as we may gravitate toward a life apart from God. Yet it is always his will that each person will come to the revelation that a life without God is vanity, like chasing after the wind.

The ways of the world may look enticing and promise "happily ever after." We might believe that impressing people is more important than helping them. However, sooner or later, people seeking to fill the "God space" with carnal things will arrive at a crisis of conscience, feeling empty and devoid of meaning. It is this death of self that is the seed for new life in Christ Jesus. This is the Good News of the Gospel.

Please take some time to look through the books of Solomon and glean wisdom from his words. You will be richly blessed as you continue to nurture and tend to the true spiritual treasures in life.

### Good Morning, Lord

*I'm here with my humble heart, open to your teachings and guidance about how to best use my time to help bring blessings to this world.*

---

*"'Vanity of vanities,' says the Preacher;*
*'Vanity of vanities, all is vanity.'"*

ECCLESIASTES 1:2 (WEB)

## BE A SERVANT OF ALL

The competitive belief is that if you come out ahead, you are better than others. Be careful with this belief, because the ego may prompt us to ignore God's guidance. The ego wants recognition, and it wants to be esteemed highly.

In Mark 9:35, Jesus sits down with his disciples and says, "Whoever wants to be first must take last place and be the servant of everyone else." Jesus is saying that if you want to be first in the Kingdom of God, then serve all those around you. Don't look for others to serve *you* and put you on a pedestal. Aim to serve *them*, in humility.

The desire to have a position of power and authority can be subtle. You may not even realize that your motives are skewed until you later get a glimpse of the reality. Don't start that new business or take that job because you want to make a lot of money, but because you want to help others. Let your motives be to care about people and to put them first.

It's an attitude of the heart, dear one. Are we seeking to be loving servants of all? Or is the furtive desire to be known, seen, and admired lurking underneath the surface? This is something to be on guard against, so check your heart with the Lord consistently.

May we all aspire to live with a servant's heart—from there, great things always fall into place.

### ∽ Good Morning, Lord ∾

*Please help me follow you instead of the voice of the ego.*
*Please help me stay focused upon true priorities*
*instead of chasing after idle fantasies.*

*"Whoever of you wants to become first*
*among you, shall be bondservant of all."*

MARK 10:44 (WEB)

## PERSISTENCE IN PRAYER

Some people are hesitant to pray because they don't think they know how. The thing is, prayer is simply talking from your heart to God. It requires no formal education. I love the way Jesus explains it in Luke 11. Just after Jesus speaks the famous Lord's Prayer, he tells a parable in the hopes of teaching his disciples about persistence in prayer.

Imagine that your best friend shows up starving at your door at midnight. You have no food, so you go to another friend's house down the road. This friend says no: "It's late, the kids are sleeping, and I'm not waking up the whole household." At this point, some would give up, but most would ask again. Your friend would likely get up eventually.

This is a lesson about tenacity—it pays off. Jesus goes on to say when you want something, keep asking, keep seeking, keep knocking!

You want to know how to pray? Be persistent. Yes, you can offer one prayer, believe you receive an answer, and move on. But there's something to be said for persistence, too. It's not about a right versus wrong way; there are different ways to pray, just like there are different ways you talk with your close friends.

Dear one, sometimes persistence is required. It doesn't take eloquent words either. Simply convey how you feel. Give yourself permission to talk with God just like you would on behalf of a friend in need asking for food.

### *Good Morning, Lord*

*Thank you for our heart-to-heart prayerful conversations and for these times when I can really feel and hear your presence and guidance.*

*"And so I tell you, keep on asking, and you will receive what you ask for. Keep on seeking, and you will find. Keep on knocking, and the door will be opened to you."*

LUKE 11:9

# PRAY IN PRIVACY

Connecting with the presence of God's powerful love is a deeply personal and emotionally intimate experience. When we pray in private, it's possible to further our connection with God even more. Joining in prayers with others is also a beautiful way to gain emotional and spiritual closeness with our community. However, we must ensure that our motives for praying aloud are sincere—not to show off to others.

In Matthew 6, Jesus is saying that when you pray, do not be like the hypocrites. They love to be seen in public speaking eloquent, well-thought-out prayers before God not so much to glorify their Heavenly Father as to be seen and admired by men. Instead, when you desire to pray and connect with God, go into seclusion, where no one sees you. Connect with your Heavenly Father there in that private place because then your full attention will be on conversing with him alone, for the sole purpose of sharing the moment. It's personal, purposeful, and intimate.

Yes, certainly pray in public when the time calls for it, but do not neglect withdrawing from the world and seeking that intimate time with your Father one-on-one. As you go about your day, keep this in mind: God desires intimacy with each person.

My prayer is that you continue to deepen your relationship with the Lord, cultivating an intimacy that richly blesses you.

*Good Morning, Lord*

*I am drawing close to you and baring my most vulnerable thoughts and feelings. For you see me as I truly am, and you are helping me reveal my God-created self instead of the egoic self.*

---

*"But when you pray, go away by yourself, shut the door behind you, and pray to your Father in private. Then your Father, who sees everything, will reward you."*

MATTHEW 6:6

## MORE OF JESUS, LESS OF ME

Spiritual maturity is what we're after. Throughout your life, I imagine that you have been walking your path, or perhaps various paths, seeking to know yourself and God better.

Sometimes, we'll hear children exclaim, "I can't wait to be an adult! I can't wait to grow up!" We probably felt like this when we were young, too. There's something in each of us that yearns for maturity. After all, expansion does the soul good!

As followers of Jesus, we're encouraged to establish ourselves maturely in the faith. We're to grow in grace and discernment, applying spiritual truth to our lives. But what does this really mean? Does being spiritually mature mean that we perform many good works in the world? Is it the ability to recite many scriptures by heart? Do we ever reach full maturity?

Our actions may indicate a level of spiritual maturity, but works alone don't define our level of faith or maturity. As you know, there are plenty of people who do good works with ulterior motives or a heart full of pride.

"More of Jesus equals less of me" is a powerful affirmation for quieting the ego and surrendering to God's amazing will and glory. As long as that kind of equation is our truth, we know we're maturing. Dear one, my prayer is that you continue to grow in grace, love, compassion, and servanthood unto Jesus Christ. That his Spirit takes up full residence in you so that his will is done more and more.

### Good Morning, Lord

*The more I surrender my ego to the Holy Trinity, the more room there is for you to reside within and work through me. Please help me let go, surrendering to your love.*

---

*"So, dear brothers and sisters, work hard to prove that you really are among those God has called and chosen. Do these things, and you will never fall away."*

2 PETER 1:10

# Have Faith

*Have faith.* Sometimes easier said than done, right? When you're in the midst of desperation and darkness, the last thing you need is for someone to tell you to keep the faith.

Yet faith is *exactly* what we need during those frightening moments. A beautiful truth is that faith is the foundation of miracles and the doorway to deliverance. Another beautiful truth is that we don't have to conjure up faith or try to control whether we have it or not. We have divine help to *increase* our faith, no matter what's going on around us. This is one of the most important prayers that we can make.

Calling upon God to fan the flames of belief, hope, optimism, and faith can be a life-changing step. The other side of this, though, is having faith in the specific solution that God devises. It's about trusting that God's infinite wisdom is taking care of all the details and knows the best way to resolve your situation. The answer to your prayer may differ from your expectations, yet it will be the optimal resolution when you look back on it.

### Good Morning, Lord

*I need your help, please. I feel stressed and nervous, and my faith is shaken. Please send your Holy Spirit to lift me up, and help me stop trying to control everything by myself. I know I can't do this alone, so I give it to you, with my heart and arms open to gratefully receiving your blessings.*

*"The Lord is my strength and shield.
I trust him with all my heart.
He helps me, and my heart is filled with joy.
I burst out in songs of thanksgiving."*

**Psalm 28:7**

# FAMILY IN CHRIST

True friendship is constant, a treasure we can bank on through thick and thin. We are bound by our common interests and the affection we bear each other. Over many years of camaraderie, we have a history of experiences that we cherish.

We know the good, the bad, and the ugly about a close friend, and they know the same about us—and we love each other anyway! The strength of our bond is based on mutual empathy, and we would do anything for a lifelong friend. It's very similar to a marriage vow: we promise to love each other in sickness and in health, for better or for worse, for richer or for poorer, until death us do part.

If we consider ourselves children of God, then we agree we are therefore brothers and sisters through him, our Father. Just as with our earthly parents and siblings, we are inclined—by the nature of our relationship—to love, support, and share each other's burdens.

Take time today to thank God for the love of your friends, family, and brothers and sisters through Christ, who will always be there for you.

### Good Morning, Lord

*I feel that you are my family, and my best friend who is there for me always, 24 hours a day, seven days a week. My heart is filled with gratitude for all that you do and are!*

*"A friend is always loyal, and a brother is born to help in time of need."*

PROVERBS 17:17

# GOD FIGHTS FOR US

When faced with challenges or times of uncertainty, we often worry about what's going to happen. As much as we want to have faith that God is in control, doubts creep in and we need reassurance that he is there to see us through.

When the frightened Israelites were being chased by the Egyptians, they lost trust in Moses and asked him why he brought them out of Egypt. In despair, they cried, "It's better to be a slave in Egypt than a corpse in the wilderness" (Exodus 14:12). Sometimes it seems easier to give up and resign ourselves to bad things that happen in our lives, thinking that we've met our fate and must suffer through it.

But Moses wasn't having any of that attitude! He'd spoken with God, and he had a plan: Moses was going to lift his hands over the water, and God would part the sea so the Israelites could walk through to the other side. Moses told the people not to worry, because God had the situation under control . . . And he did!

The clear message is that God is on your side, and he will fight for you. You just have to be patient and let him do his thing. It's easy to become afraid and give up hope, and it's tempting to think we are in control and can manage without him. Fortunately, he is there for us *always*. In times of doubt, say the words: *Be calm. Be still. God is here.*

### Good Morning, Lord

*Thank you for protecting and defending me, ensuring that if I follow your guidance, I will be safe.*

*"The Lord himself will fight for you. Just stay calm."*

**EXODUS 14:14**

# A Chosen Vessel

Job is a beautiful book, giving a wonderful look at the essence of this prophet's being. It begins as a model portrait of a successful, spiritually grown man. Job was loved by his community, and he had a close relationship with God. His life seemed blessed beyond measure, until he was hit with seemingly unending tragedy. Due to a battle going on in the heavens, Job lost his family, possessions, and health. His perfect life was shattered in a very short time.

Little did he know that God's plan remained intact. As Job wrestled with his great loss, his core was hollowed out of anything not of God. A chosen vessel, so to speak. God is always on the lookout for faithful servants through whom he can effortlessly pour out his great love. This doesn't mean that you must suffer tragedy and loss to be a chosen vessel of the Lord, but God does require that we "die" to our bodily lusts or egoic desires in order to walk pure in his sight.

There is a purification process during spiritual maturation, which isn't always easy. It's a choice every believer has to make. We discover that those bodily and egoic desires were all based upon fears, and we didn't really want or need those things anyway.

Surrender your heart to God, emptied of self, so he can fill you up. He desires that you allow the great love he has for you to flow through you, blessing you and also blessing the world.

### Good Morning, Lord

*Thank you for transforming my desires to be aligned with divine will. Instead of wishing to impress others, I now only desire that which brings blessings.*

*"God is mighty, but he does not despise anyone! He is mighty in both power and understanding."*

Job 36:5

## JESUS IS THE TRUTH

All of us value the truth. In John 14:6, Jesus says that *he* is truth—not a particular religion or set of rules. He is *truth*. He is the One sent from God to humanity to show the way. To be the truth that leads people to everlasting life.

There are those who think Jesus was just a good man, and some who think he was a myth. All sorts of false accusations have been leveled against Jesus, but the Word says he is truth. He is God's Son and Prophet sent to teach humanity how they can gain access to God and his Kingdom. He was different, marked to serve his Father and humanity in humility and love.

The scriptures point to Jesus Christ, the truth, sent to set captives free and establish a new way of life. I believe without a shadow of a doubt that Jesus is the truth that can radically change the world. His ways can mend hearts, open eyes, restore communities, refresh the weary, and unite the world. He has left us a map into his Kingdom of light and love.

If you don't already know the real Jesus of Nazareth, my prayer is that you come to know him in a personal way. He is open to anyone and everyone who calls to him, without exception. My prayer for you is that you feel and experience his real presence, and that through him you will enjoy wholeness—mind, body, and spirit.

### Good Morning, Lord

*Thank you for being in my life and for being there for everyone who asks for you. Please let me know how I can spread the Good News to those who need you in their lives.*

*"Jesus told him, 'I am the way, the truth, and the life. No one can come to the Father except through me.'"*

JOHN 14:6

# BE HOLY

Coming to know Jesus in a personal way opens the door to salvation, or stepping into the Kingdom of Heaven. The Bible talks about *justification*, essentially meaning that we have been justified through faith in Jesus Christ. It's "just as if" we've never acted out in the fleshly or corrupted nature.

The Bible also talks about *sanctification*, which means "setting apart." We have been made righteous in Christ. We can stand before God right and innocent. We've been justified by faith and have the invitation to become sanctified, or set apart for the Lord.

God's forgiveness is not to be used as justification for continuing to walk apart from him. In 1 Peter 1:15, this disciple says, "But now you must be holy in everything you do, just as God who chose you is holy." To walk before the Lord holy means to do so with the life of Jesus in us and Spirit leading us. It is allowing the work of sanctification to be realized on a daily basis. It means doing the right thing, as God guides us, and resisting temptation to fulfill the bodily lusts. It's living your life purposefully, in such a way that it glorifies God.

May we aim to be holy before the Lord, set apart for him and his purposes, and walk in righteousness, justification, and sanctification before him!

### Good Morning, Lord

*You always know the right thing to do and say. I ask that you show me how to discern what is God's will and what is the ego's willfulness. Please adjust my moral compass in the direction of God. Please help me be so filled with you that I automatically think, speak, and take action according to God's will.*

---

*"For the Scriptures say, 'You must be holy because I am holy.'"*

1 PETER 1:16

# The Good Samaritan

The parable of the Good Samaritan is a prime example of kindness. Its message, if lived out, can effect radical change for good in the world.

In the story, we learn of a man who had been robbed and beaten on the road to Jericho. The first to come across the scene, a priest, who you would think knew a little bit about compassion, had no time for the hurting man. He could not even be bothered to stop and think about how he might help.

The second to find the man, a Levite, paused to look at him. He saw the need. He may have even contemplated whether he should help, but ultimately he passed him as well.

Then the Good Samaritan came along. He saw the injured man and took it upon himself to mercifully do what needed to be done. Compassionately, he washed the man's wounds, helped him to a safe inn, and paid for it out of his own pocket.

Compassion puts all things aside and does the right thing. You are called to be a Good Samaritan to those you encounter daily. Keep focused on opportunities to help at home, work, and the community. Keep your eyes open. It could be to serve people, animals, or any good cause. Ask the Lord for guidance and discernment.

Make kindness a part of your lifestyle. May we all be Good Samaritans caring for those in need.

## Good Morning, Lord

*I pray to be less self-centered, and more God-centered.*
*Please show me how I can be a Good Samaritan to those in need.*

*"'Now which of these three would you say was a neighbor*
*to the man who was attacked by bandits?' Jesus asked.*
*The man replied, 'The one who showed him mercy.'*
*Then Jesus said, 'Yes, now go and do the same.'"*

Luke 10:36–37

## Reach Out to the Oppressed

In the first chapter of Isaiah, God explains that he's had enough of burnt offerings, pious meetings, and meaningless gifts. These displays of vain devotion and sacrifice are not what God desires. He wants us to "learn to do good" (Isaiah 1:17).

We must follow a strict moral code and be ethical in our words and deeds, and make every effort to be honest, faithful, and pure. God asks us to reach out and seek justice, to become involved in helping others who are oppressed. That entails going out of our comfort zone in our interactions with people, but that is where the true sacrifice enters the picture.

We can't just sit back, believing our monetary donation to the church or a charity is all that is required of us. We may also be called upon to take care of the physical and emotional needs of our brothers and sisters. This could be making a decision to stand up for someone you see being bullied, visiting a person who is lonely, volunteering at a charity, feeding the hungry, and looking for any way that you can to relieve another's burden.

Romans 12:1 states, "Give your bodies to God. . . . Let them be a living and holy sacrifice." God doesn't want a burnt offering as a sacrifice. He wants *you*—to be his witness in the way you live.

### ∽ *Good Morning, Lord* ∽

*Please help me overcome my resistances to living a truly helpful life.*
*I am giving you my fears and nervousness about getting involved,*
*and I commit to following your guidance as to how*
*I can be of spiritual service.*

---

*"Learn to do good. Seek justice. Help the oppressed.*
*Defend the cause of orphans. Fight for the rights of widows."*

Isaiah 1:17

## TRUST GOD FOR SAFETY

We can go through life afraid of many things. We don't know what the future holds for us and our loved ones, and we often surrender to the fears.

Fear can be a trap, as stated in Proverbs 29:25, because if we allow it to control our lives, then we succumb to the dread and the panic. If we live in a constant state of worry, we cannot live the life God intends for us. He wants us to be happy and secure in his love for us.

This isn't to say that bad things will never happen to us if we follow God's Word. We can't always avoid unfortunate events, but we have his assurance that he will be there for us, through the good times and the bad times.

When we put our trust in God, we're able to face legitimate emotional and physical uncertainties and deal with them in a healthy state of mind. Psalm 23:4 sums it up: "Even when I walk through the darkest valley, I will not be afraid, for you are close beside me. Your rod and your staff protect and comfort me."

Our faith in God will comfort us in times of distress, and remind us that he will provide the answers and we can live a peaceful existence. Turn any fears over to God and know that they are in his hands.

### Good Morning, Lord

*Please help me release my fears, including the fears I'm unaware of. Instead of feeling uncertain about future, I pray that I become certain of God and filled with trust and faith.*

"Fearing people is a dangerous trap,
but trusting the Lord means safety."

PROVERBS 29:25

# FORGIVE

Forgive others as God has forgiven you—it sounds easy, right? As much as we'd like to think the best of others, the reality is that people hurt people intentionally and unintentionally all the time.

It's all right to have a righteous indignation for intentional harm. Jesus did his share of rebuking and standing up for righteousness. However, as Christ followers, we are instructed to forgive, just as Jesus forgave when he was sentenced to death. However, forgiving doesn't mean that you are agreeing with or condoning someone's hurtful actions.

Repressed anger is toxic. If you walk around with unforgiveness in your heart, bitterness takes root. That bitterness can ultimately act as a poison, robbing you of peace, joy, love, relationships, and dreams.

The Word says that we should respond to others with the same grace that God has given us. If we don't, then a bitter spirit can arise, which will harm not only us but also others. People who walk around bitter can readily project their anger or resentment. Therefore, God asks all to willingly forgive and release their hurt to him. Do not take judgment into your own hands. Just as Jesus forgave all, so are you to forgive others.

It may be challenging. It may seem impossible. Ask God to help you release that bitterness and heal your wounded heart. Ask God for the grace to forgive anyone who has hurt or offended you or others, just as he forgives us.

### ∼ *Good Morning, Lord* ∼

*Please help me forgive so that I may purge myself of anger
and bitterness, and find inner peace.*

---

*"Make allowance for each other's faults, and
forgive anyone who offends you. Remember,
the Lord forgave you, so you must forgive others."*

COLOSSIANS 3:13

## ALLOW FRIENDS TO HELP

When God created Adam, he said, "It is not good for the man to be alone" (Genesis 2:18). So he created Eve to be with him—to journey together. We weren't meant to navigate life all on our own. God is a relational God, and he made us relational people. Isolating ourselves can spiral us into depression and loneliness.

If you're struggling, you want to have at least one friend to call on. One who will say, "I'm going to believe for you. Pray for you. I'm going to uphold you in this frustrating time. I am here for you." We all need go-to friends like that. In fact, the Word says that when desperate people give up on God, their friends should stick with them (Job 6:14).

If you don't currently have a close friend, it's time to cultivate one. Go to places with like-minded people, such as a church, Bible study, volunteer group, or clubs or classes related to your interests. And, as the truism says, "To have a good friend, be a good friend." Cultivate friendships in which you're there for one another. At the same time, be willing to reach out when you're in a tough place.

Be mindful of this, dear one. Be there for others, and allow them to be there for you. This is my prayer for you, darling.

### ⟨⟨⟨ Good Morning, Lord ⟩⟩⟩

*You are my best friend, and I ask that you guide me to healthy and supportive people. Please help me heal any fears, nervousness, shame, or feelings of unworthiness that could block me from developing deep friendships.*

*"One should be kind to a fainting friend, but you accuse me without any fear of the Almighty."*

JOB 6:14

# THE PRODIGAL SON

There was a wealthy man who had two sons. His youngest son went to him and asked to receive his inheritance early. The father granted his request, and that son left home to travel the world, doing whatever he pleased. Before long, he ended up broke, and humbly returned home.

The father rejoiced over his son's return and threw a big celebration! The older son, who'd been working in the fields, came home to find a party going on. When he learned the reason, he got upset. No one had ever thrown him such a party. Why should his brother get such treatment after his bad behavior?

His father explained that when his youngest son left, it was as if he'd died. But when he came home, it was like he'd come back from the dead! He wanted to celebrate this with all he had!

This story, known as the parable of the prodigal son, is found in Luke 15. Jesus likens the younger son to those who are separated from God. They have gone their own way but end up broken and empty, desiring again the love of the Father. Heavenly Father, who loves unconditionally, rejoices over anyone who comes to him in humility and repentance.

Dear one, no matter how long you've been gone or what you've been doing, God is *always* going to rejoice when his children come back to him. Oh, sister or brother in Christ, he is indeed a loving Father.

## Good Morning, Lord

*Please lead me back upon the solid path of truth and God's will.*
*Help me value all the true gifts and love offered*
*to me as God's beloved child.*

---

*"We had to celebrate this happy day. For your brother was dead and has come back to life! He was lost, but now he is found!"*

LUKE 15:32

# THE WORD IS TRUTH

The Bible was written by 40 authors over a period of almost 2,000 years. Throughout, it points to Jesus Christ as Savior. Across all the authors and eras, the Bible's central message of God's eternal plan stays consistent.

The Bible is useful as we journey through this life, full of practical instructions and advice. Yes, it is full of spiritual revelation and mystery, but it also provides us with clear guidelines on how to confront everyday problems like anger or resolving conflict; how to handle finances, relationships, stress, and so on; and ways to cultivate joy.

Some people get turned off by parts of the Bible that don't seem to make sense or that describe culturally archaic practices, so they don't read the passages that contain wisdom. In a sense, they throw the baby out with the bathwater. Fortunately, today there are many versions of the Bible with easier-to-understand translations.

While God doesn't need everyone to be a Bible scholar, there are treasures in the Word and practical guidelines for everyday life. My hope is that you will cultivate joy in reading through the Word. Allow it to transform you by the power of the Holy Spirit and give you hope in time with sorrow, joy in times of despair, and strength in times of weakness. Take it in a few pages at a time, and watch how Holy Spirit reveals wisdom and truth!

## Good Morning, Lord

*I think of you as my professor of spiritual truth, guiding my learning. Please show me how to study the Bible and gain the most insights from this valuable resource—the Word of God.*

*"You have been taught the holy Scriptures from childhood, and they have given you the wisdom to receive the salvation that comes by trusting in Christ Jesus."*

2 TIMOTHY 3:15

## LET LOVE RULE YOUR HEART

The book of Romans, written by the apostle Paul, is described as the "Gospel of the Righteousness of God" by various scholars. If you wish to know how God lovingly desires you to live, take some time and read through chapters 12 to 16, as a life lived in Christ can model such characteristics.

The central theme in all the instructions is love. Paul counsels us to love others without judgment, show brotherly affection, be generous to those in need, spend time with the lonely, be there for those who are struggling, and more. Essentially, he sums it all up and says, "You shall love your neighbor as yourself"—*neighbor* meaning anyone.

He counsels to love your friends and love your enemies. Love those who treat you well and those who roll their eyes at you. Love everyone! Living as a follower of Jesus assures you a loving relationship with God. You're walking in the Kingdom of light and love. Now, go and love others with that gushing river of love!

Paul also describes the reality that in Christ, you are justified and sanctified. Now, as you have been freely given to, so should you give to others. It's really much simpler than some make it out to be.

Dear one, take some time to pore over the book of Romans. Glean wisdom from Paul's instruction. As you go about your day, please let love rule and reign in your heart.

### Good Morning, Lord

*Thank you for clearly guiding my ways, helping me be a living example and conduit of pure and unconditional divine love.*

---

*"Whatever other commandments there are, are all summed up in this saying, namely, 'You shall love your neighbor as yourself.'"*

ROMANS 13:9 (WEB)

# DIG DEEP TO FIND THE LIVING WATER

Have you ever wondered why plants can live in the desert when there's so little water? One strategy is that they grow deeper roots to tap into the earth's underground water supply rather than relying upon rain. God created these plants with the ability to adapt to their conditions and, dear one, God makes us the exact same way.

Think about when you're in a dry period of life. Maybe you're faced with a particular challenge or just feeling depressed or apathetic. You need the water of God's grace because you're withering up. Now, you have some choices. You can look to outer sources (hope for rain clouds) or you can go within and look toward God (dig deep). Jeremiah 7:5–8 puts it like this:

> Cursed are those who put their trust in mere humans, who rely on human strength and turn their hearts away from the Lord. They are like stunted shrubs in the desert. . . . But blessed are those who trust in the Lord and have made the Lord their hope and confidence. They are like trees planted along a riverbank, with roots that reach deep into the water. Such trees are not bothered by the heat or worried by long months of drought. Their leaves stay green, and they never stop producing fruit.

The message is clear. In those dry seasons, go within, dig deep, and trust that you'll find God's Living Water supply that's always there. Then you'll be refreshed. Your branches and leaves will flourish. You'll sustain yourself and bear fruit for others to enjoy.

## Good Morning, Lord

*Please replenish my enthusiasm, energy levels, and motivation.*
*Help me, please, to dig deep, rooting myself in your infinite love.*

---

*"O Lord, if you heal me, I will be truly healed; if you save me,*
*I will be truly saved. My praises are for you alone!"*

JEREMIAH 17:14

# GOD CALLS YOU OUT OF DARKNESS

I've had to step out of my comfort zone many times in my life and blindly take leaps of faith as God guides me—as he guides all of us.

Looking back, I can see how God leads us out of those dark times in our lives, holding our hands and ushering us back into his light. He also gives us mile-marker signs along the way, to reassure and comfort us with the knowledge that we're heading in the right direction.

Isaiah 45:3 says God will give us treasures hidden in the darkness and secret riches. Why? So that we may know that it was he who drew us up and out of that darkness, holding the lantern for us all along the way.

This is encouraging, especially if you're going through a period of darkness. Or perhaps you need to step out of your comfort zone in order to change up your circumstances. Today, dear one, please turn to the book of Isaiah and meditate on this scripture. Almighty God will give you treasures and riches, stored in the dark or secret places, so that you may know that he is with you.

## Good Morning, Lord

*May you help me and all others find our way out of the darkness and into God's warm, loving light.*

---

*"And I will give you treasures hidden in the darkness—secret riches. I will do this so you may know that I am the Lord, the God of Israel, the one who calls you by name."*

ISAIAH 45:3

# Your Heart Creates Your Words

The news seems to focus upon all the negative things that are occurring. As such, you'll have a decision to make as to whether you're going to *respond* negatively. Will you criticize? Feel afraid? Complain?

Every day we make the choice to react in a positive or negative way to any circumstance we find ourselves in. Even if there are plenty of horrific things going on in the world, there is still so much good going on, too. The nonprofit organization transforming millions of lives. The person buying lunch for the homeless. The mother providing extra care to the neighborhood kids who come from unstable homes. There are many good-hearted people bringing God's Kingdom of light to the planet.

The Word says what comes out of your heart begins in the heart, so it's important to know what state your heart is in. In other words, what is your heart focused upon: finding fault or finding God?

Prayer can lend your heart a more positive and loving way of viewing life's challenges. Fill your heart with God's love so that you'll automatically be thinking and speaking things that will build you up and those around you.

## Good Morning, Lord

*I pray that my heart and mind are completely filled with God's love so that I bring a healed perception to the world.*

*"But the things which proceed out of the mouth come out of the heart."*

**Matthew 15:18 (WEB)**

# REMEMBER YOUR DIVINE HERITAGE!

Sometimes we forget who we are and why we're here. This spiritual amnesia can lead to depression or feeling lost, without meaning or purpose. That's when we believe that the material world is the real world, failing to remember that the spiritual world is what is true and lasting.

In case you've forgotten, this is who you really are: You are God's beloved child, made in God's image and likeness, as Genesis 1:27 reminds us. All the power, goodness, and love of God is your true spiritual identity.

There's nothing weak or wimpy in God's nature, nor in yours. You are powerful, strong, and courageous. And because you're the creation of the Creator, you're also creative. You have access to the infinite wisdom of God's mind, which supplies you with guidance on any question.

## *Good Morning, Lord*

*Please keep reminding me that you are my true parent who loves me unconditionally. Please help me claim my spiritual heritage and inheritance from you, and enjoy being one of God's beloved children, passing along these blessings to others who've forgotten who they are.*

*"See how very much our Father loves us, for he calls us his children, and that is what we are! But the people who belong to this world don't recognize that we are God's children because they don't know him."*

1 JOHN 3:1

## RELATIONSHIPS AS MIRRORS

Relationships are a hot topic. I'm the first to admit that no matter how much faith you have, romantic relationships can stretch you, sometimes even break you. Is that God's will? I presume no, but I also know that some mighty big life lessons are learned in and through relationships.

I hear a lot of people talk about seeking their soul mate. If you believe there's only one person whom God designed for you, you may spend years and years searching for that perfect person and perhaps never find them. The reality is there *is* no perfect person, but there are many people with the characteristics you'd like in a partner.

Some people don't feel fulfilled unless they're in a relationship, believing that their partner should complete them. This can set you up for disappointment. God desires that we find our "completeness" in him. Then, from there, we can add to a relationship rather than simply take. A person can't fulfill you at the deep, spiritual level, the way you truly desire.

God is all for romantic relationships. He uses relationships to help us learn valuable lessons about ourselves, others, and unconditional love. Relationships are mirrors; just as God mirrors to us his unconditional love, so our relationships with a partner can do the same.

It won't always be easy, darling. Have an open heart, lean on God, and allow him to help you cultivate an amazing, God-centered relationship.

### ᔕ *Good Morning, Lord* ᔐ

*I rely on you to fulfill me and show me how worthy I am of amazing, blessed love. May I always glean the wisdom found in God's Word about relationships.*

---

*"Those who know your name trust in you, for you, O Lord, do not abandon those who search for you."*

PSALM 9:10

## SUCCESS OR SIGNIFICANCE?

Here's a thought-provoking question for you: *Do you feel that you are going after* success *or going after* significance *in your decision making?*

Significance is about meaningfulness and making a positive difference in the world. Success is fantastic, but success that comes from a self-centered approach can feel empty and hollow once you achieve it. You could have the whole world admiring you, but unless you know deep inside that you're making a positive difference in the world, all that admiration won't bring happiness.

Significance matters. When you work toward meaning and significance, you're already a success! This doesn't necessarily mean you are deemed a success in the eyes of the world. In fact, very few may ever hear your name. Think of the missionaries who go off to care for those in need, and those who serve at the homeless shelter or clean the church after services. Think of the ones who turn down job opportunities with huge salaries so they can instead have the time for volunteer work.

There's this image of success out there that may look appealing, but in and of itself it may cause you to feel empty. I find that the happiest people are those who have a strong faith in God and who live a life where they feel significant by serving others in some way, whether it's loved ones, customers, the homeless, or whomever. God working through us—this is our prayer!

### Good Morning, Lord

*Please help me stay focused upon what really matters, and contribute as much as I can. I ask that you help me keep blinders on to "success" so that I'm not distracted by or attracted to superficiality.*

*"And what do you benefit if you gain the whole world but lose your own soul? Is anything worth more than your soul?"*

MATTHEW 16:26

## INVITE GOD IN CONTINUALLY

Chances are, you rely on yourself to accomplish many things in life. You have certain responsibilities to uphold, so you take the time and energy to tend to them. Occasionally you may run into a situation where you need help, in which case you ask someone to assist you. This is all good and well. Reaching out for help is wise.

But what about God? Does your self-sufficiency push him out, or do you still invite him in—even for the everyday tasks you can easily accomplish? Since Holy Spirit lives within you, your connection with God is always in place. God is never far away. In fact, he's within *all* the time. But perhaps you're not consciously acknowledging his presence throughout the day. You may wake up in the morning and offer him a few moments of your time, but then you may not really think about him until you're back in bed, ready to fall asleep.

Dear one, God desires that you include him in all the things you do throughout your day. From the little things, like making your breakfast in the morning, to the big things, like making a major decision.

Today, as you go about your day, keep your connection with the Heavenly Father open. Invite him to be a part of every moment, every decision, every word, and every action. He's your constant companion, and when you set an intention to continually recognize him as such, you'll feel different. Your days will feel different. And this, darling, will bless you greatly.

### ⌒ *Good Morning, Lord* ⌒

*I'm so happy that you're always with me and I'm never alone.*
*Now my prayer is to stay aware of your presence,*
*and so feel consistently safe and loved.*

*"And God has given us his Spirit as proof
that we live in him and he in us."*

1 JOHN 4:13

## MAKE TIME TO LISTEN

*Praying* is talking to God, and *meditating* is listening to God's answers. Both are necessary.

Has life seemed noisy and chaotic lately? Have you felt blocked or stuck? Does it seem like your prayers aren't being answered? God answers every question and prayer; however, it does involve us listening. It also involves us taking charge and creatively figuring out how to have quiet time alone to think.

I'm always inspired by the stories of how Jesus would go into the wilderness to fast and pray. He'd listen to God's guidance before returning back to his teaching and healing. He created this time for God, and we can all model ourselves after his example. There's a need to create a quiet space to listen. For example, you might spend time in prayer and meditation as you're falling asleep or as you first wake up. Get up early or spend your lunch hour on a walking meditation. Turn off electronics and close your eyes to tune within.

What ways have you discovered to create quiet time? You can get really inventive in brainstorming where and how to retreat into silence with God.

### Good Morning, Lord

*I know that I need to hear your guidance, and I ask for your assistance in quieting my mind. Please help me trust, hear, understand, and follow your guidance.*

*"Show me the right path, O Lord; point out the road for me to follow. Lead me by your truth and teach me, for you are the God who saves me."*

PSALM 25:4–5

# THE COURAGE TO STAND FOR GOD

The apostle Paul had a way with words, spreading the Good News of the Gospel. However, his words sometimes stirred up anger among the crowds. In the book of Acts, for example, everything was going fine with Paul's talk in Jerusalem until he said that God had called him to teach the Gentiles. This didn't go over well with the mostly Jewish audience. Forty men were so upset, they made a vow to fast until Paul was captured, with the intent to kill him.

But God had a way out for Paul. His young nephew overheard the evil plot and got word to him. Fortunately, the Roman commander in charge then got wind of this and took it upon himself to sneak Paul away in the middle of the night. His life was spared, and he continued to preach the Gospel.

How courageous of that young boy to speak up! Surely, he feared for his own life by going up against this angry, determined group of men. But God knew. God had the whole thing under control.

God sent Paul to preach to the Gentiles all over his region and stood by him along the way. He also gave that boy courage to stand up against corruption and darkness. So, too, God calls *us* to courageously stand against corruption, and he will protect us along our way. Trust in him, dear one, and continue showing up as a bright light in the world! We are making such a positive impact!

## ~ Good Morning, Lord ~

*Thank you for giving me the courage and strength to stand up and speak out to make a positive difference.*

---

*"That night the Lord appeared to Paul and said, 'Be encouraged, Paul. Just as you have been a witness to me here in Jerusalem, you must preach the Good News in Rome as well.'"*

ACTS 23:11

## BLESSED ARE THE MEEK

Jesus said during his Sermon on the Mount that the meek will inherit the earth, but what did he mean? Contrary to what some think, it does not mean weak or passive. *Meekness* is best defined as gentleness, mildness, and humility.

Moses is a model portrait of a meek man. In fact, the Word says he was the meekest person on the planet. When certain people caused him grief, he chose to bear it instead of lashing out. He didn't let others walk all over him. Instead, he possessed an inner strength and humility that most simply couldn't maintain. He gave his troubles to God, then trusted and followed God's guidance.

When Jesus talked about the meek inheriting the earth, he meant they would be able to experience the peace and joy that comes with inheriting the Kingdom of God. The meek tend to rely on God and walk humbly. They're not concerned about what others think; they're concerned about what *God* thinks.

Who are the meek today? Those who serve God and others in humility. Those who refuse to bicker about issues, confident in their own beliefs. Those who don't think of themselves as better than others. Those who trust God over their own eyes and ears. Remember how Jesus washed the disciples' feet? How many leaders today would stoop to do that?

Meekness is a virtue that we can embody in our daily lives. Let's be mindful to embrace it, dear one. Let's inherit the earth together.

### Good Morning, Lord

*I pray to be like you, firm in my faith in God yet balanced with gentleness, thoughtfulness, kindness, and compassion. May I be strong and loving simultaneously.*

*"Blessed are the meek: for they shall inherit the earth."*

MATTHEW 5:5 (ASV)

# Enthusiastically Serve the Lord

Feeling overwhelmed, a woman named Karen told her minister that despite all her involvement in the church, she was spiritually drained. She had lost her fervor and passion for serving the Lord. She taught Sunday school, sang in the choir, and chaired numerous committees. Through all these activities, she honestly thought that she was serving the Lord.

Her minister remarked that her service was commendable, but perhaps she had been more focused on serving the needs of the *church* rather than on growing in relationship to God. He suggested that she go home and seek an intimate relationship, one-on-one, with God. Rest, and refresh herself in the Lord.

She did. Later, Karen decided to volunteer at a women's shelter. She didn't preach to the women, but instead listened and offered her love and acceptance. She prayed for each person silently and with them, if they were receptive. She began to feel God's Spirit inside her as never before. Her enthusiasm for serving the Lord was renewed.

Dear one, we need to do more than think positive thoughts, read inspirational messages, or squeeze in two minutes of prayerful meditation while we're in the car.

When you're passionate about serving God, his Spirit shines through you to others. If you're lagging in diligence, pray that the Lord will direct your path to find specific ways that you can renew your excitement and maintain fervor in your spiritual life. As you do, you will both give and receive blessings.

### Good Morning, Lord

*Please fan the flames of my passion to serve,
and help me be diligent with my spiritual practices.*

*"Never be lazy, but work hard
and serve the Lord enthusiastically."*

Romans 12:11

## PRESSED, YET NOT CRUSHED

There is a story about a demonstration involving a large jar, rocks in a variety of sizes, and sand. A jar filled to the top with large rocks is presented to an audience, who agrees that it is full—no more large stones will fit. The presenter then adds small rocks to the jar, which fit nicely between the larger ones. The audience agrees the jar is full now. The presenter then pours sand into the jar, filling every last nook. Now, surely, the jar can be considered full. But wait—there's more! The demonstrator pours water into the jar, finally filling the jar to completion.

We are the rocks, of various shapes and sizes, and we fit into a vessel of God's design. We are, as described in 2 Corinthians 4:8, pressed on every side but not crushed. The sand that traces a path around all the rocks represents God's firm foundation in our lives. It flows among us and binds us together in a gentle manner, and prevents us from being "forsaken, struck down" by temptations or by lower energy. Finally, the water, which symbolizes God's Holy Spirit, is poured into our vessel and fills every crevice of our lives with love, wisdom, and comfort.

Even when you think you are full to the brim, there is more that God wants for you. He promises that even when you feel "pressed on every side," you will know that his Spirit is supporting you, flowing in and around every aspect of your life, and you will have strength to carry on.

### ⤳ *Good Morning, Lord* ⤲

*Please fill me up with so much love that I am full to the brim, with plenty to spare and share with others.*

---

*"We now have this light shining in our hearts, but we ourselves are like fragile clay jars containing this great treasure. This makes it clear that our great power is from God, not from ourselves. We are pressed on every side by troubles, but we are not crushed. We are perplexed, but not driven to despair."*

2 CORINTHIANS 4:7–8

# USE YOUR BLESSINGS WISELY

Unfortunately, in today's world, we never seem to have enough, especially when we see our friends enjoying the very thing we desire. The grass always seems greener on the other side of the fence.

There should be no judgment cast on those who have a lot of possessions. We don't know what goes on in their lives and why they make certain choices. We need to be more concerned about our own choices. Rather than covet our neighbor's "greener grass," we should nurture our own. It's likely we will realize that with a little attention, our lawn—and our life—can be beautiful, too.

We need to be aware of coveting a possession versus seeking the things we actually need, and not be swayed by the pursuit an abundance of things we think will enhance our lives. When we keep our lives simple and try not to be caught up in the trappings of the world, we will discover the freedom of not being stressed about what we don't have. We learn to appreciate the things we *do* have. Plus, a simplified lifestyle can result in extra funds to save or to use to bless others.

When we listen to God's Word, we know he provides for our needs, and the disposition of the rest of the blessings he has given us are a matter of personal accountability. Dear one, use your blessings wisely.

### Good Morning, Lord

*Please help me transform all my jealous feelings into gratitude for what I already have. I trust that if I am supposed to have something, you will bring me to it.*

---

*"Beware! Guard against every kind of greed.*
*Life is not measured by how much you own."*

LUKE 12:15

# GOD NEVER ABANDONS YOU

Abandonment fears can lead to nervousness about being rejected. Most of us have felt abandoned by at least one person. Unhealed abandonment issues can lead to low self-esteem and feelings of unworthiness. You may end up in toxic relationships repeatedly. A therapist or support group can help you discover the basis of abandonment issues, allowing you to talk about your pain, grief, and begin healing.

God is the ultimate therapist who can help you forgive and heal those deep wounds that are holding you back. There's a tendency for those who feel abandoned to shy away from God. They're hurt and angry. There may be a twinge of resentment toward God. *How could you have let that happen, God? How come you weren't there to protect me?*

Dear one, God has always been there. You've been connected with God from time immemorial. Unfortunately, free will causes people to do things that hurt others. In Genesis 25, God heard the voice of Hagar's son, who had been abandoned by his father, and ended up blessing him abundantly. He hears you, too. He will lead you to the right person who can assist you with emotional healing.

My prayer, dear one, is that you'll feel the deep love that God has for you and know that he *has* never and *will* never abandon you.

### ❧ Good Morning, Lord ❧

*Thank you for staying by my side and loving me throughout my life.
Please help me to love and respect myself and to choose
and nurture healthy, long-lasting relationships.*

---

*"But God heard the boy crying, and the angel of God called to Hagar
from heaven, 'Hagar, what's wrong? Do not be afraid!
God has heard the boy crying as he lies there.'"*

GENESIS 21:17

# GOD HELPS YOU PASS THE TEST

If there were no tests in schools, students might not be inclined to learn the material. Tests motivate people to study. Teachers use tests to gauge whether students are understanding and retaining the lessons. In the same way, life sometimes presents tests to give us the opportunity to learn lessons, too.

Do you think you've learned more lessons when life was going along easily or when you've had to face an obstacle and figure out how to get past it? Most people admit to learning valuable life lessons during challenges. And if they don't understand the life lesson, the same experience usually repeats itself until they realize the role they're playing in creating or going along with this pattern. Through all the tests and challenges, God is right there to encourage and support you.

God is all about living life to the fullest. Jesus led by example, experiencing so much in his short life on the planet. And Holy Spirit loves to enjoy every experience with you. So go, dear one. Live your life the way you desire, relying on God and trusting that even when tests come, he'll whisper every answer in your ear. Please don't worry: you'll pass the test!

## ∞ *Good Morning, Lord* ∞

*Thank you for tutoring me about life. I sense you loving, caring, and shielding me, especially during the challenging times, when I feel you holding me even closer.*

*"God is our refuge and strength, always ready to help in times of trouble."*

**PSALM 46:1**

# DON'T BE AFRAID

Everyone experiences fear at one time or another. Whether it's anxiety keeping someone stuck in a rut, or worry disrupting their sleep, fear reduces our enjoyment of life. But if we can come to an understanding of what fear really is, we'll be more apt to free ourselves to live the kind of life God intends for us.

Many believe that fear originates from the enemy, ego, or the lower energies. Fear appears when we allow pessimistic thoughts to influence our beliefs and emotions. It can wreak havoc on our central nervous system and limit our ability to function.

Fear is the opposite of faith. God desires that his children live by faith in him, and he's provided his protection so that we don't need to live in a state of fear.

Throughout the Word, God speaks often on how we can face and overcome fear through him: 1 John 4:18 says, "Such love has no fear, because perfect love expels all fear. If we are afraid, it is for fear of punishment, and this shows that we have not fully experienced his perfect love." In addition, please look up 2 Timothy 1:7, Psalm 56:3, and Isaiah 41:10. These, among many other scriptures, can help you combat fear in your life, putting it in its place and trusting God in everything.

The writers of the Bible experienced fear just the same as you and I, and they included their messages of hope so that we can also rise above and overcome it with God's help. Fear no more, dear one.

### ∽ *Good Morning, Lord* ∽

*I pray to replace fear with faith, and anxiety with peace.*
*Thank you for guiding me to choose my thoughts wisely.*

---

*"Tell those who have a fearful heart, 'Be strong.*
*Don't be afraid. Behold, your God will come with vengeance,*
*God's retribution. He will come and save you.'"*

ISAIAH 35:4 (WEB)

## PEACE AS A LIFESTYLE

Peace is a lifestyle that can be learned. You may have grown up in a home where there was chaos, and perhaps it was frightening at times. Perhaps you never really felt a sense of peace and safety. But the good news is that you can learn through applying biblical principles and coming to the realization that God's Spirit dwells within you to calm your nervous system, bringing you peace.

Apostle Paul talks about the Lord being the Master of Peace. He prayed that believers would live in peace among each other and have peace in their lives continually. Those who've learned to tap into faith in God have prayer as an effective resource for manifesting peace in such situations.

In Isaiah 9, Jesus is called the Prince of Peace. Have you ever sat by a stream or river and just felt incredible peace as you listened to the water gently flow? Paul tells the Philippians that the peace of God, the kind of peace that passes all understanding, will guard your heart and mind.

Dear one, let us commit to making peace a lifestyle, and an automatic healthy habit. To turn to God in every circumstance, asking Holy Spirit to bring us peaceful feelings as we completely trust him.

### Good Morning, Lord

*I love the idea of developing a new healthy habit of turning to prayer as soon as worrisome thoughts arise. This shows me that I don't have to struggle with fear single-handedly because I have your support readily available. Thank you!*

*"May God our Father and the Lord Jesus Christ give you grace and peace."*

EPHESIANS 1:2

## THE ART OF DECLUTTERING

A cluttered life can lead to anxiety and annoyance. If you've ever had trouble finding something in an untidy room, you've probably become frustrated. Having a large amount of "stuff" to go through can also distract you from your priorities.

In addition to "things" that clutter, there's also clutter in the mind. So many thoughts about the past, present, or future are swirling in there that it can lead to frustration, depression, worry, and fear. So how do we address clutter in our lives?

First, you must be willing to be honest with yourself. Is your house disordered? Is your mind? Do you have a tough time letting go of things? If so, it's time to make a commitment to *simplify your life*. It's time to get with the Lord and ask for discernment. Look at your home; sift through your belongings with the Lord. Listen for his Spirit and be willing to part with those things you no longer need. Chances are, someone else would be blessed to receive the items.

In the same way, ask God to help you declutter your mind. Ask him to help you take time consistently to sit in silence before him. Direct your attention to Jesus and let your thoughts wash away.

The apostle Paul speaks of "the simplicity that is in Christ" (2 Corinthians 11:3). May this be our aim as well. Simple in Christ and clutter-free!

### ❦ *Good Morning, Lord* ❦

*Please help me simplify my life, and to declutter physically and mentally. Help me say no to distractions, and yes to being able to breathe easy.*

---

*"We have depended on God's grace, not on our own human wisdom. That is how we have conducted ourselves before the world, and especially toward you."*

2 CORINTHIANS 1:12

# GOD WILL HEAL THOSE ISSUES

Recurring issues are spiritual teachers in disguise, helping us learn about ourselves. They teach us how we played a role in agreeing to the dance of repetitive issues with money, relationships, jobs, housing, and so forth.

If you're tired of repeatedly struggling, the Holy Spirit empowers you to choose a more peaceful pattern. This begins with having the courage to see how your choices led to the original pattern. Usually those choices are a form of being stuck in a loop of replaying old emotional wounds. God will lead you out of this cycle.

Until you face it, navigate it, heal it, and learn lessons from it, it will probably keep showing up. The good news, dear one, is that God really wants to help you with this. Now, you may think that God should instantly take care of that for you, but it doesn't always work that way. Think of the athlete who wants to win a race. Sure, he could ask God to make him the fastest person, but then he wouldn't learn valuable lessons, such as dedication, perseverance, hard work, sweat, grind, and faith.

In the same way, God wants to help you deal with those recurring issues, yet he's not going to do all the work for you. He may show you the way or bring people into your life to assist you. He promises to help you as you move forward. And you will rejoice and feel satisfied when you follow God's lead to uncover and heal those unresolved issues.

### Good Morning, Lord

*You are my therapist who helps me understand why I act the way that I do, for the purpose of making healthier future choices.*

*"'I will give you back your health and heal your wounds,' says the Lord."*

**JEREMIAH 30:17**

## Spiritual Wisdom and Insight

In Ephesians 1, Paul prays for the believers, asking God to give them the spiritual wisdom and insight so that they may know him. Paul wasn't talking about a mystical wisdom, but a deep knowing and concrete principles that they could put into practice as they became more intimately familiar with the Lord.

He prayed that their understanding be enlightened and that they be able to see God and life with their spiritual eyes. Why? So they would know all that is available for them as a follower of Jesus Christ, living in the Kingdom of God: this new Kingdom that Jesus talked about and invited people to enjoy.

Paul prayed that they would come to know Christ personally and gain an understanding of God's will for their lives, while leaning upon the power of the Holy Spirit. He prayed that they would receive insight into how God works and how they could use biblical truth to navigate a wonderful life, even amid pain and suffering.

Dear one, we can also ask God for insight so that our eyes may be continually opened to know him in greater ways. That we may read the Word and receive wisdom. The kind of wisdom that the world cannot give us. The kind of understanding that goes beyond the human mind.

This is my prayer for you, darling, that the eyes of your understanding continue to be enlightened.

### Good Morning, Lord

*Thank you for sitting with me and revealing the truths that I need to learn. May my mind and heart be open to epiphanies of revelation.*

*"I have not stopped thanking God for you. I pray for you constantly, asking God, the glorious Father of our Lord Jesus Christ, to give you spiritual wisdom and insight so that you might grow in your knowledge of God."*

Ephesians 1:16–17

# HOME IN GOD

Pulling up in the driveway of your home feels so good. Even for those who love to travel, it still sets your heart at ease. It feels good to be among familiarity and the comfort of your own space. Home just feels good.

Have you ever been gone for so long that you just keep thinking, *I just want to go home?* Then once you get home, you breathe a big sigh of relief. You sink into the couch or lie down on your bed, offering gratitude for your resting place. This is exactly what it feels like when we come home to God in our awareness. It's the most comfortable *and* comforting experience in the world.

Dear one, when you get to that place where you feel completely at home with God, you relax fully in his presence and allow his love to embrace you. Don't get me wrong—you still have the greatest reverence and awe for him. Yet, because you love him and you know he loves you, there is a comfort level when you spend time praying and talking with him. You want nothing at that moment except to enjoy the natural environment that is in him.

This type of relationship with the Lord exists. If you're not experiencing it, know that God is waiting for you. He's left the light on and has prepared a warm, cozy place just for you. Go ahead, darling. Make your way home.

## ∽ *Good Morning, Lord* ∼

*Your warm love helps me relax and be my true self.*
*With you, I feel at ease. I know that I can share my*
*deepest feelings with you and trust you with my life.*

---

*"I love your sanctuary, Lord, the place*
*where your glorious presence dwells."*

PSALM 26:8

## KINDNESS TO ALL

It's easy to reach out to friends and family members with whom you have a good relationship. It can be a little more challenging to socialize with those you've just met. In fact, many find meeting new people to be anxiety provoking. Quite honestly, some just don't want to be bothered getting to know people who they feel are "lower" than they are.

In Luke 14, Jesus advises that if someone invites you to a feast, take not the best seats but the ones that no one else will want to sit in. If you throw a party, don't invite only your friends and family; invite the poor, the lame, and the blind. Invite those whom you wouldn't normally associate with. He tells the Pharisees that if they do this, then they will be blessed, because those are the people who cannot repay them. He admonishes them to be unselfish and kind to all and to associate with the lowly. In doing so, they may not be glorified by man, but they will be even better rewarded by God.

Dear one, consider those who are outside of your sphere of influence. Reach out to those whom others may not consider. Ask the Lord whom you can reach out to this week. Volunteer. Bless others with your time and energy. Step out of your comfort zone in the love of Jesus Christ. God will take note, darling. He always does.

### ⟣⟩ *Good Morning, Lord* ⟨⟢

*Please help me have the compassion, sensitivity, courage,
and time to connect with lonely people who need friendship.*

---

*"But when you make a feast, ask the poor,
the maimed, the lame, or the blind."*

LUKE 14:13 (WEB)

# CHOOSE JOY OVER DISAPPOINTMENT

It's natural to feel disappointed *momentarily*. If we stay disappointed too long, however, that feeling can turn into self-pity, bitterness, or depression. So how should we deal with this emotion when it comes?

First, be honest with yourself about your feelings. Neither stuff them down nor dwell on them. Admit your feelings, then give them to God. Hand it off to the One who knows what to do with it. Some people write down how they're feeling, and then discard or burn the paper to symbolize their letting it go.

When you can accept the fact that things aren't always going to go the way you want, you'll be able to let go of disappointment much faster. Say to yourself, "Okay, God, that didn't go the way I'd hoped. It's disappointing, but I'm trusting that you are in control. I know I can let this feeling go and replace it with hope and faith." Often, you'll discover that God has something better in store for you.

You have emotions, but *you* are not your emotions. God, as Creator of our entire being, can help us overcome negative feelings or send us a qualified counselor to help. Disappointment, sadness, or depression doesn't have to oppress you. Look to God's promises that assure you that you can rejoice in him even when things don't go as planned. He will take that disappointment or mourning, dear one, help you learn from it, and turn your feelings into joy.

## Good Morning, Lord

*I am opening my heart so that you can see all my emotions. Please help me sort through the feelings that are distracting me from joyful and purposeful living. I wish to stop living in the shadows and turn my life toward your light.*

"Weeping may last through the night,
but joy comes with the morning."

PSALM 30:5

# Let God Contend with Conflict

Throughout many of the chapters in Psalms, you'll find David praising God. In Psalm 5, David was overwhelmed and perplexed by his numerous enemies yet trusted God implicitly. As he prayed, he requested a straight and narrow path for him to follow. David knew that he had a legitimate cause and that God, in his righteousness, would understand and dispense justice.

David was passionate about God. In Psalm 5:7, David acknowledges God's abundant love and kindness, and expresses his willingness to worship in reverence. He trusts that God will recognize his faithfulness and provide relief from his misery by delivering him from his enemies.

As Christ followers, we don't like to think that we have enemies. Throughout the Bible, we've been instructed to love one another, and it's nice to believe that everyone thinks this way. The harsh reality is that there may be people who don't like us, create havoc and drama, and even want to cause us harm. We should try to mend these stressful relationships, but that's not always possible. In many situations, all we can do is pray.

When you are troubled, distressed about unjust treatment from others, and uncertain what you should do, follow David's example and ask God to direct your path. God will resolve conflict in his time, but in the interim, he will give you comfort and see you through.

### ∽ Good Morning, Lord ∽

*Please shield me from unnecessary conflict and from those who would wish me harm. Please lead me to peaceful resolutions and the safety of your mighty strength.*

---

*"But let all who take refuge in you rejoice; let them sing joyful praises forever. Spread your protection over them, that all who love your name may be filled with joy. For you bless the godly, O Lord; you surround them with your shield of love."*

Psalm 5:11–12

# WITNESS THE LIGHT

In aerial formations, one plane is positioned outside the group to help guide and protect the leader. The pilot of this aircraft, known as a wingman, is secondary to the designated front-runner and supports him in any way he can.

John the Baptist was Jesus's wingman. As John the Baptist was paving the way for Jesus, there were questions about whether John was himself the Messiah who had been foretold. John never failed to tell people that he was *not* the Messiah, and that he was just there to introduce Jesus: "Someone is coming after me who is far greater than I am, for he existed long before me" (John 1:15).

John was a valiant witness to God's love, setting the stage for Jesus to come after him, sent "to tell about the light so that everyone might believe because of his testimony" (John 1:7). John was not the light and never claimed to be. He was a man sent before Jesus to prepare the way for God to shine his light, and he took his responsibility very seriously. Like John, we can testify of Jesus!

Dear one, when you commit yourself to God and bear witness to his Love, you will also pave the way for others to come to know the light!

## Good Morning, Lord

*Please shine your light to me and through me,
so that I may be like a lighthouse to help others find you.*

*"John himself was not the light; he was
simply a witness to tell about the light."*

JOHN 1:8

# GOD THINKS YOU'RE BEAUTIFUL

So many people really don't like themselves much. They try, but deep down something causes them to feel like they are bad or worthless. In fact, people don't even realize that they feel this way, yet some of their present issues stem from their disapproval of themselves.

*Self-worth.* It's a common topic, yet a large number still don't feel worthy of their own love. Oftentimes, they seek to feel worthy through others, and this is the root of plenty of relationship problems.

Dear one, do you feel as if you love yourself? I don't mean in a conceited way, but in a pure and humble way. Do you love yourself with the kind of love that you hold for your cherished family members or friends? It's easy to judge yourself for a variety of reasons, but God wants you to know he never looks at any of those reasons—and you never have to earn his approval. He created you as a beautiful soul. He even carefully chose the earthly body "suit" you'd be wearing on this planet! He finds you stunning.

He calls you worthy. He finds you amazing. He never sees an imperfection or flaw, and he invites you to view yourself the same way. God always extends acceptance and unconditional love, darling. Read through Psalm 139 and note how King David ponders God's creation of each soul. My prayer is that you see yourself through his eyes!

## ✑ *Good Morning, Lord* ✑

*Thank you for loving me unconditionally, and showing
me how to love myself in a healthy and egoless way.*

*"How amazing are the deeds of the Lord!
All who delight in him should ponder them."*

PSALM 111:2

# GOD IN YOU IS GREATER

Imagine God is the ocean and you are a wave. As a wave, you are part of the ocean. As a child of God, you are immersed *in* God. You are part *of* God. You're not separate. Just like the ocean manifests itself as a wave, God expresses himself through you.

The first book of John 4:4 says that God in us is greater than anything in the world. God's Spirit in us is greater than *anything* we come up against in the world. We are not left to fend for ourselves. The wave is always a part of the ocean; we are always a part of God. The Word says that we are in God and God is in us. It's oneness. It's unity. It's a sure thing that nothing in the world is greater than that. Whether it's lower energies or ego, or darkness, it has no power over us.

Other people, problems, and obstacles have no power over you if you stand against them in God. Now, this revelation may take some time and contemplation. Therefore, it's important to meditate on scripture. You can adapt the verse from John to say to yourself as often as you can: "Greater is he that is in me, than he that is in the world." In other words, God in you is greater than anything or anyone in the world, so you have nothing to fear or worry about!

You have the greater One living in you, darling. Let this bring you comfort and confidence as you go about your day.

*Good Morning, Lord*

*Thank you for continually reminding me that*
*I am loved, watched over, empowered, and strong.*

*"But you belong to God, my dear children. You have already won a victory over those people, because the Spirit who lives in you is greater than the spirit who lives in the world."*

1 JOHN 4:4

## GOD LOVES WHO YOU ARE

Just like God made different types of flowers so that we could enjoy a vibrant bouquet, so too did he make each of us uniquely and thoughtfully. Every part of you is evidence of God's ingenuity and love, as you were specifically made for your life purpose. We each have our own personalities, interests, desires, and hardwiring—and it's all wonderful. The key is to love your uniqueness.

It takes courage to stand up and authentically be who you are. To not allow the thoughts or words of others to sway you into pretending that you're someone different. It's that kind of courage that God will cultivate in you when you ask. God desires that you find your security in him, not in the approval of others.

We can aim to conform to the image of Jesus regarding character, values, and morals, but we do not have to conform to images that the world throws out there. If you are an introvert who loves to read books and take hikes, then proudly be that stay-at-home, book-loving, nature-enjoying soul. If you're a free spirit who can barely sit still for 10 minutes, then proudly roam the world being *that* soul.

God designed you incomparable, and he has already charted the path for you to walk. Embrace your uniqueness in God and courageously show up in the world as *you*. Individually and together, we can all shine bright as distinctive children of God's Kingdom of light.

P.S. I love you exactly as you are.

### Good Morning, Lord

*Thank you for helping me to not only accept but also appreciate myself for who I am as God purposely created me.*

---

*"Then God looked over all he had made, and he saw that it was very good!"*

GENESIS 1:31

# Let God Be the Judge

If you've been abused in any form, my heart goes out to you. If there's one person who understands the grief associated with abuse, it's Jesus. Jesus, in his human nature, surely felt negative emotions toward his abusers, but he never retaliated. He left such judgment to his Father and instead opted to forgive.

This is how healing begins: realizing that vindication cannot mend a broken spirit. Rather, forgiveness and going to God with your pain will allow him to begin restoring you.

Healing also begins when you have boundaries and say, "No more." It's acknowledging that abuse is occurring and taking the necessary steps to get away from it. If you or a loved one is suffering abuse, commit to doing what it takes to break that cycle. God will lead you, but know that there are resources in your community to assist you as well. Find a safe person to talk to so that you can begin your healing journey with support. God desires that you enjoy healthy relationships, and he will help you heal your spirit if it has been broken down by abuse, including guiding you to a talented counselor.

The first Epistle of Peter says don't repay evil for evil or insult for insult. Take care to remove yourself from any abusive situation, but leave vindication to God. We can trust that he will know what to do.

Dear one, I pray for courage to rise within you by the power of the Holy Spirit, that you allow the healing process to begin, keep protecting yourself, and trust that God will contend with those who have abused you.

### ❧ *Good Morning, Lord* ❧

*May your sweet love envelop me in a protective blanket of divine insulation, helping heal my heart so that I may trust again.*

---

*"Instead, be kind to each other, tenderhearted, forgiving one another, just as God through Christ has forgiven you."*

Ephesians 4:32

## PRAY FOR THE CHILDREN

Every parent wishes the best for their children, whether they're little or grown. If you're not a parent, chances are that you have other children in your life you care about. I make it a habit to pray for my children regularly. I trust that God is working all things out for their benefit and highest good. Now, there's really no right or wrong way to pray, but I have found it helpful to use scripture as I do so.

The following are prayers I've created based on scripture, which you might offer on behalf of the children in your life. Print these out or memorize them, and recite them regularly, silently or out loud. Do whatever you feel led to do, dear one. I pray for the highest good for you and your children.

- *My children are strong and courageous. They know that God is with them wherever they go.* (Joshua 1:9)

- *My children are content with what they have. Their needs are met in Christ Jesus.* (Hebrews 13:5, Philippians 4:19)

- *My children serve the Lord faithfully. They love him with all their heart, soul, mind, and strength.* (1 Samuel 12:24, Mark 12:30)

- *My children have godly wisdom, and rely on God when making decisions.* (James 1:5)

- *My children walk in the Spirit, bearing all the fruits of the Spirit: love, joy, peace, patience, kindness, goodness, faith, gentleness, and self-control.* (Galatians 5:22–23)

### Good Morning, Lord

*You know how much I care about my children
and all the children of the world, just as you do.
Please guide me as to how I can best help them.*

*"May the Lord bless you and protect you."*

NUMBERS 6:24

# CUT TIES WITH MOCKERS

Have you known any troublemakers in your life? Those who enjoy stirring the pot of drama for their own entertainment? We've all encountered someone with that antagonist spirit. The Bible calls such a person a "mocker" or "scorner," itching to debate, argue, yell, and be contrarian. But what do you do when someone in your circle of friends or family carries on like this?

If we look at the Word, Proverbs 22:10 says to cut ties with the mocker. Let them go. Now, this does seem rather harsh, so let's ponder the wisdom within this proverb. A quarrelsome, arrogant, self-centered person likes to create havoc. They don't care for authority and are not usually teachable. Their pride blinds them to the conflict or harm they cause with their words and actions—or, if they see it, they just don't care.

Yes, there's probably a sad reason why they act this way. And if they would get some good trauma counseling, they could heal in time. But if they don't see a problem with their behavior or refuse to get help, you may need to distance yourself from them. Pray for them, but don't hurt yourself by spending unnecessary time with them.

Mockers do not model the character of Jesus. In fact, throughout the Bible, God speaks against them. But as the Word suggests, when you drive out the mockers, the strife will cease, which is actually a simple solution. And you deserve to have peaceful relationships, dear one.

## ❧ *Good Morning, Lord* ❧

*I would love to have peaceful relationships, filled with mutual respect, gentleness, and sensitivity. Thank you for helping me make space for such relationships by releasing those who represent the opposite from my life.*

---

*"Throw out the mocker, and fighting goes, too.
Quarrels and insults will disappear."*

**PROVERBS 22:10**

## SELFLESS LOVE

The world could use more selfless love. As a follower of Jesus, you've made a commitment to live in his ways. The Word says that those who live in the Kingdom of God or light no longer walk in the darkness.

The battle between selfishness and selflessness is won when we consciously decide to live in the power of God's Spirit daily. Being selfless 100 percent of the time can feel challenging. The lower energies can be very persuasive, but the power of prayer can liberate us from the pull of selfishness.

We are here to serve as God guides us, and being selfless is actually the true path to happiness. And yet there's a balance, as we must also care for our own needs so that we will stay healthy and energetic over a long lifetime of service. It's the difference between meeting our *needs* and obsessing about *wants*.

We can seek not only our own well-being but also reach out to others in love. Many people are hurting, lonely, and in need. The Lord always seeks those who put selfish desires aside and clothe themselves in selfless love. It's something that you must consciously make a commitment to, because you won't always feel like it. You may have to leave your comfort zone. However, the rewards in Christ are incredible.

My prayer for you, dear one, is that you embrace God's kind of selfless love, blessing others along your life journey. In doing so, I just know you'll be richly rewarded, too!

### Good Morning, Lord

*The more I talk with you daily, the more I find myself modeling your helping, healing, and teaching actions wherever there's a need.*

---

*"[Love] doesn't behave itself inappropriately, doesn't seek its own way, is not provoked, takes no account of evil."*

1 CORINTHIANS 13:5 (WEB)

# THE PARABLE OF THE TALENTS

God has blessed everyone with various talents and a measure of faith to help us develop our gifts. It's our obligation to take our gifts and cultivate them, to show our appreciation to God. In Matthew 25, we read the parable of a man who gave three of his servants *talents* (silver), according to their ability. Later, the servant who was given five talents and the one given two talents showed their master they had invested those coins wisely. As a reward for their wise investments, they were given more coins and the praise "Well done, good and faithful servant. You have been faithful over a few things, I will set you over many things."

This lesson shows us that when we accept God's gifts and nurture them, we will be blessed with more. Some people might be afraid to use their talents. The third servant in the parable, who was given one talent, was afraid to lose the money, so instead of investing the coin, he hid it. When his boss realized that he hadn't done anything with the gift, it was taken from him.

Practice, polish, and use the talents God gave to you, dear one. Use your gifts to help make the world a better place. Share your talents to inspire and uplift others, and God will give you more.

## *Good Morning, Lord*

*Please help me recognize and appreciate my gifts and talents, and use them in a way that brings blessings to the world.*

*"God has given each of you a gift from his great variety of spiritual gifts. Use them well to serve one another."*

1 PETER 4:10

# FATHER, FORGIVE THEM

"Father, forgive them." These words were spoken when Jesus was nailed to a cross, enduring an agonizing death. His garments were taken, and the soldiers mocked him. Under these circumstances, unforgiveness would be understandable. If Jesus could ask God to forgive these people, even to the extent of excusing them by saying they didn't know what they were doing, then we should be able to forgive *anyone* for *anything*.

When we're hurt by someone or something that happens in any kind of relationship, forgiveness is an important part of healing. When we are willing to forgive, it's also possible to mend the relationship and reestablish trust (as long as the other person doesn't repeat their hurtful actions). There are circumstances, such as abuse or physical violence, where it would not be healthy to attempt to restore a relationship, but forgiveness is still necessary. We have every right to despise what was done to us, but when the abuser is forgiven, they receive our mercy—the same mercy that God gives to *us*.

Forgiving doesn't mean that you agree with the action, but that you no longer choose to carry around toxic anger within yourself. It might take time to heal a damaged relationship and restore trust, but often it's a matter of one person extending an olive branch, offering forgiveness and a peaceful resolution. Jesus set the bar high when he asked God to forgive the people who crucified him. Remember his example, if you ever feel that you can't forgive someone.

### Good Morning, Lord

*I'd love to purge and purify myself of repressed anger, and I ask for your help in doing so. Please guide me upon the path of forgiveness so that I can be free from emotional burdens.*

*"Jesus said, 'Father, forgive them, for they don't know what they are doing.'"*

LUKE 23:34

# A Little Rest and Relaxation Goes a Long Way

*Relax.* You've worked hard and deserve to rest. So, why don't you take some moments to relax and trust God? Just move to the passenger seat, metaphorically, and let Jesus take the wheel. The idea here is to create more space in your life for good old-fashioned rest and relaxation, and allow more space for God to help you. The truth is that God can do more for you in minutes than you can do in months!

You may have been striving for years to make your dreams come true, yet still feel lacking. My advice? Just relax a bit and trust God. He always knows what he's doing, and when you completely lean on him, he'll work magic. Jesus said you can move a mountain with your faith, so have faith that your responsibilities and dreams can be fulfilled in a more peaceful and relaxing way.

The next time you find yourself exhausted, pushing, striving, and trying to "do it all," take a step back. Take a deep breath, and relax. Go for a walk with the dog. Get away with your family for a weekend. Read a book. Take a nap or a bubble bath. Go with the flow.

It's time to trust God totally. Listen for his wisdom. That epiphany he gives you could be the breakthrough you need! God can help manifest whatever it is you're trying to bring to fruition. Above all, have faith in the Lord, who cares for you.

## Good Morning, Lord

*I need a breather, and I pray for your creative solutions in figuring out how I can rest more and learn to relax and enjoy my day while still meeting my responsibilities.*

---

*"Take my yoke upon you. Let me teach you, because I am humble and gentle at heart, and you will find rest for your souls."*

**Matthew 11:29**

# No Fear of People

Do you find it challenging to say no? Do you avoid conflict, or try to keep everyone happy? If so, you're not alone. There are plenty of "people-pleasers" who struggle with such fears. People-pleasing, also known as *codependency*, can run you ragged and cause issues in your relationships with others, yourself, and God.

Proverbs 29:25 says the fear of man is a "dangerous trap." Now, you may not necessarily "fear" man in the sense that you will be harmed, but you may fear rejection or disapproval by someone. Trying to please people is an exercise in futility and can keep you from living your own truth.

The antidote? Journey within to tap into Holy Spirit. Ask him to show you why you're working so hard to please others. Are you overcompensating for feelings of worthlessness? Are you addicted to approval? God will help you begin healing, which may include his guiding you to a compassionate counselor.

To overcome people-pleasing, make it a habit to check in with yourself before agreeing to another request or doing additional things for others. Yes, God wants you to serve and practice kindness, but if your motive is fear-based validation, you'll end up draining yourself time and time again.

Have silent conversations with your teacher, the Holy Spirit. Pray and listen. You are already approved of and applauded by your Heavenly Father, dear one. You can rest on that truth as you move forward, secure in the love of Almighty God.

### ❧ *Good Morning, Lord* ❧

*Please help me detach from the fear of abandonment
and heal from any people-pleasing tendencies
so that I can live and love authentically.*

---

*"Whom have you dreaded and feared, so that you lie,
and have not remembered me, nor laid it to your heart?
Haven't I held my peace for a long time, so you don't fear me?"*

Isaiah 57:11 (WEB)

## SERVE WITH YOUR GIFTS

God placed his Spirit in you when you asked Jesus Christ into your heart as your Lord and Savior. Holy Spirit is helping you to fulfill the purpose and guidance that God gives you.

As a child in God's Kingdom, you've been given abilities and talents, which he guides you to use to help those in need.

God has always asked anointed people to fulfill his purposes. If you read through the Bible, you'll see men and women using the gifts God has given them to accomplish much for his glory. There are also inspiring stories from modern times of people stepping up to help others.

Dear one, God has placed specific gifts in you. He wants you to discover what the gifts are, and use them to be a blessing to the world. You might be one among a million people who can sing, but no one can do so exactly like you. You may have a gift to write beautiful poems that will stir the hearts of readers. You may have the gift to teach, or to help others heal. God's gifts come in countless varieties!

God wants to stand tall in you. He wants you to connect with your strengths and talents so that you can be a blessing to the world. Are you ready to be that willing vessel? Are you willing to step out? Cultivate and hone that gift? Wonderful! Let's pray this morning, friend.

### Good Morning, Lord

*Please help me discover my gifts and use them to benefit others. Help me locate my strengths and use them for your glory. I trust you, Lord.*

*"Work willingly at whatever you do, as though you were working for the Lord rather than for people."*

COLOSSIANS 3:23

## GOD'S DAILY SUSTENANCE

God promises to nourish us spiritually, as he's always willing to feed us his Living Bread. Today, let's discuss what bread means for those in the Kingdom of God.

First, bread is a representation of the Word of God. When the Israelites were crossing the desert on their way to Canaan, God provided them with *manna*, which fed them, but they complained about it, wanting more. What they failed to understand was that the manna represented more than just food; it was actually the Words of God in the form of food. It was physical and spiritual sustenance.

Second, bread is a representation of the necessities of life—the things that we need for our daily survival to ensure that we will be all right. It is a provision. At the same time, Proverbs 14 reminds us that we must work to get our "bread." If we're lazy, there won't be any to bring to the table. Yes, God provides, but we must do our part, too.

Bread also represents salvation and spiritual nourishment. Jesus said he is the bread of life. At the Last Supper, he takes bread, divides it, gives each disciple a piece, and says, "Eat, for this is my body." In the Lord's Prayer, the phrase "give us our daily bread" signifies that we are to ask God for what sustains us physically and spiritually.

Dear one, God wants you to rely upon him for your daily needs, whether physical, mental, emotional, or spiritual. Go to him, relying on him to send you the "manna" to get you through each day.

### Good Morning, Lord

*Thank you for being the bread of life, my true friend and confidant, during those moments when I feel insecure about myself and my future. Thank you for filling my heart with what I really need: love.*

---

*"Give us today our daily bread."*

MATTHEW 6:11 (WEB)

# HAVE FAITH . . .

All throughout the Gospels are stories of Jesus's miraculous healings. He instantly healed people with paralysis and chronic illness, brought the dead back to life, and restored eyesight to the blind. Repeatedly Jesus said that these healings were because of the faith of the person that they would be healed.

In one famous passage, a woman with a chronic bleeding condition was convinced that if she could just touch Jesus's clothing, she'd be healed—so she did, and she was! Yet Jesus took no credit for the healing. Instead, he said to her, "Daughter, your faith has made you well. Go in peace. Your suffering is over" (Mark 5:34).

Science shows that medicine has differing curative effects, depending upon whether the person believes in it and their doctor. Faith is a powerful healer!

Calling upon Jesus for healing is helpful for reducing worries and tension that exacerbate illness, and for increasing healthy feelings of peace, faith, and confidence.

## Good Morning, Lord

*Thank you for replacing my fears with faith, and helping me be confident, optimistic, and hopeful. I relax in the knowledge that you love me, care about my health, and are supporting and guiding me.*

*"But when Jesus heard what had happened, he said to Jairus, 'Don't be afraid. Just have faith, and she will be healed.'"*

LUKE 8:50

## LIVE AND LOVE ON PURPOSE

What is the purpose of life? God's Word says that it's to love with a constant, conscious, action-oriented kind of love, helping others achieve their true potential in Christ. By loving and expecting nothing in return, we glorify God and life feels purposeful.

Giving God's kind of love, according to the Word, is essential to our purpose and truly is an act of worship. When we give, without thinking about what it does for us, we are rewarded by the Lord through his blessing. It also blesses others! Giving ought to be cheerful, voluntary, and for the right reasons.

We all can include a little more kindness in our lives, and be a loving, giving role model. For example, practice empathy regularly. Put yourself in the shoes of others to understand their feelings, and be there for them. Practice forgiveness. Turn the other cheek. Be patient when others are having a meltdown. Leave judgment to God. Repay insult with blessing. Write out a check to charity. Go on a mission trip. Invite the in-laws over for dinner. Sit on the floor and play with your child. Be love.

Dear one, we all can incorporate love a little bit more, so let's be mindful of this as we go about the day. Be the love you want to see in the world!

### Good Morning, Lord

*Please help me be less self-involved and more other-involved.*
*Please teach and show me how to be more thoughtful*
*in a way that is healthy and balanced.*

*"So now I am giving you a new commandment: Love each other.*
*Just as I have loved you, you should love each other."*

JOHN 13:34

## DESPERATE TIMES

When we look at Psalm 143, we see King David in a desperate state. At the end of his rope, he expresses his distress, completely broken open before the Lord. He wasn't wearing a mask nor concerned about what his prayer sounded like. Simply baring who he is, seeking the Lord's attention, he says: "Hear my prayer, O Lord; listen to my plea! Answer me because you are faithful and righteous. Don't put your servant on trial" (Psalm 143:1–2). He continues, "Come quickly, Lord, and answer me, for my depression deepens. Don't turn away from me, or I will die" (Psalm 143:7).

Have you ever been in such a state, suffering in the depths of depression or fear? God is all you have, and you're praying with fervor and passion. You plead, grabbing on to Jesus with all your strength, knowing he will pull you out of that darkness and embrace you as a father embraces his child.

David was not afraid to ask God to come through quickly. He trusted that if he was persistent and prayed passionately and diligently, the Lord would answer. He remembered what God has already done for him and knew he would do it again.

Dear one, this is how you can go to God, too. Whatever you are struggling with, go to God with your petition, just as David did, in fervent prayer. Trust that he will help you in the best way.

### ❧ *Good Morning, Lord* ❧

*Please hear these prayers and take them to our Father on my behalf:* [describe the situation you need help with, pouring out all your fears and other emotions].

*"Therefore, my spirit is overwhelmed within me.*
*My heart within me is desolate."*

**PSALM 143:4 (WEB)**

# THE CRIES OF THE POOR

Two men were walking down the street and came upon a beggar. One of the men reached into his pocket and pulled out a few dollars for the bedraggled man. The other shook his head in disbelief and told the first man, "You shouldn't waste your money giving it to a bum like that. He's just going to spend it on drugs."

The man turned to his companion and said, "Yes, you might be right, but that's not my problem. You see, God will consider that man based on what he does with his money, and he will consider me on what I do with mine. When I see someone who needs help and I feel God prompting me to act, I know I will be held accountable for whether I follow his Spirit or not."

It's often challenging to know where to direct our donations to those less fortunate. On the one hand, our heart goes out to the individual. On the other hand, our judgment suspects that our charity might be spent on alcohol or drugs. This story reminds us that judgments about poor people should not keep us from helping them. We only need to help as God specifically guides us.

God answers prayers by calling helpful people such as yourself into loving and charitable action. And one day if you find yourself in a position of need, he will also answer *your* prayers by sending them to you.

### Good Morning, Lord

*Please guide my charitable donations so that they are truly helpful. I trust you to show me whom to help and to teach me how I may best do so. Please also help me keep my thoughts aligned with divine love.*

*"Those who shut their ears to the cries of the poor will be ignored in their own time of need."*

PROVERBS 21:13

## ZACCHAEUS MEETS JESUS

As much as people like to judge others and predict whether God will accept them, Jesus makes it clear that he came with the intent to redeem all. In Luke 19, we find the story of Zacchaeus, a wealthy tax collector. When Jesus was on his way to Jericho, Zacchaeus wanted to catch a glimpse him, so he ran ahead and climbed up in a sycamore tree.

When Jesus saw Zacchaeus, he told him to come down so he could visit with him at the man's house. Zacchaeus was excited, but the others were upset that Jesus would stay with a "corrupt" tax collector. Zacchaeus, honored to be with Jesus, tells him that from that day on, he'll give much money to the poor and pay back those he'd stolen from. Jesus gladly forgives Zacchaeus, telling him that he came to seek that which was lost.

The story is another great example of how Jesus chose to associate with those who weren't necessarily living with high morals and strong values. The assumed "righteous crowd" murmured and complained that Jesus passed up spending time with them. But Jesus had a plan. He took the opportunity to show that he came to give any and all the chance to have a relationship with him. He was interested in spending time with anybody regardless of their past beliefs or actions.

Just as Zacchaeus got to meet Jesus, so everyone today has that same choice. Perhaps you've already made it, dear one, and that is wonderful. We can rejoice on that account. We pray that everyone who needs help will choose to call upon Jesus and meet him in a personal way.

### ⤞ *Good Morning, Lord* ⤝

*Please help me be open-minded and compassionate like you. Guide me, please, to care more about helping others than I care about my reputation. Let me be a pure and true servant of God.*

---

*"For the Son of Man came to seek and save those who are lost."*

LUKE 19:10

# OPEN THE WINDOWS OF HEAVEN

When you think of your finances, are you met with feelings of despair or worry? What about in your day-to-day life? Worry about money is called a "scarcity mentality," which can easily take a toll on you. Thankfully, we serve a God of abundance, who is never lacking and is more than enough.

But what *is* abundance, and how do we receive it?

The Bible states that God *can* supply abundantly, not that he *will*. It is up to us, as children of God and followers of our faith, to trust and believe that he can provide for us in the ways we need. Most of the time, it also requires us to quietly listen to God's guidance to take positive action. We must serve a purpose, and then our purpose will serve us.

Isn't it so relieving to know and have faith that no matter how perilous the times, when we seek God, he will always have our back? He will always give to us that which we cannot give to ourselves, if only we have the courage to seek his face and believe.

Believe in God's promises, and trust the ideas that he gives to you—for example, to start a new business, finish a creative project, or make a contribution to the world in some other way. You may need to take a leap of faith, but if you follow God's guidance, your needs will be supplied.

## Good Morning, Lord

*I need your help, please, in learning how to responsibly manage my finances and practice discernment about my spending habits. Please teach me how to live simply and frugally so that I can focus upon serving a purpose as you guide me.*

*"'Bring all the tithes into the storehouse so there will be enough food in my Temple. If you do,' says the Lord of Heaven's Armies, 'I will open the windows of heaven for you. I will pour out a blessing so great you won't have enough room to take it in!'"*

MALACHI 3:10

# WRITE THE VISION

As described in the Old Testament, the prophet Habakkuk went to God, discouraged that God wasn't working fast enough on his behalf. God told him to write the vision that he received from the Lord and pass it on so others might know the plan, too.

It is our spiritual duty to create quiet time to listen so that we may follow the path laid out for us by God. He has given each of us unique gifts and talents in order to bless others with the love that comes with letting God into our lives. To write the "vision" might mean that we need to write out God's vision for ourselves, so that we may take actionable steps toward realizing it.

For a different approach to this scripture, what if it means that we should write down our personal testimony? Instead of being ashamed of our past failures, heartaches, and frustrations, can we turn them into a story about how we overcame obstacles, loss, and failure by our faith in God? Maybe by sharing our story of faith, we will bless and uplift others.

By combining the two interpretations, not only can we follow the plan God has made for us but also give a good dose of encouragement to others. God doesn't want us to wait until we've got it all figured out before we follow him or share with others. He wants us to come to him while we're still struggling, hurting, or lost so that he may lead us and fill us with his beautiful love and peace.

## ❧ *Good Morning, Lord* ❧

*Please use the story of my life, with all that I've suffered and struggled, in a way that may inspire others and offer an example of what—or what not—to do.*

*"Write my answer plainly on tablets, so that a runner can carry the correct message to others. This vision is for a future time. It describes the end, and it will be fulfilled. If it seems slow in coming, wait patiently, for it will surely take place. It will not be delayed."*

HABAKKUK 2:2–3

## VICTORY IN THE PRAISE

Every victory is preceded by a well-carried-out plan, accompanied by skill, wisdom, and more. In biblical times, it was no different for Joshua in conquering Jericho.

When Joshua, instructed by God to take over the city of Jericho, saw the towering walls, he knew he was up against a powerful army. He needed a plan, and he needed God's help. The plan God laid out for him was quite unconventional. He told Joshua that he and his men should march around the walls of the city once a day for six days, completely silently. On the seventh day, they were to march around the city seven times, and then the priests were to blow their trumpets. At the same time, the people were to shout praises to God for the victory. Then the city walls would fall, and they could go in and take over.

Imagine the faith they must have had to do what the Lord said. Those walls looked impenetrable. But they believed the word of God, following through with his plan, and the walls fell as they praised and shouted to the Lord.

What obstacles are you facing, dear one? Do they look insurmountable? May your faith rise as you lean on God to give you a plan for victory. May you praise and shout with a thankful heart now, believing that victory is already yours. Let the story of the battle of Jericho increase your faith today, and may you follow the Lord with courage as he leads the way.

### Good Morning, Lord

*Please, Lord, help me have faith and focus upon you instead of worrying about obstacles. I pray that you reach into my mind and heart and pull out my fears and faithlessness, so that I can be entirely trusting and filled with grace.*

*"The seventh time around, as the priests sounded the long blast on their horns, Joshua commanded the people, 'Shout! For the Lord has given you the town!'"*

JOSHUA 6:16

## SACRIFICIAL GIVING

Would you be willing to give every penny you have to the Lord's work? That's exactly what an unnamed woman did in Mark 12. Jesus, ever observant, took note that this poor widow put her last two coins in the treasury as an offering to the Lord. Jesus pulled his disciples aside and told them that the poor widow had given a better offering because she gave out of her poverty, while the rich gave out of their abundance.

See, many people equate big donations with approval from God. Some might think they are better than the poor, and that God favors them more because they give more. But God is not looking at the size of the offerings. He's looking at the heart and the intentions behind the donation. A $5 tithe from someone who only has $10 may be more valuable than a $1,000 tithe from someone who has $1 million. It's not so much the *amount* as it is the *intent* and size of the heart that gives.

Perhaps it's not a financial donation but a time donation that you offer. Whatever you can give, give with a grateful heart unto the Lord. Give from a place of love and service to God and humanity. God desires that everyone be "givers," clothed with compassion and generosity, as so many people and organizations in the world are in need. Dear one, as you give, may you be blessed in so many glorious ways.

### ❧ *Good Morning, Lord* ❧

*Please show me where and how I can be of the most help, and I will do so. Thank you for helping me overcome my insecurities, my fears, and any ego issues about volunteering, as I don't want to waste any more of life on meaningless or selfish activities.*

*"This poor widow has given more than all the others who are making contributions."*

MARK 12:43

# PARABLE OF THE DISHONEST MANAGER

In the parable of the dishonest manager, detailed in Luke 16, a wealthy businessman discovers that his steward has been untrustworthy, so he demands an account of the records. The manager then goes to each of the debtors and offers to reduce their debt in half, hoping that gratitude for this generosity would lead to a job after he was fired. Surprisingly, the master commends him. Why would he be praised for being shrewd and dishonest?

Jesus explains that he's not condoning the dishonest behavior. The man went to great lengths planning ahead, being strategic about his life. Such foresight is a good quality to have and act upon. Jesus goes on to say that if you are faithful in little, you'll be faithful over much. He's essentially saying that believers should be "street-smart," as the shrewd worker was, but also honest. The honest heart will serve the Lord, not money.

The things done in the dark will be exposed by the light. In this parable, Jesus was talking to men who loved money more than God. They certainly didn't like the moral of the story and scoffed at him. Jesus said he knew their hearts, and as always, he tells stories to try to get people to understand his ways.

Money is necessary and can do so much good in the world, but the Word says we can't have two masters. The love of money pulls people into dark places. Dear one, my prayer is that you remain a good steward of what the Lord blesses you with financially, as you serve the Lord with all that you have.

## ⌘ *Good Morning, Lord* ⌘

*Please help me have a healthy attitude about money and other resources, neither loving nor fearing them. Please help me appreciate and utilize my resources wisely as you guide me.*

---

*"No one can serve two masters. For you will hate one and love the other; you will be devoted to one and despise the other. You cannot serve God and be enslaved to money."*

LUKE 16:13

## NEVER ALONE IN SUFFERING

Depression affects many people. Even if you don't struggle with it, you probably know someone who does. Some might think that because Jesus came to deliver people out of darkness, those who follow him would never fall into depression, but that's not the case. Plenty of Christ followers struggle with it. Those who do should not be made to feel like they don't have enough faith nor should they be judged in any way. Rather, they ought to be loved with the kind of love that Christ brings to life in hearts.

Some of King David's prayers to the Lord depict a man suffering in extreme darkness. He was at his wits' end, crying out to the Lord for deliverance. God didn't judge him. Rather, God heard his cries and stayed with him. Many times, God delivered him. God never promised a life free from suffering, but he has promised to never give us more than we can bear.

We don't always know why depression lingers on for some despite them doing all they know to do medically and trusting the Lord. But we don't have to understand. We simply need to make a choice to stand beside them patiently, lift them up unto the Lord, encourage them to get appropriate help, and love them just as God loves them and us.

The Word says that our inner spirits are being renewed each day. Let this be our prayer for those suffering in depression, that God renew their spirit each day, lifting their souls. And may we make it our aim to help them bear their pain, letting them know they are not alone.

### ⟶ *Good Morning, Lord* ⟵

*I am praying for everyone who suffers from depression,
and ask you to guide me as to how I can help. Please reach
into my heart and allow me to be a bright light who inspires others.*

*"That is why we never give up. Though our bodies
are dying, our spirits are being renewed every day."*

2 CORINTHIANS 4:16

# BE QUICK TO REPENT

Love the Lord with all your heart, mind, soul, and strength, and love others, too. These are the "laws" of God, which are certainly not unreasonable. As a follower of Jesus, we've willingly entered his Kingdom of light. As such, we make it our aim to be light and love to the world.

But what if you miss the mark? What if you have a bad day and lose your temper, or gossip, are selfish, or hold judgmental thoughts? When you act out of your ego, going against God's ways, chances are that you'll feel bad about it afterward.

The Holy Spirit in you will tug on your heart, and you'll feel it. This is a process known as the "Holy Spirit's conviction." After a while, you welcome being convicted by Holy Spirit, because you recognize that it's part of your spiritual growth and learning.

Now you have the chance to ignore it, or you can simply acknowledge your words or behavior and ask God to forgive you. God wants his children close to him, and continued acts of disobedience can make you feel separate from God. Of course, God will forgive you when you go to him in repentance. He dusts you off and essentially says, "Go, child. Pick up where you left off."

## Good Morning, Lord

*Thank you for shepherding me along the straight and narrow path, and helping me take action according to God's will.*

*"For the kind of sorrow God wants us to experience leads us away from sin and results in salvation. There's no regret for that kind of sorrow. But worldly sorrow, which lacks repentance, results in spiritual death."*

2 CORINTHIANS 7:10

# THE BLESSINGS OF SELF-CONTROL

*Get your act together.* Perhaps you've heard this a time or two throughout your life. The control of self implies a battle between your ego and your true self whom God created. The ego will try to distract you from following your God-given guidance by tempting you with an addiction or introducing doubt into your mind. Recognize when your ego is running the show, and then pray for divine intervention.

It says in Proverbs 25 that a person without self-control is like a city with broken-down walls. It won't serve you well. Lack of self-control can cause you to experience struggles that could have been avoided had you displayed restraint.

So just how do we begin exercising more self-control? Use willpower? Dear one, willpower is great, but sometimes it takes more to tame the "flesh." It's a job for the Holy Spirit, who can help so that things don't *get* out of control. Those who exercise self-control tend to feel better and are more prone to experience success in life.

Maybe you're going overboard when it comes to food or alcohol or your spending habits. Take some time to consider how you're doing in these areas, and if you notice you're lacking self-control, pray and ask Spirit to help you do better. If you feel led, get some counseling for the issue. God desires that you allow his Spirit to rule and reign, not the ego. This is my prayer for you too, darling.

### Good Morning, Lord

*Please help me! I keep getting distracted by thoughts and feelings that have nothing to do with my priorities and everything to do with the ego. Please help me be guided only by divine love, not by the ego's willfulness. Please help me be focused and peaceful.*

*"A person without self-control is like a city with broken-down walls."*

PROVERBS 25:28

# LORD, HELP MY UNBELIEF

In Mark 9, Jesus comes across his disciples and a large crowd. A father had brought his deaf, mute boy to the disciples in the hopes that they could heal him, as he was under the possession of dark spirits. He had been tormented since childhood, and sometimes the spirits would try to get him to jump into water or fire to harm himself.

When those spirits saw Jesus, they caused that boy to go into an epileptic fit. The father asked Jesus to heal his boy if he could. Jesus, noticing that he used the word *if*, said to the man, "If you can believe, all things are possible to him who believes" (Mark 9:23).

The father, aware of his weak faith, asked him to please help his unbelief. The man was honest with Jesus. He was believing to the best of his ability, but he asked Jesus to help him to have even greater faith. Jesus healed that boy, no doubt helping increase his father's faith significantly that day.

Are you ever lacking in faith at times? Do you want to believe with all your heart, but sometimes doubt creeps in? Jesus knows, and he's willing to help according to God's will and timing. Miracles still occur today all over the world, dear one. God says everything is possible to those who believe. Stand strong in your faith, and if unbelief appears, simply cry out to God to help.

## Good Morning, Lord

*I want to have strong faith, but it wavers at times.*
*Can you please help me believe and trust?*

---

*"Immediately the father of the child cried out*
*with tears, 'I believe. Help my unbelief!'"*

MARK 9:24 (WEB)

# God's Attributes

Throughout the Bible, God reveals characteristics that show just how powerful and great he is. For a clearer picture of who God is, take some time to study the long list of attributes found in the Word. For a brief introduction, God is:

- *Sovereign.* This means that God is in control of everything (including giving us free will over our own choices).
- *Omniscient,* meaning he knows everything there is to know.
- *Omnipresent,* meaning he's everywhere.
- *Jehovah-Jireh,* which means Provider. God has always provided and will always provide for his people.
- *Jehovah-Shalom,* meaning "peace." God wants his children to feel peaceful, no matter what.
- *Elohim,* meaning "power," one of the names for God. He is the all-powerful God who creates and sustains.
- *YHWH/YAHWEH/JEHOVAH.* This name represents God's immediate presence.
- *Adonai,* meaning "Lord." This word was used instead of YHWH, because the Jewish people thought that YHWH was too sacred to speak.
- *The Rock, the Ancient of Days, Most High, Lord of Hosts, Shepherd,* and so many more.

Dear one, God is not just one thing; he is more than we can even comprehend. Take some time to meditate on God's attributes and names. As you'll see, his greatness is worthy to be praised and adored forevermore.

## Good Morning, Lord

*I stand in awe of the Holy Trinity: God the Father, Jesus the Son, and the Holy Spirit, who are my real and entire world.*

*"I will proclaim the name of the Lord; how glorious is our God!"*

DEUTERONOMY 32:3

## BE STRONG AND COURAGEOUS

*I can't do it. I'm afraid. What if I fail? What if I get rejected? I don't know how to do it.* These types of doubts go through many people's minds when they desire something but are afraid to move forward. When you're facing a frightening situation, call on God and ask him to fill you with courage, and he will.

When the Israelites were headed to the Promised Land, God told Joshua to be strong and courageous, for he is with him and has chosen him to lead everyone in. Essentially, God was telling Joshua that he understood his concerns, but God is bigger than any concern. God chose Joshua to lead his people into the land flowing with milk and honey, which means it was prosperous and safe to dwell in.

Dear one, this is what God desires for you, too. Whatever you aspire to, he is with you. He will give you courage to move forward, even if it's just a tiny step. Oftentimes, when you take that first step, God puts things into motion quickly. He sees your faith and your trust in him, and this pleases him.

God promises to be with you. This ought to help you feel more confident no matter what. Do you have a dream you've been putting off? Is there something you want to do but are afraid of failing at? Are you stuck? Be strong and courageous, dear one, in the power of the almighty Lord! He desires to lead you to *your* promised land!

### ◁ *Good Morning, Lord* ▷

*I dream of being filled with faith and courage, yet I find myself stopped by worry. Please help me trust and have the courage to take the positive actions that I'm divinely guided to take. Please reassure me that you are watching over me.*

---

*"Then the Lord commissioned Joshua son of Nun with these words: 'Be strong and courageous, for you must bring the people of Israel into the land I swore to give them. I will be with you.'"*

DEUTERONOMY 31:23

# CHOOSE LIFE

The choices you make affect more than just yourself. Your choices can affect your immediate family and society in general. Sometimes, you may not think you *have* a choice in a matter, but God wants you to know that you *always* do.

Yes, we have dozens of choices to make each day. What to eat, where to go, what to read, whom to talk with, and so on. But when we choose God first and foremost, we're choosing life, love, peace, light, joy, and more. As we do, he promises to give us many years in our promised land. In the Kingdom of light and love. When we choose God, we opt for health, true happiness, and blessings, rather than misery. We hear his voice, instead of chasing after the temptations in the world, which promise happiness but only lead to emptiness and sorrow.

Today, dear one, choose life. Choose God. Keep him front and center in your heart, listen for his voice, and he will lead and guide you into goodness and blessings. He will help you walk in his Spirit, bearing plentiful fruit for his Kingdom. Enjoy God's kind of life!

## Good Morning, Lord

*Hooray! I have finally learned to choose you instead of the distractions that have pulled me down in the past. With you as my steady guide, I am assured of true happiness no matter what's going on around me.*

*"Oh, that you would choose life, so that you and your descendants might live!"*

DEUTERONOMY 30:19

## GO AND MAKE DISCIPLES

When you've got something good, don't you just want to share it? Jesus feels the same way. He has something amazing to share—the peace and joy that comes along with living in his Kingdom. Jesus wanted to give everything to his disciples, and he also wanted them to share the Good News with others. Essentially, he said, "Go, teach others what I have taught you. Visit with them, share with them, baptize them into my Kingdom. Freely you have received; now freely give." You may have heard this described as the Great Commission.

As believers in Jesus Christ and the message of salvation, we are instructed to share the Good News of the Gospel with those we encounter. Some, such as missionaries and pastors, are called to do this as their full-time job. But every believer is commissioned to share the Good News. Let those who are feeling lost and separated from God know that there is a way to reconnect with him. Offer healing for the sick. Comfort for the hurting. In the power of the Holy Spirit, we are to *be* imitators of Christ in our everyday lives. How exciting!

Dear one, as Jesus commissioned his disciples to become apostles, so too are you to go into your world and show up as God's light and love bearer, sharing the wonderful news that all can enter into the Kingdom of God! All are welcome! You've been given the authority through the Holy Spirit, darling. Go, in that power, knowing that God is with you every step of the way.

### ⮜⮜⮜ *Good Morning, Lord* ⮞⮞⮞

*I want to speak of you, yet I am afraid of people's reactions. Please guide my teaching work so that I can reach out most effectively.*

---

*"Therefore, go and make disciples of all the nations, baptizing them in the name of the Father and the Son and the Holy Spirit. Teach these new disciples to obey all the commands I have given you. And be sure of this: I am with you always, even to the end of the age."*

MATTHEW 28:19–20

# Your Faith Has Healed You

Struggling with a persistent illness can wear you down. It can certainly make you feel desperate, willing to do whatever it takes just to be healed and feel well.

It was no different in Jesus's day. A woman who had a bleeding disorder approached Jesus for a healing. She was an outcast, considered "unclean" according to Mosaic law. But she was desperate and weary and didn't care that she could be arrested just for showing up. She was going after her healing from the Healing Master himself!

Surely she wondered about how she'd reach him among the large crowd. *If I can just touch the hem of his garment, I'll be healed,* she thought. She believed with all her might that this would be enough for his healing power to flow into her body.

As she touched the bottom part of his robe, Jesus paused. He'd felt power leave him. He felt her faith extract power from him! He said, "Who touched my clothes?" The woman, trembling, told him everything. He said, "Your faith has made you well."

How incredible! Jesus wasn't concerned about the law. He marveled at her faith. His compassion always shined bright, even for the outcasts and less fortunate.

Dear one, you too can touch the hem of Jesus's garments with your faith. You too can grab hold of him and receive his healing power. It is your faith that makes you whole in mind, body, and spirit. Go to Jesus today with your requests, as he knows when great faith touches him!

## Good Morning, Lord

*I have such faith in you, and I'm desperately pleading with you to help me with [describe situation], as I know without doubt that you can resolve this. Thank you!*

*"[Jesus] said to her, 'Daughter, your faith has made you well. Go in peace. Your suffering is over.'"*

MARK 5:34

# Persist in Patience

Waiting can be difficult at times, especially when there's something you need so desperately. It can be easy to grow impatient and start to believe that God isn't paying attention to your prayers. You may believe that God ought to resolve your situation more quickly. Yet the Lord really does work in mysterious ways. Some prayers aren't answered as we'd hoped because God has a better plan for us.

We just need to trust in the Lord and have faith that he's interceding in our lives, and ultimately everything will work out for the best. This can be hard to remember when we're waiting for a cure, true love, an answer, a miracle, and so forth.

If you look through the Bible, you can see many examples of patience. Sometimes hundreds of years passed before prayers were answered, but there was always a lesson and a reason. Reading the Bible and adopting a bird's-eye view on these situations, you find it easier to see objectively and understand why the time needed to pass, why God planned events the way he did.

Dear one, when you're growing impatient waiting on God, ask him to help you be patient. Turn the situation completely over to him, trusting that he's got a plan. Ask him to reveal any insights or lessons he'd like you to learn in the meantime. God is with you, and he's aware, even if it feels like he isn't.

 *Good Morning, Lord*

*Please hear my prayer, Lord! I need your help to increase my faith and patience, and trust that my prayers are being answered.*

*"So Jacob worked seven years to pay for Rachel. But his love for her was so strong that it seemed to him but a few days."*

**Genesis 29:20**

# Come Close to God

What does it mean to be intimate with God? First, let's talk about what intimacy with God does *not* look like. Being the loudest at worship during church service is not necessarily intimacy, nor is it going to every Bible study group. These can be great things, but they don't constitute intimacy.

Dear one, God desires intimacy. He wants your whole heart—all the broken, scattered pieces, along with the most beautiful, joyful ones. The great news is that God wants *all* his children to have an intimate relationship with him; no one is left out. The secret to being truly intimate with God lies in creating your own quiet space within to share the deepest parts of yourself regularly. Your desires, needs, fears, aspirations—everything! He's the One who can see into the furthest recesses of your being and be lovingly present with you without any judgment.

To grow in intimacy, spend time alone with God. Speak from your heart to him, either silently or aloud. Be sure to listen, as both speaking and listening are equally important. God has always been there, but when you come close to him—in all your vulnerability and complete honesty before him—you can feel his presence more. It's a divine exchange.

I invite you to let him into the darkest corners of your heart, and practice intimacy. Make a commitment, just like you'd make a commitment to anyone you're seeking to become more intimate with. He wants to come close to you, and he's waiting on you to make the first move.

### ∼ Good Morning, Lord ∼

*My heart aches to know you on a closer level. I pray to have a deeply personal relationship with you. Yet I fear drawing near to you, and I need your help, Lord, to get quiet and open up.*

---

*"Come close to God, and God will come close to you. . . . Purify your hearts, for your loyalty is divided between God and the world."*

JAMES 4:8

# THE SPIRIT OF TRUTH

Father, Son, and Holy Spirit are all equally God in the Holy Trinity, and none is more important or powerful than another. They are like water, steam, and ice—all forms of the same substance.

When we first made a choice to follow Jesus, get baptized, and enter into his Kingdom, the Holy Spirit began to dwell within our hearts. See, the Holy Spirit is not just a feeling or emotion. He is a living teacher who helps guide us to learn how to live our lives in a godly manner. The Holy Spirit also convicts us in case we act in a way that displeases God. He communicates with us, empowers us to do God's will, intervenes, is always with us, and connects us to God and Jesus.

When Jesus ascended, he sent his Spirit to continue to do the work of his Father in the world. Jesus could only do so much in the flesh, going about teaching and raising up others, but his Spirit is available to everyone and can be everywhere to empower believers and continue building God's Kingdom here on Earth.

Dear one, just as you can build a relationship with God, so too can you build a relationship with Holy Spirit. Know that he is always with you, to lead you, guide you, and empower you to live a powerful life in Christ Jesus. If you've not yet invited Holy Spirit in, do so today. He wants to be a present reality in your life.

## Good Morning, Lord

*Thank you for sending Holy Spirit to all of us, to show us the way to God's Kingdom of Heaven. Thank you, Holy Spirit, for clearly teaching me what I need to learn.*

---

*"When the Spirit of truth comes, he will guide you into all truth. He will not speak on his own but will tell you what he has heard. He will tell you about the future."*

JOHN 16:13

# EXTRAVAGANT WORSHIP

People worship God in all different ways. Psalm 29:2 says that we should "honor the Lord for the glory of his name. Worship the Lord in the splendor of his holiness." So some light candles, some raise their hands, some sing, some sit quietly. Others might worship in extravagant ways, such as in the story in Mark 14.

While Jesus was dining at the house of Simon, a man who'd had leprosy, a woman came to Jesus with an alabaster jar of very expensive perfume. She poured the perfume over Jesus's head, worshipping him with all her heart. The spectators were upset. They thought that what she did was foolish—she could have sold it and given that money to the poor. But Jesus praised the woman, saying, "She has done what she could and has anointed my body for burial ahead of time" (Mark 14:8). To him, her act of worship was wonderful, and he was moved.

Even today, grand gestures are often deemed foolish. There are those who think there should be limits on the amount of money, time, and adoration one ought to give. But Jesus welcomes all worship done with a grateful heart. If Spirit is leading you to perform an extravagant act of worship by donating your time, talents, or resources, go for it. It's between you and Jesus, dear one, and no one else.

God invites worshippers to step out of the box and live a personal relationship with him, lovingly worshipping as they are led. My prayer is that all of us cultivate such a heart that worships the Lord extravagantly.

## ⤚ *Good Morning, Lord* ⤚

*I want to focus upon you with wonderful creativity.*
*I am inspired to show my gratitude and love in a beautiful way.*

*"While [Jesus] was eating, a woman came in with a beautiful alabaster jar of expensive perfume made from essence of nard. She broke open the jar and poured the perfume over his head."*

**MARK 14:3**

# NO LONGER ENSLAVED

Have you ever felt like you were a slave to something or someone harmful? Addicts are enslaved to their drug of choice. Criminals may feel enslaved to their life of crime. Codependents may feel enslaved to abusive people. Workers may feel enslaved to a low-paying job. These forms of slavery prevent people from experiencing freedom, but Jesus came to set people free. This is part of the Good News he brings.

When a person makes a choice to follow the ways of Jesus and enter into his Kingdom, they're set free from a life enslaved by corruption. When you choose to make Jesus your master, you can walk out of any cage you've been locked in, to enjoy life in light and love.

Being a slave to anything is not God's will. That's why he freed the Israelites from slavery. If you're going to be enslaved at all, be "enslaved"—of your freewill choice—to Jesus Christ, who promises a life of freedom, unconditional love, and eternal goodness. Christ came to save that which was lost, to rescue that which was imprisoned. How exciting is that?

Dear one, if you feel enslaved to something other than Jesus, my prayer is that you recognize that he came to set you free. He desires that you live life out of bondage. Go to him and ask for help. Ask for revelation or insight as to what's keeping you enslaved. Turn your attention to God, for your answers and freedom come from him. Allow him to set you free today, friend. You deserve a life of freedom!

## Good Morning, Lord

*Please turn the key in the lock of my self-made prison, dear Lord, and set me free. You are the one who can show me a better way of living and lead me to feel safe being free.*

*"And remember, if you were a slave when the Lord called you, you are now free in the Lord."*

1 CORINTHIANS 7:22

## PRAY FOR YOUR PARTNER

I've noticed that couples who pray for one another tend to have less friction. When they make a commitment to put God first, even above their marriage, and take the time to intentionally pray for each other, fewer issues arise.

So many people *want* to pray consistently for their partner but don't always follow through. But I believe that if you make a commitment to pray regularly for your partner and your relationship, you'll notice a change for the better. You'll notice a change in your own heart and perhaps a change in your partner.

Today I'd like to leave you with several affirmative prayers for your partner. If you're single, you can say these prayers for the future partner to whom God is leading you. Add to these prayers as you wish, as there's no right or wrong. Prayer is simply you affirming and conversing with God.

*I pray that my partner embraces righteousness,*
*walking in ways that glorify God.*
*I pray that my partner cultivates a sensitivity to Holy Spirit,*
*hearing his voice easily and obeying him fully.*
*I pray that my partner be firmly committed*
*to the Lord and our relationship.*
*I pray for my partner to live in divine health*
*mentally, emotionally, spiritually, and physically.*

Dear one, *my* prayer is that you make a commitment to pray for your partner and relationship regularly. I pray that both of you enjoy a beautiful lifelong partnership that glorifies God.

### Good Morning, Lord

*Thank you for uplifting, purifying, and healing my partnership so*
*that we may be equally watched over by your love.*

---

*"The earnest prayer of a righteous person has great power and*
*produces wonderful results."*

JAMES 5:16

# SOUND WISDOM

Have you ever had someone come to you for advice? Perhaps you gave them your best counsel, yet they chose to ignore it. There are many who desire wisdom but are resistant to receiving it. They'd rather follow their own path, which may involve following lower energy. A lot of teenagers and young adults do this. While they would do well to heed the good advice of their elders, there's something rebellious in them that wants to do it *their* way. In truth, that's how many people learn valuable lessons in life.

God admonishes us to have a teachable spirit: "The wise are glad to be instructed, but babbling fools fall flat on their faces" (Proverbs 10:8). Those who are sensible consult with wise people, consider the advice they're given, and put it into practice. But the foolish in heart will disregard solid advice, doing their own thing for prideful reasons.

There are plenty of times in life when we need wisdom. You likely know a person who will sit with you and share their wisdom when you're in need. Dear one, take heart and listen to those who have learned valuable lessons in life. Don't allow ego or pride to rule you. Ask the Lord to direct you to those people or resources you need. As you do, life will go much smoother, and one day *you* will be the one offering the same wisdom to others.

### Good Morning, Lord

*Please help me be humble enough to ask for and accept the wisdom of my respected elders. Please allow me to squelch the voice of the ego, and more clearly hear and follow God's will.*

---

*"The words of the godly encourage many, but fools are destroyed by their lack of common sense."*

PROVERBS 10:21

# No More Comparison

Our culture promotes comparison. We so easily evaluate ourselves on the basis of others. There's an old adage, "Don't compare your insides with other people's outsides." Remember that everyone has insecurities, even when they look confident.

Living the kind of life where you continually compare yourself to others will set you up for disappointment. Whether the comparison involves your job, children, house, financial status, weight, intelligence, or spirituality, it can bring you down. Instead of accepting yourself for where you are, you set the bar so high that you always come up short.

Yes, you should have goals and intentions, and want more in your life. But when you measure yourself against others, you're not able to create momentum from a healthy place. You'll try to move forward while hampered by an unhealthy feeling of lack. Remove yourself from the lineup, and give yourself permission to accept yourself as you are.

God accepts you right where you are. If there's any comparison going on, compare yourself to Jesus Christ. Set the intent to become more like him and be less concerned about others. This will help you experience more joy and peace. So what if the neighbor's yard looks better than yours? So what if your sister makes more money than you? What does it really matter? It only means something if you put an attachment there.

Dear one, put an end to comparison today. God loves and accepts you exactly as you are.

## Good Morning, Lord

*I am tired of feeling inadequate and second-best.*
*I pray for my heart to be healed so I can feel good about myself.*

---

*"This is what the Lord says: 'Don't let the wise boast in*
*their wisdom, or the powerful boast in their power,*
*or the rich boast in their riches.'"*

JEREMIAH 9:23

# Serve Jesus's Brothers and Sisters

Jesus came proclaiming the Good News that humankind no longer had to walk in darkness, separated from God, but could now become spiritually renewed and enter the Kingdom of light that dwells within. Yet this life is more than just enjoying what God has given us; it's also about freely giving to others out of love and compassion.

In Matthew 25, Jesus talks about the Kingdom of Heaven and what it's like. He reminds people that the talents given to each person ought to be used to glorify God and serve others. Jesus teaches how one day the Lord will weigh the works that believers have done. He says blessed are those who fed him when he hungered, gave him drink when he thirsted, tended to his needs. The crowd was puzzled, as they'd never seen him in need. Jesus goes on to say that if they did this to one of the least of his brothers, then they'd done it to him.

Essentially, Jesus was teaching that there are always people in need. If a believer can turn a blind eye to all of that, it's like the believer is turning a blind eye to Jesus himself; these people are just as important as he is.

I know this is a touchy subject for some. It's easy to find many excuses as to why we cannot help. But Jesus challenges this type of thinking, knowing that if he were in need, people would be jumping at the chance to serve. Dear one, my prayer is that we all likewise serve the neediest among us.

## Good Morning, Lord

*Thank you for prompting me to consider how I spend my time and resources. May I jump at the chance to serve those in need around the world.*

---

*"I tell you the truth, when you did it to one of the least of these my brothers and sisters, you were doing it to me!"*

Matthew 25:40

# SAY YES TO GOD

Some people think that if they choose to follow the ways of Jesus, their lives will become boring. They worry they won't have any more fun, yet this is far from the truth. Yes, God will call upon those engaging in corrupt behavior to walk a different path. But the reason God requires this is because such beliefs or behaviors sever the connection between him and us.

God is holy, and those who engage in unrighteous acts are not walking holy. Therefore, they're not able to fully enter into God's Kingdom in right standing. At the same time, God does not require perfection. If he were after perfection, we'd all be in trouble. What God does require is an honest effort to follow the ways and teachings of Jesus on a consistent basis. It's a heart issue. Giving up things like addiction or hurtful words or behaviors is beneficial to you and society. Living a life clothed in compassion, humility, service, and charity not only benefits you; it benefits humankind.

God desires that your will align with his. He loves a pliable heart so that he can mold it and shape it into a God-loving heart. He desires that you let go of things that would hold you back from his presence.

To live a life in the freedom of Jesus Christ requires that you let go and trust God in every area. This is true freedom. Just say yes to God and his ways, dear one. A life lived for the glory of the Lord is far from boring. In fact, it's an extraordinary adventure!

## ☙ *Good Morning, Lord* ❧

*I am surrendering my old ways and asking for a makeover of my life so that it is aligned with God's will. Please help me make this change peacefully and gently.*

---

*"He died for everyone so that those who receive his new life will no longer live for themselves. Instead, they will live for Christ, who died and was raised for them."*

2 CORINTHIANS 5:15

# The War between Body and Spirit

Are there times in life when you do those things you don't want to do? You know it's not God's will, but there you go, doing it anyway. Do you want to do those things that are pleasing to God but don't follow through? Paul understood. He was no different from you or me. He writes about the corrupt nature of the body's cravings, and how it can feel like a war going on between flesh and spirit. At times, you may feel like a wretched man or woman, but praise God for Jesus Christ and the Holy Spirit, who can certainly help us to win that battle.

Paul addresses this, saying, "I want to do what is good, but I don't. I don't want to do what is wrong, but I do it anyway" (Romans 7:19). He sees his flesh warring against his mind and bringing him into captivity or corruption. He's frustrated and asks who will deliver him. Of course, the answer is Jesus Christ.

Part of growing spiritually is learning valuable lessons. By yourself, you usually end up only going so far. The struggle is real, dear one, between the flesh and the spirit, but the Word of God assures us that there's a power available to us to end the struggle. Put on the armor of God, and trust that Holy Spirit will continue to help you as you ask. And should you falter, get right back up on God's path. He's always there waiting to walk with you.

### ✐ *Good Morning, Lord* ✐

*Oh, how I desire to be free of addictive cravings that pull
me away from you! Here, Lord, please take these cravings
and distill them down to their essence—underlying fears—
so that I may face and be free of the ungodly pull.*

---

*"I love God's law with all my heart. But there is another power
within me that is at war with my mind. This power makes me a
slave to the sin that is still within me. . . . Who will free me from
this . . . ? Thank God! The answer is in Jesus Christ our Lord."*

ROMANS 7:22–25

# Bloom Beautiful

Have you ever looked at a flower bud, noticing that it's about to open and bloom for all the world to see? Some might pass by and think nothing of it. However, if you're a flower lover, an expectancy and joy will arise within you, because you know that the bud signifies the bloom is fast approaching.

In the same way, a new believer is like that flower bud. It's already lovely; it just hasn't bloomed yet to display its beauty for all to see. Just as it takes time for a flower to open, it takes time for us to blossom.

Beauty comes from within. It's not outer appearances such as your physical attributes, what kind of work you do, or how much you've accomplished. Authentic beauty comes from a deep-down connection with the Divine. And just as a flower will attract bees and butterflies, so too does the beauty that arises from the Lord attract those who are seeking God.

So, dear one, keep this in mind, whether you're a new believer or seasoned in the faith. You may still be a bud, or you may be in full bloom. Recognize the stage you're in and be joyful in it. It takes time to grow, to bloom bright for the Lord. But rest in the assurance that you're indeed connected to the Source, revealing a kind of beauty that can only come from the Lord. Bloom vibrantly, darling, and showcase your unique beauty for all to see.

## Good Morning, Lord

*Let me appreciate how far I've come in my spiritual understanding since I accepted you as my Lord and Savior. Life is more blissful now, and I have a deeper sense of peace thanks to your profound love and care.*

*"I am the spring crocus blooming on the Sharon Plain, the lily of the valley."*

SONG OF SOLOMON 2:1

# DO NOT COVET

Will the things you want most in life bring you happiness? Really think about the top three things that you feel will make you feel happier. I imagine many people will have similar desires: a loving partner, health, financial security, more free time, and so forth. Truly, these desires could add pleasure to your life. However, are they really a key to long-term happiness?

Some material cravings stem from selfishness and envy. Perhaps you're bored and craving something new. Or maybe you believe that if others are impressed with you, they will love you more. When you want something, take it to the Lord. Ask him to reveal whether you desire it to gratify the ego or whether it will help you become closer to the Lord.

To covet something is to desire to possess it. It's a craving or wanting in a particularly strong way. Now, desiring things isn't bad, but pay attention, because the ego is sly. In no time, you could be thinking that new "thing" will solve all your problems and have you swimming in bliss, but it may cause you stress, distract you from your priorities, and bring disappointment, because nothing material lives up to the fantasy—not to mention your craving may not be God's will.

Be watchful, for the world is full of amazing things, but "things" won't fulfill you—only an intimate relationship with the Lord will. Seek him first, darling, and ask his opinion before grabbing at that next material desire.

## ‿✑ *Good Morning, Lord* ✑‿

*It feels like the ego is trying to sabotage my beautiful path beside you, with all these time-wasting, expensive distractions. I pray for your help in guiding me to stay focused upon that which really matters. Don't allow me to stray, dear Lord!*

*"You must not covet your neighbor's house or land . . . or anything else that belongs to your neighbor."*

DEUTERONOMY 5:21

# FEEL GOD WITH YOU AT ALL TIMES

While it's natural to feel lonely at times, in truth we're never alone. God walks with us through the good and challenging times in life. Not only does he walk with us, but he also loves us in ways incomprehensible to the human brain. The Father gave his only Son for us, so that we could inherit his Kingdom in all its light and bliss. Jesus gave his life so that we might be forgiven, saved from the darkness, and receive the powerful Holy Spirit.

What, in all creation, has ever been a more loving act? How could anyone love us more than God can? This is what we need to remember in times of loneliness and disappointment. That no matter how our brothers and sisters treat us—no matter how much has been taken from us—no one can ever take away the love that God has for us.

Even though at times you may feel broken or unworthy, God crowns you whole and worthy regardless. Worthy of his extraordinary love. Worthy of an intimate relationship with him. He understands that you're feeling lonely. He sees your broken heart, fears, doubts, and issues, and he's right there with you.

In the times when you feel alone, remind yourself that God is a breath away. Feel him move within you. Feel his arms wrap around you tenderly, letting you know that he cares. Know that you're loved by the most powerful, most important Source of love and life imaginable—not just today but every day, for eternity. You and God are partners forever and ever. Now that's something to rejoice about!

## ⟨ Good Morning, Lord ⟩

*Thank you for demonstrating the ultimate act of love by surrendering your earthly life to save us. I pray that I never lose sight of your love, and that I am constantly aware of and grateful for you.*

---

*"For God so loved the world, that he gave his one and only Son, that whoever believes in him should not perish, but have eternal life."*

JOHN 3:16 (WEB)

# SEARCH ME, GOD

"Search me, God, and know my heart." This was the heartfelt prayer of King David. Humbled, he asked God to search the innermost parts of his being and let him know what he finds. David wanted to walk holy before his God, and he was aware that sometimes he could deceive himself, whereas God is never deceived. God knows all and sees all. His spotlight can show if there's the merest scratch of corruption marring the heart.

Why would we pray such a prayer? Because to live a life unto God is to aim for holiness. It is to be beacons of light and vessels of love to bring hope and healing to a hurting world. David, despite missing God's mark more than once, continued to go to God in humility. David asked God to search his heart and show him what areas were not pleasing to the Lord so that he could address those areas.

David asked that God would lead him on the path of holiness so that he could dwell in the house of the Lord, so that he might dwell in the Lord's presence and gaze upon his beauty. There's a deep hunger that can arise for the Lord and his presence. This is my prayer for you, dear one, that you will pray as David did:

*Search my heart, God, and know me.*
*See if there's anything in me that is keeping me from you.*
*Lead me into the path of righteousness, for your sake,*
*oh God. In Jesus's name, I pray.*

### Good Morning, Lord

*I want to be completely honest, authentic, vulnerable, humble,*
*open, and transparent with you so that you can see everything*
*I think and feel. Please help me be purified so that*
*I'm in alignment with God's loving truth.*

*"Search me, God, and know my heart.*
*Try me, and know my thoughts."*

PSALM 139:23 (WEB)

## STICK TO GOD'S BUDGET

There's a popular song titled "Love Makes the World Go 'Round." While God's love certainly *does* make the world go 'round, a lot of people still believe that *money* makes it go 'round.

The truth is that money is necessary for supplying our earthly needs, so let's discuss biblical principles and guidance concerning finances. First, God desires that his children be good stewards of the finances they receive. This means creating a budget and being responsible so you can support yourself. Many financial issues are not due to lack of income but rather a failure to be wise with your money. Fortunately, there are many resources that teach financial principles.

The Word of God has so much to say about finances. If you're looking for wisdom, turn to the Word. Study it. God's financial system is different. He desires that people look to him as their Source, and honor him with what they receive.

God doesn't want people to suffer in lack. What he does desire is a group of people who commit to being godly stewards. Not storing up treasures for themselves and turning a blind eye to those in need, but rather listening to Holy Spirit, who leads people to give from their abundance. It is possible to be debt-free and bless others when you start living by God's biblical principles regarding money. My prayer is that you will study this topic extensively so you can live with financial freedom and bless those in need.

### ⤜⟶ *Good Morning, Lord* ⟵⤛

*I feel like I ask you for so much, and here I go again. I know that I've been irresponsible with my income, and I need help with self-control and guidance about charitable giving. Thank you, Lord, for stewarding me through this often-confusing part of my life.*

*"Whoever gives to the poor will lack nothing, but those who close their eyes to poverty will be cursed."*

PROVERBS 28:27

# STORE GOD'S WORD INSIDE

God's desire is that we store his Words within, calling on us to "cherish my law in your hearts" (Isaiah 51:7). While it's an inward commitment, we're reassured by outward symbols to remind us to keep him present.

As we follow the path God intends, we immerse ourselves in his Word, keeping scriptures around us to teach our children and remind us of his promises. In Deuteronomy 11:20, we read: "Write them on the doorposts of your house and on your gates." Many Christians display this well-known scripture at the entrance to their home: "But as for me and my family, we will serve the Lord" (Joshua 24:15).

Symbolic gestures provide reminders of our commitment to God. Many people wear a cross as a display of their faith and to keep God close to their heart for comfort. Some people declare their faith with an *ichthys*, or "Jesus fish," on the back of their car.

While there's nothing wrong with these outward signs of your dedication to God, the most vital thing is to absorb God's Word and let his Spirit dwell inside you, where it will be a part of how you live and breathe each day. When you keep his words within you, nothing can take them away from you.

## Good Morning, Lord

*May I always stay motivated to connect with you all throughout each day, and to store your loving guidance in my heart.*

---

*"If you carefully obey the commands I am giving you today, and if you love the Lord your God and serve him with all your heart and soul, then he will send the rains in their proper seasons."*

DEUTERONOMY 11:13–14

# GOD'S REQUIREMENTS

What does God require of us? This question we find in Deuteronomy 10, along with some answers that can encourage all of us:

- *Fear God.* This does not mean to be afraid but rather to have reverence and respect for his authority over us. He made us; he guides us. We honor God by being humble and submitting to him.

- *Love God.* God is our Father, and we have assurance that he will take care of our needs, just as our earthly parents do. Over time, our relationship grows, and we connect with God as our friend as well as our Father.

- *Serve God.* We can serve in a begrudging manner or with joy. In return for his love for us, we should serve God with all our admiration for him, displaying enthusiasm and generosity in everything we do in his name.

- *Obey God's commands and decrees.* We can't expect to live without rules or guidelines to follow, and God has given us directions that will help us keep on his path.

God doesn't want you to suffer or be unhappy. By following his guidelines, you will strengthen your relationship with him and be blessed for your obedience to his Word.

## Good Morning, Lord

*I pray that you will help me know that your commandments are ultimately what will bring me the lasting happiness I crave. Please help me let go of control issues, and accept being helped.*

---

*"And now, Israel, what does the Lord your God require of you? He requires only that you fear the Lord your God, and live in a way that pleases him, and love him and serve him with all your heart and soul. And you must always obey the Lord's commands and decrees that I am giving you today for your own good."*

DEUTERONOMY 10:12–13

# THE COVENANT WITH GOD

A covenant is a promise or a pledge, but it tends to hold more weight. Covenants were common forms of agreement in ancient days. God initiated covenants at various times in Israel's history. It began with Noah, to whom God promised never to cause a great flood to come wipe out the world again, signaling that covenant with the rainbow.

God made a covenant with Abraham to lead Israel. In Genesis 12, God told Abraham to gather his family and leave town to set out for a land that God would show him—the Promised Land. God told him that if he followed his ways, he would bless Israel with great favor.

Notice the clause in the covenant, "if." *If* Israel fully committed to following God's ways, *then* they would experience the blessings and be a blessing to the world. If they turned away from the Lord, he would remove his favor from the nation.

In the same way, through Christ, we are in covenant with God today, but the clause still holds true. "If" we commit to following God's ways, then he will pour out his favor and blessings, not just for our benefit but for others', too. Why doesn't God just do this automatically? God gives us, as freewill creatures, the choice to love him wholeheartedly. He delights when we choose to do so.

Dear one, my prayer is that you commit your ways unto God, who desires to shine brightly through you. Offer the Lord your entire heart, making a commitment to uphold your end of the covenant in Christ Jesus. As you do, know that God will certainly uphold his end of the covenant.

### ⌒⌒ *Good Morning, Lord* ⌒⌒

*Please let this be the day when I completely trust and surrender to God's will. Help me release my resistance and follow you.*

*"All the families on earth will be blessed through you."*

GENESIS 12:3

# Hungry for Wisdom

In the days of the Old Testament, the Queen of Sheba had heard all about how wise Solomon was and how blessed he was by the Lord. You can hear amazing things about a person, but it's usually not until you meet them and have a conversation that you really gauge what they're about. So she took a trip to visit him. She realized just how incredible this man was after witnessing his wisdom in action and seeing the favor of the Lord upon his household. She gave praise to God for placing him in such a position of power.

Dear one, this is what God desires from us. That our lives be marked with godly character and favor. That people be inspired by our lives. That people would want to sit and converse with us because they are drawn to God in us. They want to know if we're the real deal.

If someone were to come to your home and have a discussion, would they be more apt to glorify God after getting to know you and seeing how you are blessed? I don't mean just with material things, but spiritually. Your peaceful, loving, meek, compassionate, godly spirit. Surely God puts us all in positions where we can be an example of Jesus to those around us.

There are a lot of people who, like the Queen of Sheba, are hungry for answers to their most pressing life questions. May we be people to whom they can come and receive an impartation of Jesus.

## Good Morning, Lord

*I am so deeply inspired by you that I commit
to live my life to be an inspiration to others.*

---

*"I didn't believe what was said until I arrived here and saw it with my own eyes. In fact, I had not heard the half of it! Your wisdom and prosperity are far beyond what I was told."*

**1 Kings 10:7**

## SOLOMON'S DEMISE

King Solomon was blessed and favored by the Lord, and he spent many years serving the Lord wholeheartedly. But as he grew older, he began turning his heart away from God and onto women. He had a wandering eye and no problem following it.

Solomon's heart grew far from the Lord in his old age. Some of those women influenced him to actions that were displeasing to God, such as building temples to pagan idols. It's an all-too-familiar story where great wealth and power negatively influences one's relationship with the Lord. Some people forget that it was God who blessed them with the success. Sometimes ego or selfishness gets in the way, which can be the cause of their downfall, just as it was for Solomon.

At the same time, this is a firm reminder that we should pick our partners carefully. If you are fully devoted to God and a godly lifestyle is important to you, then when you are seeking a mate, this should be high on your priority list. Do not count on changing someone. If you happen to now be with someone who does not follow the ways of Jesus, you can certainly pray for them and be patient.

Dear one, stay committed to the Lord and resist the temptation to compromise. Remember where your blessings have come from. When the grass looks greener on the other side, turn back to yours and water your own grass. God desires that you keep your eyes fixed on him, even unto your last breath. This, darling, is my prayer for you this morning.

### *Good Morning, Lord*

*I need your help in staying focused, dear Lord. If you ever find me wandering away from you, please shepherd me back!*

---

*"In Solomon's old age, they turned his heart to worship other gods instead of being completely faithful to the Lord his God, as his father, David, had been."*

**1 KINGS 11:4**

## DELIVERANCE IN BLEAK TIMES

In the story of Exodus, the Israelites were under rule by the Egyptians as slaves for many years. The Pharaoh started to fear that the numbers of Israelites would grow enough to overpower the Egyptians, so to curb the population, he ordered that the male babies be killed. To save Moses, his mother put him in a basket and let him float down the Nile River, hoping that one of the Egyptians would find and raise him. As part of God's plan, Pharaoh's daughter found Moses. Later Moses would be instrumental in saving the Israelites from the Egyptians.

Just as the Egyptians feared the potential power of the Israelites, there are lower energies and enemies in the spiritual realms that fear your power in the Lord Jesus Christ. There is a heavenly war going on. There's darkness and light, but God always has a path of deliverance and victory for his children. Just as he had a plan for Moses when life looked very bleak, he has a plan for you as well.

You may feel like you're pinned up against the wall. You may feel as if the enemy has the upper hand in an area. But remember this story and many other stories throughout the Bible where God delivers his people. God can take your situation and turn it into a mighty victory in his time. He is orchestrating it right now. Trust and listen as he leads you and know that he is always defending you in the heavenly realms. Hold on, dear one, and believe that your deliverance is at hand.

### Good Morning, Lord

*Please help me believe and keep going. I know that God is stronger than any negativity, but it would surely help if you would send me some signs that I am on the right path. Thank you for filling me with faith and for protecting my loved ones and me.*

*"The princess named him Moses, for she explained,*
*'I lifted him out of the water.'"*

EXODUS 2:10

## Blessed Are You Who Believe

*I'll believe it when I see it.* It's a common saying, and it was true for Thomas in the New Testament. When Jesus had risen from the dead and appeared to some of the disciples, Thomas hadn't been there. The disciples tried to assure him of the truth, but Thomas said he must see the nail marks in his hands and the scar on his side. This is where the popular phrase "doubting Thomas" comes from.

Now, maybe Thomas just didn't want to get his hopes up. I think we can all relate to being skeptical to protect our hearts. When Jesus showed up to Thomas, he in essence said, "Here are my hands. Touch them. Go ahead and believe." Of course, then Thomas believed and went on to share the Good News of the Gospel with many people.

Jesus told Thomas that he commended him for believing, but he also said, "Blessed are those who believe without seeing me" (John 20:29). This still applies to us today. Those of us who have not yet consciously experienced Jesus's presence and still believe that he's real and alive are blessed. Even though we may not see Jesus physically today, God always gives us the proof that we need deep in our hearts to know that Jesus is alive.

If you're doubting, dear one, ask God to reveal the living Christ to you and help you to overcome skepticism. There's a blessing involved in those who believe and have not yet seen. Have eyes to see, darling. Jesus is alive!

### ⤜ *Good Morning, Lord* ⤛

*Oh, how I'd love to be 100 percent believing, to have pure faith with not one shred of doubt. What a blessing that would be! If it's possible for me, Lord, please increase my faith.*

---

*"Then Jesus told him, 'You believe because you have seen me. Blessed are those who believe without seeing me.'"*

JOHN 20:29

# THE DAY OF PENTECOST

While Jesus walked his earthly ministry, he made it clear that he had to ascend so that he could send his Spirit upon the earth to continue his work in his believers. After Jesus had risen from the dead and ascended to his Father, 120 believers got together to pray and wait for the Holy Spirit that Jesus promised.

At the time, it was the Jewish feast of Pentecost, and a lot of people were in the area. When the Spirit filled them, there were signs and miracles. People saw visions of fire above the heads of those who received the Holy Spirit, symbolizing his power and presence upon them. Some of them spoke in languages that they had never learned. Peter shared powerfully in the power of the Spirit, and many people came to the Lord that day. The day of Pentecost began a new era for the church.

Jesus has given us access to his Spirit, which is powerful. The Spirit's presence within you can be the difference between sharing a message where people are bored and where they are moved to tears or feeling immense love from the Father.

The Holy Spirit desires to dwell within every believer. The Spirit's motive is to bring people closer to the Lord, awakening their spirits to the reality of the Kingdom of God. If you have not received the baptism of the Holy Spirit, ask the Lord for this gift. Then believe that you are indeed filled with and can walk in the same power that Jesus did!

## Good Morning, Lord

*Good morning, Holy Spirit, please come to me and fill me with your indwelling passion, crystal clear wisdom, and blissful love.*

---

*"Then, what looked like flames or tongues of fire appeared and settled on each of them. And everyone present was filled with the Holy Spirit and began speaking in other languages, as the Holy Spirit gave them this ability."*

ACTS 2:3–4

# THE SPIRIT POURED OUT FOR ALL

On the day of Pentecost, Peter announced that this was what the prophet Joel spoke of: In the last days, God would pour out his Spirit on everyone. Signs and wonders would occur, and all would prophesy, see visions, and dream dreams. He emphasized that *all* would have direct access to God—Jews and Gentiles alike. Everyone, everywhere!

Perhaps you have had a vision or heard a word from the Lord that you felt compelled to share. Maybe you've had dreams that you feel are directly from the Lord. The presence of the Holy Spirit upon the earth and within us today gives us all a direct link to God. We're able to tap into the mind of God. Some people are more apt to hear the voice of the Lord, while others may be more inclined to see visions. There are many ways the Lord reveals himself to his people.

On the day of Pentecost, thousands decided to follow Jesus and received the Holy Spirit. Every day around the world, people are hearing the Good News of the Gospel and making that same decision. It's easy to get caught up in the mundane everyday routine and forget about sharing the Good News with those who haven't heard or those who are seeking answers.

My prayer is that we will be mindful each day to listen for the Word of the Lord, be filled with his Spirit, and watch for dreams and visions from him. The world is hungry for inspiration, dear one. May we boldly proclaim it in love.

### ❧ *Good Morning, Lord* ❧

*Please reveal your teachings to me in my heart*
*so that I may help others receive your Good News.*

---

*"'In the last days,' God says, 'I will pour out my Spirit upon all people. Your sons and daughters will prophesy. Your young men will see visions, and your old men will dream dreams.'"*

ACTS 2:17

# GET SOME REST

Your body needs rest, and your heart needs quiet time for reflection and contemplation. These needs can't be ignored because of a busy schedule—they are musts, not optional. As a caring, sensitive person, you naturally want to help others to be happy and healthy. But please don't exclude yourself.

When I first became a psychotherapist in my early 30s, I wondered where all the older therapists were. I soon discovered that counselors and other professional helpers have a high burnout rate. This burnout also applies to those who care for their family or do volunteer work.

Without balance—and getting some rest—we won't be as effective in helping others, and we won't be happy ourselves. And if you needed help, wouldn't you feel better receiving it from a happy person instead of from someone who's unhappy and burned-out?

There's a good reason why one of the Ten Commandments is to take a day of rest—we need it! While very few people observe the Sabbath, it's still a reminder to slow down, rest, and ask for guidance and help from the Lord. And there's also a good reason why Jesus asked his disciples to follow him and get some rest in Mark 6:31 and Matthew 11:28.

May *you* follow Jesus and get some rest, dear one!

*Good Morning, Lord*

*Please help me slow down, remind me
to breathe, and relieve me of guilt as I rest.*

---

*"Dear friend, I hope all is well with you and that you
are as healthy in body as you are strong in spirit."*

3 JOHN 1:2

## OBSERVE SABBATH REST

After God created the heavens and the earth, the Word says that he rested on the seventh day. If God chose to rest, we—God's creations—also need to do so. Time away from work is valuable. It allows us the chance to refresh, enjoy the company of loved ones and the Lord, and do things that we enjoy.

The Sabbath day made it into the Ten Commandments. The Israelites had a strict set of rules regarding the Sabbath, and today many still follow such rules. We are not under an obligation from the law to observe the Sabbath like in the old Covenant, but observing it can prove valuable in our lives.

To observe the Sabbath means to take a day each week and not do any work. It doesn't mean that you shouldn't cook meals and tidy up after yourself, but we are encouraged to take it easy. If you're part of a community of believers, meet with them for fellowship. Make time in the Lord's presence in his Word and in prayer. Plan a fun day with loved ones, or minister to the lonely or sick. Read an inspiring book. Sit in nature and journal. Whatever helps you refresh and feel revived, do that.

In today's world, busyness is often expected and rewarded, and sometimes it's challenging to turn the motor off. But God is advising that one day a week you shut it all down. I think you'll be thrilled by the results!

### ➥ Good Morning, Lord ➥

*I would love to observe the Sabbath, and I ask for your help in doing so. Please show me how to change my schedule so that I can truly rest.*

---

*"Remember to observe the Sabbath day by keeping it holy."*

EXODUS 20:8

# GIVE YOUR WORRIES TO GOD

The ego habitually worries about the future, which is draining and demoralizing. Worry keeps us from enjoying our day, wrecks our health, and makes us second-guess following God's divine guidance.

It's *how* we deal with worry that matters most. Our thoughts and words have the power to create and attract, meaning that worry can create and attract what we worry about. So it's essential to notice worries and not allow them to fester or grow. Just as we'd take action if there were an infestation in our home, so too must we take action in the face of an influx of worrisome thoughts or feelings.

The remedy is prayer, which lifts our thoughts and feelings to the holy strength and power of God. There is no worry or fear in love, and love keeps us safe.

### Good Morning, Lord

*Here are my worries: [describe them]. I gladly give them to you now. I don't like this feeling of being afraid, and I ask that you remind me of your presence and the safety of my loved ones and me and our world.*

*"For you didn't receive the spirit of bondage again to fear, but you received the Spirit of adoption, by whom we cry, 'Abba! Father!'"*

ROMANS 8:15 (WEB)

# A SOLID FOUNDATION

Relationships are a wonderful way to experience the kind of love that God has for us. But when families are built on the foundation of the ways of the world, there's a good chance that the foundation will start to crumble when struggles come. The house might not fall for years, but with each harsh word and conflict swept under the carpet, cracks form in that foundation.

When you put God first in your relationship, those cracks are less likely to form. It doesn't mean that you'll never experience struggles or conflict; you will. But when God is first, he will lend strength to the foundation so that it will be able to withstand pressure.

What does it look like to have God first in your family? Does it mean going to church together? Praying together? This will look different for each family. It's really a heart issue. It's getting with your partner and having a discussion about what this might look like. It's putting it out there on the table and coming to an agreement that you all want God first in your relationship. It's modeling the character of Jesus in front of your children. It's taking the commitment to seek the ways of God first in your own life and in your family seriously.

We all know that many relationships don't work out, even among those who love and serve God with all their heart. God can help you build a strong foundation, though. My prayer is that you'll honor the Lord individually and as a family. That you'll enjoy a fruitful and joyous relationship with your partner and loved ones.

### Good Morning, Lord

*I pray for healing in my marriage and family. Please help us unite harmoniously in joy, love, and a sense of joined purpose.*

*"Unless the Lord builds a house, the work of the builders is wasted."*

PSALM 127:1

# WE ARE SOJOURNERS

Dear one, we are sojourners. This physical planet is not our eternal home.

Now, I know that this isn't always comforting to hear, because so many people fear death. However, I assure you that you, the real *you*, will never die. The real you, your soul, will live on forever in God's Kingdom. As you journey in this life, keep in mind that it is a learning experience, an adventure, and an opportunity to help others.

Instead of thinking about how fleeting this life can be, perhaps we can get excited about the reality of eternity. Life in God's Kingdom without the trappings of the fleshly body. Illuminated spiritual beings in the presence of God 24-7, experiencing unconditional, unfathomable love. Now that's something to get excited about!

Yes, this earthly life is important, and we ought to focus on living an upright life honoring God and helping others. At the same time, let's focus on the fact that we are pilgrims in this land—visitors. We truly are spiritual beings in a suit made of flesh, on an earthly journey. The land in which we will rest forever will be free from heartache, suffering, and labor.

My hope is that upon your last breath as a human, instead of fearing the unknown, you can rejoice in the reality that your spirit will live on and on in the glorious presence of the Lord.

### Good Morning, Lord

*Please show me how to fully embrace life,
both here on the earth and also in heaven.*

---

*"For you have been born again, but not to a life
that will quickly end. Your new life will last forever
because it comes from the eternal, living word of God."*

**1 PETER 1:23**

## No Partiality

Have you given your power to others? Does *your* mood get affected by the moods of those around you? How much of your day is dedicated to thinking or worrying about others? Or taking care of another person?

We need people. We're encouraged to connect with all people, showing no favor to one over another. We were not meant to journey alone. However, we're also not meant to be controlled by other people, lose ourselves or our sanity, or base our value upon another person's approval or attention.

Jesus showed no partiality to people. He wasn't attached in an unhealthy way to anyone but attached in a healthy way to his Father fully. He knew who he was in his Father's eyes and based his worth on that. He went up against plenty of rejection and had a host of people he tended to in ministry, but he set and kept internal boundaries. His desire for you, dear one, is that you break loose from any unhealthy dependence on others so that you can enjoy such freedom!

Dear one, if you feel as if you have given your power to others, address this with God. You may also want to seek someone who can support you who has knowledge of treating codependency, and read some helpful books on the topic. Relying on others for your personal happiness will lead you to feel frustration and pain. Turn to God and ask him to reveal his great love to you so that you can base your worth solely on him.

### Good Morning, Lord

*I'm here before you, asking you to teach me about true love within relationships, because I don't know how to feel loved. I've been trying to win people's love at my own expense, and it's draining me, Lord. Please help me, and please love me. Thank you.*

---

*"For God does not show favoritism."*

ROMANS 2:11

# UPLIFTING YOUR HEART

As much as we try to stay positive, sometimes we go through times of sadness. For some people, this sadness becomes chronic depression. Even though it can seem as though those negative feelings will never leave, it helps to remember that every storm blows over eventually.

Psalm 6 is a poignant portrait of how depression, hurt, and anxiety feels. The psalmist David describes how challenging it is to feel depressed and how beaten down you can feel. Reading through it, you'll realize that you're not alone in your deep suffering. Life can be full of challenges and unfortunate situations, and it can certainly affect your state of mind.

David tells the Lord that his soul is in great anguish. He's groaning, crying, and questioning God: *How long? How long must I endure this agony?* He knew where to take his grief. He knew God was there; even if he was silent at the moment, David knew eventually God would show up. He talks about feeling lost and broken, but he also acknowledged that God heard his prayer.

Darling, there is always someone who loves and cares for you. Your Heavenly Father wants to help you. If you've been feeling hurt, broken, or depressed, turn to God. Relax into his goodness and love. Trust him to take care of you, including guiding you to a wonderful counselor or support group.

You are worthy of love and happiness. You can make it through hurt and sadness. Know that you are worth so much, and no matter what you are facing, you do not have to confront it alone.

### ❧ Good Morning, Lord ❧

*I know that you have my best interests at heart, so I am giving you my heart for healing. I've closed it off from the overwhelming pain, and I need your help to feel safe enough to reawaken it.*

*"The Lord has heard my plea; the Lord will answer my prayer."*

PSALM 6:9

# My Heart Shall Rejoice

We all go through challenging times, and we can get so lost in our upset that we forget to pray or ask for help. In Psalm 13, David cries, "How long, Lord? How long will you ignore me?" It can feel as though God has forgotten you, as though you aren't worth anything. However, if you read the rest of the psalm, you'll see that deliverance comes. God loves you and created you with a purpose.

Today, I'd like to share some supportive prayers I created based on scriptures to help during times of darkness. You can pray for others who are struggling, too. God desires to bring you through your challenges, so exercise your faith in his Word— even when you don't feel like it.

- *God, I cast my burden on you. I know you will take care of me.* (Psalm 55:22)

- *God, I know you are with me through these murky waters. The river will not consume me. The flames will not burn me, because you are by my side. You protect and sustain me.* (Isaiah 43:2)

- *I know you hear my cries, and I wait patiently for you. I know you will show up. You'll pull me out of this slimy pit of mud, clean me off, set me upon a joyful rock, and I'll be singing songs of praise to you, God!* (Psalm 40:1–3)

Darling, you will rejoice once again. God won't let you down. There's hope and help in God's Word, and he's always loving you.

### Good Morning, Lord

*I pray that you will lift me up. Help me see and feel your light, please. Please hold me and reassure me that I am loved.*

*"But I trust in your unfailing love. I will rejoice because you have rescued me."*

PSALM 13:5

# SPEAK GOD'S WORDS

Numbers 23 and 24 tell the story of Balaam and the king of Moab, Balak. Balak was afraid that the Israelites were going to take over his land, so he sent for Balaam, a prophet, to curse the Jewish nation. At Balak's third request, God told Balaam to go, but not to speak before he heard from the Lord.

Along the path, Balaam's donkey stopped because he saw the angel the Lord had sent. Balaam beat the animal until God performed a miracle that allowed the donkey to speak and Balaam to see the angel. The angel confirmed that he should not speak until he heard from the Lord, and the donkey told Balaam to stop hurting him. When Balaam got to Moab, he told King Balak that he could not curse Israel because God had not cursed and never would curse Israel. Instead, the prophet blessed the nation.

Just as God spoke to Balaam, he desires to speak to us. He will even send us angels to deliver his messages. God told Balaam that he would not change his mind about Israel. This is a great reminder that God's promises are kept. God always has a plan, and he follows through with that plan, not taking anything back. He has blessed all nations and will continue to.

Read through the story of Balaam. See how he is changed when he encounters the angel of the Lord. One encounter with the Lord can certainly transform a person. Note how he refused to speak until he heard from the Lord. There are wonderful lessons that we can glean from this story. Dear one, God seeks those who listen for his voice, speak his words, and perform his will regularly.

## ❧ *Good Morning, Lord* ❧

*I ask that you help me understand God's will for me and forgive me for the times I've not listened. Thank you for guiding me to take action according to God's will; this is the true path to happiness.*

*"I will speak only the message that the Lord puts in my mouth."*

NUMBERS 23:12

# JOURNEY IN HEALTH

God's Word speaks to us about food and a healthier lifestyle. We are told that our body is a "temple of the Holy Spirit" that we should use to "honor God" in 1 Corinthians 6:19. Likewise, 1 Corinthians 10:31 says "whether you eat or drink, or whatever you do, do it all for the glory of God." In Genesis, God says that he's given us plants and trees for food. It is God's will that we be healthy, though he also gave us the free will to choose items that are healthy or not healthy for the body.

Granted, things are a lot different today in industrialized areas of the world. Food is among the top addictions in many nations. It's quite easy to overindulge, which can cause health issues over time. I believe that God desires that each person focus on embracing a healthier eating lifestyle in balance. He desires that we surrender cravings for unhealthy foods to him. He desires that we eat more organic fruits and vegetables, instead of processed junk food.

The truth is that turning your food habits around takes time, energy, and discipline. I assure you that God is right there, supporting and guiding you. Begin a journey to educate yourself when it comes to healthy foods. Ask God to show you his truth and help you walk in the Spirit so that you don't succumb to unhealthful cravings. Pray for help, especially with self-control, to eat of the fruits of the Spirit.

### Good Morning, Lord

*Please hear and answer my prayers to be relieved from unhealthful cravings. I do not want to succumb to the cravings, yet their power is strong. I need your strength and might, dear Lord, to return my appetite to that which God wills for me.*

*"Then God said, 'Look! I have given you every seed-bearing plant throughout the earth and all the fruit trees for your food.'"*

GENESIS 1:29

# WHAT IF I STUMBLE?

Around the holiday season, parties often offer delicious-but-unhealthful food and drink temptations. While some people are able to indulge in moderation, others will go on binges.

At times, you may stumble in a certain area and perhaps even fall. But God will always ensure you can get back up and on the path that you desire. When it comes to a healthy lifestyle, setbacks may occur, but you always have the opportunity to begin again with the Lord's blessing.

The bodies we've been blessed with are vessels unto the Lord, and he desires that we take care of those vessels when it comes to eating and drinking. But the journey to get from unhealthy to healthy eating habits may take some time. If you're concerned, know that you're not alone; help is available should you need it. There are plenty of resources, including support groups in your community, eating-disorder counselors, dietitians and nutritionists, and a plethora of online material to educate yourself.

If you look at the whole picture, you may become discouraged. Do it in bite-size pieces, darling. Your intention is progress and balance, not perfection. If this holiday season hasn't gone as you hoped regarding your eating habits, allow God to pick you up and give you strength to get back on track. Ask Holy Spirit to help you each day in choosing nutritious foods and in giving you the desire to exercise regularly. It won't be as challenging as you think, and you'll feel better all around.

## Good Morning, Lord

*Here I am again, back in the situation of succumbing to unhealthy cravings. I'm tired of the struggle. Can you please intervene? I need big help in surrendering and adjusting my appetite and cravings, and I appeal to you, Lord.*

*"Though they stumble, they will never fall, for the Lord holds them by the hand."*

PSALM 37:24

# Lose Your "Self"

Self-centeredness always leads us away from God. When a person is obsessed with the fleshly nature, they are by default not focused on the Lord. It's like we run around feeling like the "self" is lost, and try to find that self in this material world. Whether chasing after success, lovers, addictions, or other quick fixes, we gain nothing except momentary pleasure.

However, when we run after the kind of life that Jesus has offered, we gain our authentic self in the Lord. In other words, those who try to hold on to a self-centered life forsake the true life of focusing upon the Lord. But those who give up their lives for the Lord actually receive true or higher life. When we focus upon following God's will, it is then that we will find authentic, joyful, eternal life.

There's a double meaning to the word *life* here. One is in reference to this physical or temporal life, and the other to a higher or eternal life. If we go after the lower, temporal life, we lose focus upon the higher, eternal life. It's dying to the self and coming alive in the spirit.

This is God's will for us.

So many people focus on accumulating the outer things to impress others, but true life comes from a focus on the inner, the spiritual, the lasting things. Instead of trying to impress others, *bless* others. My prayer is that you continue to go within—not to the selfish ego, but to the living Christ that dwells in you. There you will find true life!

### ∾ Good Morning, Lord ∾

*What a relief it is to know that everything I need is within you!*
*That I can finally get off of the treadmill and relax in your arms,*
*while fulfilling my purpose of bringing your blessings to others.*

---

*"If you cling to your life, you will lose it;*
*but if you give up your life for me, you will find it."*

Matthew 10:39

# MAY YOU BE AT PEACE

God, being peace, created you in peace and with peace inside you. And you are here as a creator of peace yourself.

I remember going into a grocery store one time while I was traveling and seeing two people shopping who were *glowing* with peacefulness. They were so radiant, not in a look-at-me, attention-seeking way, but in an I-am-in-love-with-God way. Big, open hearts, shining bright light as they shopped.

I was stunned seeing them, and even though that was 15 years ago, I will never forget their example of our potential to go to an ordinary place like a grocery store and—without saying a word—be a spiritual teacher and healer.

This light of peacefulness comes from the pure joy of deeply connecting with God's love through prayer, meditation, and contemplation. God sends Holy Spirit to us as a personal spiritual teacher to enlighten our minds and lift our hearts to peacefulness. May you go forth today glowing with God's peacefulness, and inspire others to be at peace!

## Good Morning, Lord

*Here are all the worldly distractions that are on my mind:* [describe anything that's upsetting you]. *Thank you for teaching me how to deal with life in a peaceful way.*

*"Then you will experience God's peace, which exceeds anything we can understand. His peace will guard your hearts and minds as you live in Christ Jesus."*

PHILIPPIANS 4:7

# BE TRUE TO GOD

As a kind, gentle, and sensitive person, you may feel the energy of others trying to influence you in their favor. Perhaps someone tries to take advantage of your generous nature, or commercials try to influence your spending habits. Or perhaps you're fortunate enough to have people in your life who genuinely care about your physical or spiritual health, so they are trying to influence you in healthful ways.

Influences can come from the songs you hear, movies you watch, books you read, and people with whom you spend time. That's why it's essential for you to be strong in yourself and God about what your core values and priorities are.

Be true to yourself and God so that you won't be swayed by influences that aren't in alignment with your truth. Trying to please others by betraying your true feelings never leads to anything good, unless others are trying to influence you in a healthy way that's aligned with God's will for you.

It can be confusing knowing whom or what to trust. Fortunately, prayer can give you the strength to say no to distractions, and help you gain clarity about the best path and the next steps for you to take. Prayer can also help you have accurate discernment about the people and influences in your life.

### Good Morning, Lord

*Please let the only counsel in my head and heart be from your pure, loving wisdom, as you have the highest will for me. Please protect me from distractions and detours, and help me stay focused upon the path of love.*

---

*"Let me hear of your unfailing love each morning, for I am trusting you. Show me where to walk, for I give myself to you."*

PSALM 143:8

# LEAN ON GOD

Anything that pushes you away from the routine can shake up your sense of predictability. When you begin working on something new for yourself personally or professionally, there's a sense of walking in the unknown and unfamiliar. That's why it's important to remind yourself that God walks *with* you through your divinely guided activities. Check in with God through prayer and meditation each step of the way.

You may not know what you're doing or what's coming up next, but God does! Instead of grappling with self-confidence, have God-confidence!

When you lean on God and surrender everything to God's infinite wisdom, you can completely trust that it will work out—even if you humanly can't figure out *how* it will work out. God's miracles are far beyond human logic, yet they *are* logical because they are based upon love, which is the most logical part of earthly life.

Put your whole focus upon gratitude and faith that God has got the situation handled in the best possible way. Everything has already been worked out in spiritual truth. There's nothing to fear!

### Good Morning, Lord

*I can't do this alone, and I need your strength, support, and guidance to know what steps I should take.*

---

*"Those who listen to instruction will prosper; those who trust the Lord will be joyful."*

PROVERBS 16:20

## LET YOUR BURDENS BE LIFTED

The reason why you so often hear "Let go and let God" is because many of our struggles are caused by us trying to manage life by ourselves. Giving the situation to God lifts your burden of trying to be in charge.

Any resistance we have to asking for God's help is from the ego, which wants to control everything. Yet the ego was the one who created the problem in the first place. The ego doesn't trust anyone, not even God. Yet trust and faith are the divine prescriptions to treat life's ailments.

God's infinite wisdom brings ingenious solutions and answers in ways we couldn't have anticipated or planned. The ego is afraid to pause and listen to divine guidance, worried about what God might say. Fortunately, there's nothing to fear about true divine guidance, which always leads us on the right path.

### Good Morning, Lord

*I can't handle this situation anymore. Please help
me give it over entirely to you. I hereby relinquish
any part of me that wants to control the situation,
and I humble myself before your divine will.*

*"But when I am afraid, I will put my trust in you.
I praise God for what he has promised.
I trust in God, so why should I be afraid?
What can mere mortals do to me?"*

PSALM 56:3–4

# AUTHORITY IN JESUS

In Matthew 7:28, it says that the multitude was astonished by Jesus's teaching, for he didn't teach them like the scribes and the Pharisees, who were scholars when it came to the law, but did so with authority. He taught with conviction, passion, power, and zeal. The crowd could certainly *feel* the difference in the depths of who they were. He also spoke with an assurance that he wasn't just speaking in his own words but those of his Father in power.

Now that we have access to the Holy Spirit, we can also stand up in the world and speak with such authority, as Jesus did. This doesn't mean that we're all intended to preach to the public. But it does mean that wherever we are, whomever we're talking to, we can know our authority in Jesus Christ through the power of the Holy Spirit.

When you believe, you can step out knowing that you have victory over the circumstances in your life. That through the Word and power of the Holy Spirit, you're a conqueror in Jesus.

God himself dwells in you. When you can really get revelation of this, you will begin operating your life from a new kind of authority. A holy assurance. Jesus said that what he did in the world, we can do as well. This is my prayer for you, dear one. Go in the authority of Jesus Christ, in the power of the Holy Spirit.

## Good Morning, Lord

*Please authorize me to speak in your name, dear God, Holy Spirit, and Jesus of Nazareth, and help me accurately bring through the messages that you wish for me to share.*

---

*"When Jesus had finished saying these things, the crowds were amazed at his teaching, for he taught with real authority— quite unlike their teachers of religious law."*

MATTHEW 7:28–29

# FAITH OVERCOMES UNCERTAINTY

Life just feels loud sometimes. Whether you're hearing voices inside or outside your head, peace escapes even the calmest person at times. Do you ever feel like you're distracted by the chaos of the world? Lost among the noise? The uncertainty?

This is when Holy Spirit turns to you and essentially conveys, "Shhh. Quiet that mind, my love. The noise can fade. Let me teach you." Then he teaches you to slow down. Sit by yourself with no distractions. Take slow, deep breaths, and if you have to say something, utter a whisper. Take yourself to a calming place where God's voice can drown out all the others. Enter that place where God can shower love on you. When the world is chaotic and loud, don't partake in it. Calm your mind and listen. Listen to what is being said. Listen to silence.

You want certainty. I understand. You want life to be neat and organized. But, my dear, life doesn't fit in a box. It's too unpredictable. Instead of trying to control every aspect of your life and twisting yourself into a pretzel, trust God to lead you to a calm, peaceful place.

Sure, it can be challenging to trust God when life seems to be out of control, but if you can remember that God loves you and is always there for you, you will be okay. Faith overcomes fear. Step out in faith, darling. Calm down. Listen. This is where the rubber meets the road. Surrender control. Give your worries to God and trust his plan, that in the stillness, you'll experience abundant peace.

### ❧ *Good Morning, Lord* ❧

*Please teach me how to take care of my responsibilities with a peaceful mind. Please take away this stress and transform me into the peaceful person who I know is my real self.*

---

*"You will keep in perfect peace all who trust in you,*
*all whose thoughts are fixed on you!"*

ISAIAH 26:3

# GOD'S BEAUTIFUL GARDEN

Whether you believe the Garden of Eden to be literal or a metaphor, I imagine that all the gardens of biblical times must have been beautiful and lush before our modern age of environmental pollutants. Thankfully, people are now returning to nature and eating from the land, as God intended for us to do.

I increasingly meet people who enjoy plant-based diets, free of pesticides or processing. That's how I've been happily eating since 1996, after I received clear divine guidance to do so. If you often buy vegetables with every intention of eating them, but allow them to sit in your refrigerator too long, growing your own can motivate you to eat them more often.

I always encourage people to get outside and work—or as I call it, *play*—in their yard, if possible, as there are various associated benefits. Don't have a yard? You can grow your own organic produce in a planter on your balcony or join a co-op or a community garden.

Spending time outdoors among plants and trees is a natural way to slow down, breathe, and quiet your mind to better hear and feel God. Many people find gardening a meditative way to gain answers and insights.

If you've been wanting to do some yard work for a while, go ahead and get your hands dirty. Bring your dog and go play in the grass or enjoy a walk. Or simply sit outside and inhale the fresh air, enjoying God's amazing creation.

## Good Morning, Lord

*Thank you for the God-given delicious fruits and vegetables that nourish our health. Please guide and support my gardening activities so that I can enjoy the bounty of growing my own food.*

---

*"Build homes, and plan to stay. Plant gardens, and eat the food they produce."*

JEREMIAH 29:5

# MOVE ON

Sometimes you just have to move on. Hard as it may be in some situations, letting go can ultimately help you learn valuable lessons and grow. Now, you may be wondering, *If God tells us to hold on to faith and his promises, how are we to know if it's his will to stay put or move on?*

Good question. The truth is that it's not always easy to discern. Yes, the Lord will support you. Yes, the Lord hears you and wants the best for you, and sometimes the best thing for you is to move on. For example, if you're mistreated in a relationship, it may be time to move on. If you're in a dead-end job, consider moving on.

Is moving on always the answer? No. It's not "all or nothing." Sometimes the situation calls for us to stay and work on a solution. *Either* way requires you to hear the Lord's voice as best you can, discerning his will. It may also require you to seek professional help if you're really struggling. A seasoned counselor can help you sort out what's going on.

There were times when the Israelites had to move on, trusting that the Lord was with them. Jesus and his disciples moved on from towns where the people didn't recognize the value of his teachings.

Is there an area in your life you need to consider moving away from? Dropping? Letting go? Take it to the Lord.

### ❧ *Good Morning, Lord* ❧

*Please help me give myself permission to address this issue in light of my truth and from your perspective. I trust that you will lead and bless me, no matter what I decide.*

*"If any household or town refuses to welcome you or listen to your message, shake its dust from your feet as you leave."*

MATTHEW 10:14

# GOOD AND PERFECT GIFTS

God has given you something to add value to humanity. Maybe you have a passion for painting, writing, taking photographs, or building or inventing things. As the creation of the Creator, you are innately creative. Or maybe you've got leadership skills just waiting to be tapped. Do you see yourself on the stage teaching? Writing books? Assisting the poor? There are thousands of gifts and talents to introduce to the world.

When you really believe that God has gifted you with a certain talent, you'll move on it. A good starting point is praying for God to reveal his will and the gifts that he gave you. You don't need to figure out your life purpose on your own, as God is right here as the ultimate life coach for you. The ego always argues that you can't turn your talents into a viable career, yet God is who gave you those dreams and interests in the first place!

Dear one, your life purpose is not always about doing. Sometimes it's simply *being*: listening, praying, and delighting in those you come into contact with. What if that's your gift? What if showing up as light and love right in your own house and community is your talent?

Whether you're "being" or "doing," please listen for that inner voice prompting you to value and use the gifts that God has given you. You'll feel better, and the world will be a happier, healthier place thanks to you.

### Good Morning, Lord

*Thank you for always listening to and speaking with me!*
*I've been wondering about the best ways for me to help the world,*
*and I could really use your counsel and support, please.*

---

*"Whatever is good and perfect is a gift coming down to us*
*from God our Father, who created all the lights in the heavens.*
*He never changes or casts a shifting shadow."*

**JAMES 1:17**

# CREATE A FAITH-FILLED HOME LIFE

Jesus wants you to model him everywhere you go, including at work, at community events, and at home. Living out your faith at home will allow you to be a good witness for Jesus. If you're choosing to live righteous and holy only while you're out and about, but at home you're acting selfishly or in anger, that is not honoring the Lord. It won't do your family any good either.

God created the institution of family, and he desires that families serve him together. He encourages them to learn his Word and model his attributes in their everyday lives. Parents have the opportunity to teach their children the way of Jesus and model his kind of behavior, too.

Living out your faith in the home can help your children learn valuable lessons about love, making good choices, forgiveness, and true happiness. The Word offers wonderful guidelines and wisdom, so taking the time to teach your children Bible stories will benefit them throughout their lives.

Have conversations about God and his Word. Let your children ask questions. Make a commitment to modeling faith in your home, and allow God's love to permeate the whole family atmosphere. Honor your spouse, apologize and forgive yourself when you miss God's mark, and be a godly example. Children watch their parents, so what you say and do matters. Dear one, foster a holy home life so that God will be honored and so your family will experience the blessings of God.

## Good Morning, Lord

*I'm here seeking your guidance for my home life,*
*as we need your divine intervention and support, please,*
*to direct us on the path that God intends for us.*

---

*"So again I say, each man must love his wife as he*
*loves himself, and the wife must respect her husband."*

EPHESIANS 5:33

## No Fear in Love

Everyone wants to feel loved, yet we also have unconscious fears about love that block us from the experience we desire most. Reasons someone might fear love include the risk of getting hurt, being controlled, or experiencing disappointment. So we keep one foot on the gas pedal, and one foot on the brake—wanting love, yet fearing emotional pain.

This pattern also continues on the spiritual level, where we desire to feel the unconditional love that God has for us yet harbor fears that block our awareness of love. The fears of God's love are usually about feeling unworthy or being controlled. Facing these fears with prayer can help you release their unconscious grip on you.

Since you *are* love in spiritual truth, fearing love means fearing your true self. Conversely, healing this fear of love is the gateway to authenticity. It means loving yourself for who you are—quirks, mistakes, and all.

And when you love yourself as God loves you, you lose the fear of allowing others to love you. In fact, you stop attracting people who are self-fulfilling prophecies of your fears about love, and you instead attract gentle and trustworthy people who honor you and your relationship.

### Good Morning, Lord

*You know the contents of my heart and of my life experiences,*
*so you can understand why I'm afraid of being hurt and disappointed.*
*Please lead me past this barrier, dear Lord, and help*
*me feel safe in opening my heart to true love.*

---

*"There is no fear in love; but perfect love casts out fear."*

1 John 4:18 (WEB)

# THE ONLY POPULARITY THAT MATTERS

If you're seeking popularity with the world, living out the ways of Jesus probably won't assist in that. If you've got high standards and morals, some people may criticize, judge, or mock you. Followers of Jesus have been called radical, foolish, peculiar, and different. Sure, in your own circle, everything usually goes pretty well; people affirm your choices. But take your love, compassion, and empathetic spirit to those who have no desire to be anything like that, and you may be the unpopular one.

When you want to expose wickedness for the darkness that it is, the lower energies rebel. There were plenty of saints who were exiled and martyred on account of trying to live out the Good News of the Gospel of Jesus Christ. So what is the solution if you're criticized for your faith?

Jesus said that we are to love our enemies and pray for them. We are to respond in a loving manner. We are to keep our eyes on God, and when we find ourselves in situations where others oppose us, don't let it get us down. There is a cost in following the Lord, but it's well worth it. We're not out to win a popularity contest; we are out to love and serve humankind in the power of the Holy Spirit.

Fix your eyes on the Creator, dear one. If you experience scorn from others, receive it with grace, assured that you're doing God's will. Jesus was despised and rejected, but knowing the will of his Father, he asked that the Lord forgive them. May he serve as our model.

## Good Morning, Lord

*I will do anything for you, as I believe in you and everything you teach. I am ready to openly share my love and respect for you and your teachings with others.*

*"For they loved human praise more than the praise of God."*

JOHN 12:43

# DON'T WORRY ABOUT ANYTHING

Life is about learning and growing, which means that you'll experience a lot of changes.

You may currently be going through a change in where you live, where you work, how you eat, your health, or your relationships, your spiritual path, or another area.

Fortunately, God accompanies us upon *all* of life's journeys. He also sends an angel to lead the way, as he did for Moses and the Israelites in their exile. There's no need to struggle on your own, when heavenly help is readily available—if you'll ask for and accept it.

When you're in the dark about where you're going next, prayer will always light the path of your next step.

### Good Morning, Lord

*I need your help. This area of my life isn't working, and I surrender it to you for an overhaul. I'm letting go of trying to control or fix things on my own, and I'm putting my entire trust in you, Lord, to guide my way over the mountains of change.*

*"O my people, trust in him at all times.
Pour out your heart to him, for God is our refuge."*

**PSALM 62:8**

## LEARNING DISCERNMENT

Wouldn't it be nice if like Moses, we could talk to God face-to-face? Or sit down in person with Jesus, as did his disciples? We may not have physical manifestations like these, but we do have the very real connection of the Holy Spirit. As Jesus ascended, God sent his Holy Spirit to Earth as a comforter who teaches us about God's will.

Recognizing and understanding the divine messages, guidance, and answers from the Holy Spirit may take some time and effort, as you learn to distinguish them from your imagination or ego. To enhance discernment when it comes to God's will over your own will, there are several things that you can do:

- *Create quiet time.* It's easier to notice messages from Holy Spirit when your mind is free from noisy distractions.

- *Notice your inner truth-detector.* When God's messages come to you through Holy Spirit, you recognize it as the truth. It clicks as being an honest message.

- *Know the Word.* God's messages are biblically correct.

- *Feel the love and respect.* God's messages may be at times confrontational about our selfishness, fearfulness, and so on, yet they are always delivered with love and respect. If you receive a disrespectful message, call upon Jesus for help, because that is a sign it's not a divine message.

God desires that we commune with him and sincerely seek his will. This way, dear one, your discernment is far more apt to be accurate.

### ❦ Good Morning, Lord ❦

*Dear Holy Spirit, please teach me to accurately discern your messages so that I am guided only by God's will.*

*"I pray that your love will overflow more and more, and that you will keep on growing in knowledge and understanding."*

PHILIPPIANS 1:9

## SIT QUIETLY WITH THE LORD

Chances are, you've become distracted during your quiet time with the Lord. It can be challenging to sit still and not get sidetracked.

When you're sitting quietly with the Lord, thoughts are going to intrude periodically. Some people find it challenging to sit with an empty mind focused on the Lord for even one minute. Their minds are so used to racing with thoughts. But the good news, dear one, is that you can train your mind to rest while you maintain your focus on the Lord during quiet time. It simply takes patience and practice.

When you're sitting quietly with the Lord and a thought pops into your mind or your attention wanders, gently bring your focus back to your breath and back to the Lord. That way, you're focusing on the present moment rather than your meandering thoughts.

Let your heart swell up with affection and gratitude for God, and let him shower you with his affection, too. This divine exchange is where inner transformation can really flourish, darling, so take time daily to sit quietly with your loving Father.

### Good Morning, Lord

*I love this time we spend together, and I would love to spend more of it focused upon you. Please teach me, Lord, how to connect with you all throughout the day.*

*"Let them sit alone in silence beneath the Lord's demands."*

LAMENTATIONS 3:28

December 8

## Appreciate Your Spiritual Gifts

You have spiritual gifts God has given to you, and your gifts of creativity, sensitivity, healing, and so forth are uniquely suited for your life purpose and circumstances. Because our spiritual gifts have been personally selected for each of us by our Creator, our role is to discover, practice, polish, and honor them. The apostle Paul discussed the many ways in which we each have spiritual gifts when he wrote:

> But to each one is given the manifestation of the Spirit for the profit of all. For to one is given through the Spirit the word of wisdom, and to another the word of knowledge, according to the same Spirit; to another faith, by the same Spirit; and to another gifts of healings, by the same Spirit; and to another workings of miracles; and to another prophecy; and to another discerning of spirits; to another different kinds of languages; and to another the interpretation of languages. But the one and the same Spirit produces all of these, distributing to each one separately as he desires. (1 Corinthians 12:7–11)

Prayer can lead you to the right teacher, book, or other form of support to develop your spiritual gifts. God knows who you are, and what you're capable of. He gave you your gifts and is guiding you as to the best way to bless others through them.

### Good Morning, Lord

*Please guide me to discover my spiritual gifts and learn to use them in your service. Please help me to lose any fears about my spiritual gifts, and not misuse them or take them for granted.*

---

*"There are different kinds of spiritual gifts, but the same Spirit is the source of them all. There are different kinds of service, but we serve the same Lord. God works in different ways, but it is the same God who does the work in all of us."*

1 Corinthians 12:4–6

## ALLOW GOD TO HELP YOU

If you struggle with letting go and letting God help you, you're not alone. Many people wrestle with worry and control issues. They *want* to let go, but don't know how.

Dear one, trust and believe that your prayers have been heard and are being answered in the best way and with the best timing. The more you can surrender fears or control issues, the better everything will go.

"Letting go and letting God" means working as a team with your Creator's infinite wisdom and ingeniously creative solutions. If the world's greatest inventor offered to help you for free, wouldn't you say yes? Prayer loosens the grip of fear's talons so that you can be free to be yourself. After all, your true self already does trust. The real you believes and has faith.

Here's a helpful prayer:

*Dear God, I can't do this alone. I need your help.
And yet, I can feel resistances within myself, such as fear
of trusting that you'll help me and disbelief whether you can or
will actually answer my prayer. A part of me thinks I should just
do everything by myself, because that's what I've always done. Still,
I acknowledge that I do need help, as my way hasn't been working
well. So I need your assistance in loosening the grip of fears and
control issues. Please help me let go, release, trust, and believe.*

### Good Morning, Lord

*Your presence means so much to me, and I feel that I can tell you
anything, sharing all my fears and insecurities as well as my hopes
and dreams. You are my best friend, Lord, and I love you!*

"Commit everything you do to the Lord. Trust him, and he will help you. He will make your innocence radiate like the dawn, and the justice of your cause will shine like the noonday sun."

PSALM 37:5–6

# WISE STEWARDSHIP

---

This time of year, shopping and finances may be on your mind. I believe that money is a resource that *can* be used to honor God and fulfill his will. Sometimes it's challenging to know exactly where faith fits into the topic of finances. There are those who believe God calls everyone to a life of charity and poverty, and others who believe God promises abundant riches.

God desires that you include him in your financial portfolio. He desires that you be a steward of all resources that come your way—including money. God is not a genie who grants financial wishes, but he will guide us to make wise decisions. Sometimes it's a matter of practicing self-control with your income and following biblical financial principles. If you're not being wise with what you make, begin educating yourself and changing your spending habits. If you keep doing what you're doing, you're going to get the same results, no matter how much you pray.

Is giving financially to others God's will? Absolutely. God does not give so that we can hoard but so we can be blessed and bless others. If you live in a cycle of overspending, debt, and stress, begin praying and asking the Lord to help you get your finances together. Because when you can live within your means financially, you will certainly feel more at peace, and you'll be better able to give to others who are in need. So do consider offering charitable donations in your loved ones' names as your thoughtful Christmas gifts this year.

### Good Morning, Lord

*Thank you for partnering with me through every area of my life, including having support and sufficiency to meet my earthly needs. Please guide my earning, saving, spending, and charitable-giving activities.*

---

*"Wealth from get-rich-quick schemes quickly disappears; wealth from hard work grows over time."*

PROVERBS 13:11

# PEACEFUL HOLIDAY GATHERINGS

It's easy to feel loving when you're in a gentle setting, but how about during the holidays when you may feel stressed about family get-togethers or other relationship issues?

First, know that we are all going through these challenges together. Relationships involve the peril of conflict. It's not a matter of finding that magical conflict-free relationship, but rather of dealing with conflict in healthy ways, such as honest discussions, prayer, counseling, and assertiveness . . . If all that doesn't work, then simply walk away.

The ego wants to analyze others' egos, picking apart the reasons for a conflict. This would be fine if this method actually worked to bring about peace—but it doesn't. Analyzing someone else's ego only increases isolation, blame, judgment, and other bases of fear.

What does work is to have compassion for everyone involved with the conflict. See everyone as little children, lashing out because they're afraid. If there's an abusive situation, stay away from abusive people, direct any anger into taking positive action steps for healthy change, and pray fervently for divine intervention. Spiritually, what matters most is how you deal with the situation, always with love.

### Good Morning, Lord

*I need your help with this person, please. [Describe situation]. Please show me how to deal with this situation in healthy and loving ways. Please give me the strength to be loving, authentic, and compassionate toward everyone involved, including myself.*

*"Love is patient and kind."*

1 CORINTHIANS 13:4

## RELAX—GOD IS IN CHARGE

If you look for something to worry about, you will find it, as the mind locates whatever it's seeking. The ego says that it is keeping you safe by anticipating danger so that you can control or avoid it.

Yet does worrying really have benefits? If so, what are they? Isn't it more effective to plan for tomorrow, instead of worrying?

Whatever happens in life, God is there to help you and give you strength. If you need something, prayer will lead to great ideas, and acting on them will generate whatever you need, plus bring blessings to others.

Relaxing and having faith makes our minds more receptive to hearing God's guidance, and gives us the confidence and energy to enact the guidance. The key is to be aware of worry when it first creeps in, and then stop it in its tracks with a prayer such as this one:

*Dear God, I am worried about* [describe the situation],
*and I can't handle this alone. Here, God, please lift away*
*these worries and let me know what action I need to take . . .*
*Then please give me the courage and support to take it.*

### Good Morning, Lord

*I love that I can talk with you about my worries,*
*and that you lead me through them to the other side of fear,*
*which is complete faith and inner peace.*

---

*"That is why I tell you not to worry about everyday life—whether*
*you have enough food and drink, or enough clothes to wear.*
*Isn't life more than food, and your body more than clothing?"*

MATTHEW 6:25

# HOLD MY TONGUE

*Oh God, please help me hold my tongue.* I think we can all relate to wanting to express strong words, but we hold back to preserve the other person's feelings. We know in our hearts that God desires that we convey our truth in a kinder way. Even if we're simply talking in general about the nation or the state of the world, our choice of words makes a difference.

The psalmist David understood. He asked God to help him hold his tongue and keep him from getting even. Oftentimes, it is the mouth that will lead you down a path that could be displeasing to the Lord. You don't have to go far to hear people slandering, insulting, and verbally bashing each other.

The words we speak are powerful. Ask the Lord to help you hold your tongue or use words that will edify or "build up." Positive words may create a shift in the energy of a place and put a stop to the negativity. If you're a complainer, ask God to stop you before the words come out. When insults or criticisms are directed your way, resist the urge to respond in kind. I'm not saying that you have to be a doormat or that you cannot address the disrespect, but retaliation is not God's will.

Keep your soul filled to the brim with God's Word and walk in the power of the Spirit. Instead of returning insult for insult, you'll be able to bless others. This, dear one, will please the Lord.

### Good Morning, Lord

*You are my role model for speaking with both love and truth.*
*I wish to learn from you how to be authentic and true*
*to myself, while also being loving and compassionate.*

*"Take control of what I say, O Lord, and guard my lips."*

**PSALM 141:3**

## LOVE IS SINCERE

Being a peaceful and loving person doesn't mean allowing others to take advantage of your niceness. Yet this happens a lot when you feel confused about the definition of *loving*. This confusion leads gentle people to be "too nice" to those whose intentions *aren't* nice.

Assertiveness is being lovingly honest. It's speaking sincerely from your heart in a way that honors your own and the other person's feelings. It releases pent-up anger in constructive ways.

If you sense that someone is trying to take advantage of your niceness, the kindest thing you can do is to say no. After all, saying yes just reinforces that person's behavior, causing them to continue their exploitative ways with you and other nice people. For your own health and theirs, say no to unreasonable requests. Stop trying to rescue people who don't need or want rescuing, and instead direct your resources to those who are truly in need.

As we near Christmas, when people may be feeling stressed, it's important to practice self-care. And one of ways you care for yourself is by saying no to activities or requests that you honestly don't have the time or energy for. While it may be tempting to accept every Christmas-party invitation you receive, or volunteer for every charity committee, the truth is that you also need to consider your well-being and schedule. Say yes when it makes sense, and then know that it's okay to say no when you must. No guilt, just love.

### ⌘ *Good Morning, Lord* ⌘

*Thank you for guiding my activities and relationships
to be healthy, mutually beneficial, and authentic.*

---

*"Don't just pretend to love others. Really love them."*

ROMANS 12:9

## Accept God's Help

God is continually offering us help and support, yet it's up to us to accept these gifts. Over the years, many people have tried to convince me that they were the exception to this and that God was ignoring their prayers. Always when we looked more closely at their situation, we'd discover that it was the person who was ignoring *God's* answers to the prayers.

Every prayer is heard and answered, without exception. The answer can be subtle, though, such as your suddenly becoming inspired to take positive action or make a much-needed change. If you don't follow that guidance, you may erroneously believe that God hasn't answered you.

Just as the sun continually sends light to everyone who stands under its rays, so is God always beaming blessings to you and everyone. If you were to stand in the sunlight, though, and only look down at the shadows, you might mistakenly believe that darkness was all there is.

Look up to the light, and you'll feel and hear God's strength and support, which has always been there for you. Focus upon gratitude, count your blessings, pray from your heart, and follow your inner guidance. And open your arms to receive all the gifts that God is giving to you!

*Good Morning, Lord*

*Please help me drop my defenses, heal my fears, and be open to receiving all the gifts that you send to me—including the ones that come through other people. I truly desire to receive your help, and I need your help to be helped. Please reach into my heart and clear me of any dark thoughts or feelings so that I trust you and feel safe receiving your love.*

"When he prays to God, he will be accepted. And God will receive him with joy and restore him to good standing."

JOB 33:26

# Follow the Ultimate Teacher

There are a lot of spiritual and religious leaders today who sound amazing. They're insightful, smart, and charismatic; have written books; and can draw the crowds. It seems they have all the answers, but be careful, dear one, because they could truly be spiritually blind. In Matthew 15, Jesus says to leave such people be, because they are "blind guides."

There are those who are very attractive when it comes to principles for success, love, life, or spirituality, but be wary; some of their teachings go against God's Word. They usually teach "prosperity ministry": easy ways to pray or affirm yourself to abundance, without having to do any work except for thinking positively.

Jesus cautions us to look for those who teach sound doctrine. This is one more reason to study the Word. He also wants us to pay attention to red-flag warnings about any spiritual path or teacher.

Dear one, I encourage you to stay true to the Lord's course, backing up everything with the Word of God and the ways of Jesus. God helps those who help themselves, and no amount of positive thinking will bring you prosperity unless you also take divinely guided action. Does the teaching path honor God or elevate the ego?

Jesus is the life, truth, and the way. May our eyes always be open to the truth taught by the ultimate teacher.

### ∽ *Good Morning, Lord* ∼

*Thank you for shepherding me on my spiritual path,*
*guiding me away from false teachings, and keeping*
*me focused upon God's Word and will.*

---

*"Jesus replied, 'Every plant not planted by my heavenly Father will be*
*uprooted, so ignore them. They are blind guides leading the blind, and*
*if one blind person guides another, they will both fall into a ditch.'"*

Matthew 15:13–14

# Patiently Wait for God's Timing

One of the easiest ways to get frustrated and stressed is to try to hurry the answer to your prayer. The ego wants to be in charge and control everything, including telling God what to do and when to do it.

Have you ever experienced a delay in your prayer being answered, and when it *was* answered, you could look back and see that it couldn't have happened in a better way? This is an example of divine timing. God respects the freewill choices of everyone, so if your prayer involves other people, *their* freewill choices are a factor in the prayer being answered.

Divine timing means that our prayers are answered in the best possible way at the best possible moment. Getting frustrated or worried about *when* the prayer will be answered only delays and blocks the process.

What *does* work is to let the situation go, with a feeling of happiness and gratitude that you trust God to provide— including providing you with divine guidance to take positive action in answer to prayer. Trust in God's timing, because he knows and sees when all the factors will line up for you.

## ❧ Good Morning, Lord ❧

*Please transform my worries about the future into faith and gratitude in your almighty power to shift and heal everything. Please send your angels to protect me from negativity, and clearly guide me as to what I need to do to walk the path of grace.*

*"O Lord, I cry out to you. I will keep on pleading day by day."*

**Psalm 88:13**

# BUT I WILL TRUST IN YOU

This is the page to turn to on the days when you're really struggling—when your hope is spread thin and life feels unbearable. You've prayed. You've waited and been patient, but today you're spent. Your burden is overwhelming.

Go ahead, dear one. Cry out to the Lord. Cry out, and then sit and rest in silence. He sees your pain. He feels it, too. Parents always feel their children's pain.

He may not be able to remedy the situation right now or in the way you'd hoped, but he promises to give you strength every day. He promises you will never be alone in your suffering. If you commit to being still with him, he'll come and put his arms around you tightly and hold you. He'll send his angels to accompany and comfort you.

It's all right to let your feelings out. Tell God how you feel. He won't ignore you. He's heard it all. David expressed his raw feelings to God in Psalm 55 and goes on to say, "Who will give me wings, God? I want out of here!" David held nothing back from God. He was real and vulnerable in his misery but also in his hope.

May you feel free to go to God with your real and raw self in your distress, and sum it all up, as David did, with "but I will trust in you." God hears us in our pain, and he holds us with loving arms, dear one. Today, know that he's with you, along with my prayers. You're never alone.

## ∽ *Good Morning, Lord* ∽

*I am upset and can't see a solution to this situation.*
*I am frustrated because I want a quick fix, but I know this*
*will take time. I trust you to help me in the way that is best.*

---

*"But I will call on God, and the Lord will rescue me. Morning, noon,*
*and night I cry out in my distress, and the Lord hears my voice."*

PSALM 55:16–17

# A Gift the World Cannot Give

*There is nothing to fear.* How many times have we heard this reassurance in our spiritual studies and meditations? Yet, why do we continue to feel afraid? Much of the time, it's because we have disconnected from God's divine loving consciousness and are trying to take the journey alone. That, by the way, is the definition of *sin*.

If you were hiking in a large mountain range in a foreign country, you would go with a guide. With any wisdom, you would listen to your guide, and you would remain safe and not be afraid. In the same way, God has given you a guide who is trustworthy, strong, and supportive: the Holy Spirit, a teacher who will walk beside you like the most skillful Sherpa ever imagined.

The thing is, though, we have to keep checking in and slowing our racing thoughts enough to receive true divine guidance. When we don't check in with divine guidance, or if we ignore it and impulsively go on our own, that's when we are sinning, which leads us to feel afraid. But I promise you that if you continually talk with God, Holy Spirit, Jesus, and your guardian angels, you will enjoy walking the trails of life. Instead of being afraid of the steep cliffs and the twists and turns, you will relax and enjoy the views and everything you learn along the way. And that's a beautiful gift to you from God.

May the peace of God be with you now and always!

### Good Morning, Lord

*Please hold my hand firmly, and slow me down in my thoughts, actions, and the decisions I make. Instead of reacting impulsively or fearfully, please help me walk in peace as you divinely guide me.*

---

*"I am leaving you with a gift—peace of mind and heart. And the peace I give is a gift the world cannot give. So don't be troubled or afraid."*

**John 14:27**

# DON'T JUMP IN WITHOUT GOD

Moses led the Israelites out of Egypt through the parting of the Red Sea, and at that moment, the Israelites believed God's promise of delivery. Then their faith wavered, and "they forgot God, their Savior, who had done such great things in Egypt" (Psalm 106:21). They thought they could go it on their own from there.

This reminds me of a story about a five-year-old boy who was at the pool. Not able to swim yet, the boy put on his "swimmies"—those blow-up flotation devices that children slide on their upper arms. His dad watched him splash in shallow end, unaware that the boy was watching and yearning to join the older kids in the deep end. When his dad's back was turned, the child quickly exited the pool and defiantly pulled off the swimmies. Despite hearing his dad shouting at him to stop, he ran and flung himself into the deepest part of the pool. Of course, the dad instantly jumped in and rescued his son. They got out of the water and hugged. Then, much to everyone's surprise, the boy bolted to jump back in again!

How soon we forget when God rescues us. We think, *I got this*, and do something unwise. We take it for granted that God will be there for the really important stuff—and he is! We just have to wait and listen to his guidance and not give in to cravings and temptations, like jumping into the deep end of life without him.

### ∽ *Good Morning, Lord* ∾

*I am so grateful for your support, Lord. Please remind me to check in with you before taking action, so that I will stay on the best path.*

---

*"Yet how quickly they forgot what he had done!*
*They wouldn't wait for his counsel!*
*In the wilderness their desires ran wild,*
*testing God's patience in that dry wasteland."*

PSALM 106:13–14

# THE GREATEST ARE SERVANTS

As a follower of Christ, going out into the world and being of service is important. As we approach Christmas, thoughts about bringing joy and peace to those in need are especially strong. One of the best ways to lift your spirits is to help others.

Jesus was diligent about being that beacon of light in the world, opening eyes to the reality of his Father's Kingdom, available for all. He didn't do it alone, though. He trained up others to do this with him. He knew there were many people who hadn't heard that the Messiah had come to fulfill the prophecies and bring freedom to all people. So, he got out in the community often.

In the same way, you can get out into your community by volunteering your time. Contact your local soup kitchen. Be sure to drop money in the many charity collection buckets during the holidays. Most churches also collect toys and food for needy families to help them celebrate a merry Christmas. You can donate items in this way, or help organize the donations.

You can also make your gifts a part of charitable giving. For instance, you might give a donation to a charity in your loved ones' names and include the receipts in their Christmas cards. Many people are lonely during the holidays, so you can also volunteer to visit residents of senior centers, hospices, hospitals, and other such places.

What a beautiful way to spend Christmas—by helping others, as Jesus dedicated his life!

### ⤜ Good Morning, Lord ⤏

*I pray that I can stay filled with faith every day. Please forgive me for sinning in separating my thoughts and actions from God's will.*

---

*"The greatest among you must be a servant.*
*But those who exalt themselves will be humbled,*
*and those who humble themselves will be exalted."*

MATTHEW 23:11–12

## WISE MEN WORSHIP JESUS

This time of year is wonderful for many, yet dreaded by others. Some fall prey to the pull of materialism that surrounds the holiday season. They feel compelled to shop for countless people, spending more than they can afford. Some will run themselves ragged with decorations, parties, and other festivities.

Consumerism and materialism have stripped away a large portion of the meaning of Christmas. The true story of Christmas is all about the birth of our Savior. Christmas is a holiday, but not the holiday that many cultures make it out to be. It's a celebration of Jesus Christ.

Now, in the celebratory spirit, you do not have to go broke or stress yourself out. The very first Christmas was simple, with a focus upon honoring the Son of God. When Jesus was born, the wise men came for the sole purpose of adoring him, thanking God for sending him. If this is all *we* ever did to celebrate Christmas, it would be enough.

I encourage you during the holiday season to keep it simple. It's better to give one thoughtfully considered, inexpensive or handmade gift than dozens of expensive but meaningless ones.

Resist the urge to purchase gifts that people probably don't even need. Resist the urge to overspend, too. Have an honest conversation with your family about the true meaning of Christmas. Educate your children on the matter, and be wise. Keep your eyes on Jesus and pray about how he would like you to celebrate and honor his birth.

### Good Morning, Lord

*Please help me disentangle myself from the materialism surrounding your birthday. Instead, show me how to express love and gratitude to my loved ones during Christmas.*

---

*"Where is the newborn king of the Jews? We saw his star as it rose, and we have come to worship him."*

MATTHEW 2:2

## JOY TO THE WORLD

"Joy to the world; the Lord is come! Let Earth receive her King." No doubt you've heard this popular carol during the holiday season. Written by Isaac Watts in 1719, the exuberant song declares that every heart should prepare him room and sing.

There's been no other event that has brought so much transformation for humankind. God's Son, in the flesh, sent to humanity to redeem that which was lost. To bring those in the darkness into the light. To teach people how to connect with their Heavenly Father, not just for the future's sake but for today's sake!

Jesus came so that we can rejoice and sing now. So that we can receive our King and his Kingdom now. What an astounding reality, dear one!

The song "Joy to the World" draws from many of the psalms that portray God's redemption plan. It extolls the reality that Jesus Christ came as Savior, Healer, Protector, Teacher, King, and more. Though it's mostly sung at Christmastime, Watts wrote it with the intent that people sing it all year long, but more importantly, take the words to heart and feel the life and power in them!

Look at the lyrics to Watts's song. It will move your heart to rejoice even more during the holiday season. "Repeat the sounding joy!" Let your heart be filled with gladness and joy this holiday season, and sing joy to the world! A Savior has been born! Go tell everyone the news! Shout it from the rooftops! He rules the world with truth and grace!

### ∽ *Good Morning, Lord* ∽

*I love you! I am so grateful for you! Thank you!*

*"Shout to the Lord, all the earth;*
*break out in praise and sing for joy!"*

PSALM 98:4

## GRATITUDE UNLEASHES PEACE AND JOY

What are you grateful for? What is it that you want to offer thanks to God for this morning? Are there some things that you cherish that you'd like to take a few moments to acknowledge before the Lord? Your family? Friends? Health? Home? Pets? I imagine that there is so much you can feel good about if you focus upon your blessings.

The holidays are a wonderful time to reflect on your life and offer gratitude to God and other people. Regardless of whether you're spending the holiday season alone or with others, I encourage you to make a gratitude list and write down all the things for which you're thankful. What are you grateful for physically and spiritually?

As you celebrate the birth of Christ this holiday season, let gratitude lead you. Even if you're struggling, make that gratitude list and take it with you wherever you go. Read it ten times a day if you must. Extend gratitude to your loved ones as well, letting them know how grateful you are for them. After all, darling, a heart of gratitude can make way for peace and joy to flow into your life—and this, dear one, is my prayer for you.

### Good Morning, Lord

*I am deeply grateful for you. When I am consciously in your presence, I feel my defenses and fears melt away.*

*"Give thanks to the Lord and proclaim his greatness. Let the whole world know what he has done."*

1 CHRONICLES 16:8

## GLORY TO GOD IN THE HIGHEST

Jesus's birth is a beautiful and beloved story. Joseph and Mary traveled to Bethlehem, and while they were there, Mary gave birth to God's Son, Jesus. There was no room for them in the inn, and they retired to a stable, where Mary wrapped Jesus in swaddling clothes and laid him in a manger. Such a humble place to birth the Messiah! However, Joseph and Mary were grateful, and they welcomed the shepherds and the wise men who came to the stable to see their "Savior—yes, the Messiah, the Lord" (Luke 2:11).

The birth of Jesus was simple, and nothing extravagant was involved. The holiday was never meant to be a commercial industry. Rather, the reason we celebrate Christmas is to honor Jesus's humble birth. Like the multitude of the heavenly hosts, we praise God and give him the glory. Then and now, Jesus represents the hope of peace and goodwill among God's children.

When Jesus was born, it wasn't just earthly beings praising him. It was also the angels. Every heavenly being took note of the occasion and offered glory to God! So remember, dear one, Jesus is the reason for the season! Gather with your family this Christmas and offer glory unto the Lord for our Savior. May we celebrate his birth today, and every day.

### ⟊ Good Morning, Lord ⟋

*Happy birthday, and thank you for continuing to be with us today. I honor and give deep gratitude for all the love, caring, support, and hard work you do for each and every of us. Thank you—I love you!*

*"Suddenly, the angel was joined by a vast host of others—the armies of heaven—praising God and saying, 'Glory to God in highest heaven, and peace on earth to those with whom God is pleased.'"*

LUKE 2:13–14

## REJOICE ALL YEAR LONG

The day after Christmas can be a time of gratitude and rest. The big meals are eaten, and leftovers are enjoyed. The heavy lifting of the holidays is over, and there's a sense of relief.

For some people, though, there's a post-Christmas slump. They crash emotionally on December 26. They were very excited during the holiday season and experienced a lot of joy, but the day after, they struggle. They feel a little bit sad, not because they have the task of taking down the Christmas decorations (though that may feel tedious), but because there's just something in the air around the holiday season that they get attached to—that feeling of joy and anticipation.

If we're not careful, we can get into the habit of going after that "temporary high" that's grounded in circumstances. Those good feelings can come from shopping, holiday parties, and giving or getting presents. But God desires that we "always be full of joy in the Lord" (Philippians 4:4).

My prayer for you, dear one, is that you ground yourself every day in appreciation of our Savior, Jesus Christ. That you continue to get revelation of what it means to be in Christ, partaking in his Kingdom. Rejoice and sing songs of praise, even as you box up all those Christmas decorations. As you put them in storage, smile, knowing that the spirit of Christ remains with you all throughout the year if you allow it. Give yourself permission to sing songs of praise (and Christmas music if you wish) year-round!

### Good Morning, Lord

*Thank you for sharing your birthday with all of us around the world, that we may rejoice and give thanks for your presence and teachings!*

---

*"How my spirit rejoices in God my Savior!"*

LUKE 1:47

# A Leap of Faith

As we approach the new year, your thoughts may turn to *What's next?* You may be considering making resolutions for change, and praying for God to lead you to your own promised land.

After we pray for God's help, he often answers by giving us divine guidance about actions we are to take. Always, God guides us to actions that are positive, life-affirming, and biblically correct. This is how you can recognize that it's truly guidance from God.

One reason why we may resist following our divine guidance is the fear of the unknown. As much as we may dislike our current situation, at least it's a known commodity. This is when we feel stuck, not content with our lot but afraid of changing it.

Yet if God is divinely guiding us to make a life change, we can be sure that he wouldn't give us an idea without also offering the support to enact that idea. For example, in Exodus we find God sending an angel to help Moses follow his divine guidance to lead the Israelites out of Egypt.

We're often called to act in faith initially, and *then* the support appears. Hebrews 11:6 tells us that God is pleased when we are filled with faith. So take a leap of fate: act purely on the faith that if you listen to God, everything will work out.

 *Good Morning, Lord*

*Please continue to shine your light upon my path and show me where I'm going. Please calm my fears and worries about the future, and help me have the strength to do what you guide me to do.*

*"Faith shows the reality of what we hope for; it is the evidence of things we cannot see."*

**Hebrews 11:1**

## MAKE PRAYER A HABIT

If you struggle with having enough time for prayer, it's a habit you can break. *Lack of prayer* a habit? Yes, you can get so used to *not* taking time to pray that it becomes habitual. For example, if you've been getting up for the last 10 years and immediately logging onto your computer to catch up on the latest news, check e-mails, or scroll through social media, that has become a habit. Not praying first thing in the morning has become a habit.

If you've gone about your day busy with work, family, and friends, and have not made a concerted effort to connect with God, that has become a habit. Believing you don't have enough time to attend worship services, volunteer, or dig into the Word of God—they all become self-fulfilling stories about your schedule.

Do you know what they say about habits? Bad habits can be broken in 21 days if you are consistent with your efforts. So, essentially, if you spend 21 days not doing the "unwanted" action and doing something "wanted" instead, you'll break that undesirable habit. Granted, some say it takes longer than 21 days, and it may. It will surely depend on various factors.

So, if you want to increase your prayer time or quality time connecting with God, make a commitment to changing up your routine for at least 21 days. My prayer is that this book provides a catalyst to starting each day with prayer. Daily prayer is one of the healthiest habits out there!

### Good Morning, Lord

*My time communing with you is so precious to me. How can I make more time for prayer, meditation, and spiritual study? Please show me, Lord, and lead the way through my daily life.*

*"Keep watch and pray, so that you will not give in to temptation. For the spirit is willing, but the body is weak!"*

MATTHEW 26:41

# HOLD FORGIVENESS IN YOUR HEART

In the early days, as the New Testament church continued to grow, men and women of God went about preaching the Gospel of Jesus Christ. One such a man was Stephen. But some men did not like what Stephen was teaching, so they seized him and brought him to the authorities.

When the high priest asked Stephen if the charges against him were correct, Stephen rebuked them because they did not believe that Jesus was the Son of God. He called them "heathen at heart and deaf to the truth" (Acts 7:50). The people became very angry and dragged Stephen out of the city to stone him. Stephen, standing strong in the Lord, looked up toward heaven and saw a vision of the glory of God. As he was being stoned, he cried out for God to receive his spirit and to not hold the people's sin against them. Stephen died a martyr for Jesus Christ.

Dear one, forgiveness looks beyond the attitudes and actions of people. It sees the sacrifice Jesus made for all to come into the Kingdom of God. It sees the fallen nature of humanity and chooses to forgive them, for they know not what they do, *really*. Not at the spiritual level.

We embody Jesus most when we choose to forgive—even when it's challenging. May we hold forgiveness in our hearts today, and every day, just as Jesus, Stephen, and many others who lost their lives did living out the Gospel message. Through prayer, God will help you forgive in the healthiest of ways.

## Good Morning, Lord

*Thank you for holding my hand on the journey of forgiveness, this process of discovering and releasing my previous judgments and resentments. Thanks to you, I am finally free!*

---

*"If you forgive those who sin against you, your heavenly Father will forgive you. But if you refuse to forgive others, your Father will not forgive your sins."*

MATTHEW 6:14–15

# Run Your Race with Faith

The last letter that Paul wrote was the second Epistle to Timothy. He wrote it in Rome, knowing that his final days were at hand. His letter references the Old Testament offerings to the Lord, involving taking wine and pouring it on the altar.

Paul says in 2 Timothy 4:6 that his life has been "poured out as an offering to God." He'd fought the good fight and finished the race that was set before him. He grabbed hold of faith and held on to it throughout his mission; as such, a crown of righteousness was waiting for him in the heavens.

Dear one, will you be able to declare the same things in your last days? Will you be able to look at God and feel good about enduring hardships? Not giving up even when life's struggles and pain seemed unbearable?

Faith is believing even when you don't see. Even when the road is dark and the obstacles are huge. It's believing that as you step out, God steps with you. Not only that, he goes before you, leading the way. He sends angels to surround, accompany, and protect you.

As you continue along your journey in Christ, following his ways, spending time with his Word, and listening to Spirit's voice, this is the kind of faith that will grow in you. The kind that will help you finish your race with gladness!

Enjoy your journey. Keep the faith, today and every day. And trust that the Lord is with you every step of the way.

 *Good Morning, Lord*

*I can feel the power and strength that you bring to me.*
*I lean upon you, and any fears leave me. Please stay with me,*
*Lord, so I will continue to feel confident and filled with faith.*

---

*"I have fought the good fight, I have finished the race,*
*and I have remained faithful."*

2 Timothy 4:7

# NEW YEAR PRAISING

As we celebrate every New Year's Eve, we may experience a variety of emotions. We are saying good-bye to the old year and everything that transpired during that time. In most individuals' lives, there is a mixture of good and bad, but now we have the opportunity to put it behind us and move forward. At the other side of midnight is a new year, a fresh start, a new beginning.

This mixture of emotions toward the past and the future brings to mind Ezra 3:11–13, which tells the story of the Israelites at the site of their ruined altar. The foundation was finally being laid for a long-anticipated new temple. It was as if a new era was to begin. When the older priests and the people who remembered the first temple witnessed the new construction, they had mixed emotions. They wept from sorrow over the ruins of the lost temple, but they soon joined with the younger people in shouts of joy for the promise of a new beginning. The shouts from both grief and happiness were heard for miles.

God gives us the promise of washing away transgressions and allowing us to put our past away through his forgiveness, not only on the last day of the year but every day of our lives. Go forward into each new year filled with a spirit of shouting for joy and praising God for his gift of new beginnings.

## *Good Morning, Lord*

*Thank you for all the support you've given me this year.*
*I look forward to sharing an even better year ahead with you.*
*I love you, and I'm deeply grateful for you.*

---

*"The joyful shouting and weeping mingled together*
*in a loud noise that could be heard far in the distance."*

EZRA 3:13

# About the Author

*Doreen Virtue* graduated from Chapman University with two degrees in counseling psychology. A former psychotherapist, Doreen now gives online workshops on topics related to her books and card decks. She's the author of *The Courage to Be Creative, Don't Let Anything Dull Your Sparkle, The Miracles of Archangel Michael,* and *Loving Words from Jesus* cards, among many other works. She has appeared on *Oprah,* CNN, the BBC, *The View,* and *Good Morning America* and has been featured in newspapers and magazines worldwide.

Raised by her parents in New Thought religion, Doreen found that her spiritual path was transformed by an experience in January 2017, when she had a life-changing vision of Jesus that led her to become a baptized and confirmed born-again Christian in the Episcopal Anglican Church. Her work now focuses on gently helping people reconnect with the real Jesus, as well as running her vegan animal-rescue ranch.

For information on Doreen's work, please visit her at AngelTherapy.com or Facebook.com/DoreenVirtue444. To enroll in Doreen's video courses, please visit www.HayHouseU.com and www.EarthAngel.com.

ANGEL THERAPY ©

## Hay House Titles of Related Interest

*YOU CAN HEAL YOUR LIFE, the movie,* starring Louise Hay & Friends
(available as a 1-DVD program, an expanded
2-DVD set, and an online streaming video)
Learn more at www.hayhouse.com/louise-movie

*THE SHIFT, the movie,* starring Dr. Wayne W. Dyer
(available as a 1-DVD program, an expanded
2-DVD set, and an online streaming video)
Learn more at www.hayhouse.com/the-shift-movie

———

*FOR LOVERS OF GOD EVERYWHERE:*
*Poems of the Christian Mystics,* by Roger Housden

*HOLY SPIRIT: The Boundless Energy of God,*
by Ron Roth, Ph.D., with Peter Occhiogrosso

*PRAYER AND THE FIVE STAGES OF HEALING,*
by Ron Roth, Ph.D., with Peter Occhiogrosso

*UPLIFTING PRAYERS TO LIGHT YOUR WAY:*
*200 Invocations for Challenging Times,* by Sonia Choquette

*WRITING IN THE SAND: Jesus, Spirituality,*
*and the Soul of the Gospels,* by Thomas Moore

———

All of the above are available at your local bookstore,
or may be ordered by contacting Hay House (see next page).

We hope you enjoyed this Hay House book.
If you'd like to receive our online catalog featuring
additional information on Hay House books and products,
or if you'd like to find out more about the
Hay Foundation, please contact:

Hay House, Inc., P.O. Box 5100, Carlsbad, CA 92018-5100
(760) 431-7695 or (800) 654-5126
(760) 431-6948 (fax) or (800) 650-5115 (fax)
www.hayhouse.com® • www.hayfoundation.org

---

*Published and distributed in Australia by:* Hay House Australia Pty. Ltd.,
18/36 Ralph St., Alexandria NSW 2015 • *Phone:* 612-9669-4299
*Fax:* 612-9669-4144 • www.hayhouse.com.au

*Published and distributed in the United Kingdom by:*
Hay House UK, Ltd., Astley House, 33 Notting Hill Gate, London W11 3JQ •
*Phone:* 44-20-3675-2450 • *Fax:* 44-20-3675-2451 • www.hayhouse.co.uk

*Published and distributed in the Republic of South Africa by:*
Hay House SA (Pty), Ltd., P.O. Box 990, Witkoppen 2068
info@hayhouse.co.za • www.hayhouse.co.za

*Published in India by:* Hay House Publishers India, Muskaan Complex, Plot
No. 3, B-2, Vasant Kunj, New Delhi 110 070 • *Phone:* 91-11-4176-1620
*Fax:* 91-11-4176-1630 • www.hayhouse.co.in

*Distributed in Canada by:* Raincoast Books,
2440 Viking Way, Richmond, B.C. V6V 1N2 • *Phone:* 1-800-663-5714
*Fax:* 1-800-565-3770 • www.raincoast.com

---

ACCESS NEW KNOWLEDGE.
ANYTIME. ANYWHERE.

Learn and evolve at your own pace
from the world's leading experts.
www.hayhouseU.com